Subversions of the American Century

Subversions of the American Century

*Filipino Literature in Spanish and the
Transpacific Transformation of the United States*

Adam Lifshey

University of Michigan Press
Ann Arbor

Published in the United States of America by the
University of Michigan Press
Manufactured in the United States of America
⊗ Printed on acid-free paper
2019   2018   2017   2016   4   3   2   1

A CIP catalog record for this book is available from the British Library.

Lifshey, Adam.
    Subversions of the American century : Filipino literature in Spanish and the
transpacific transformation of the United States / Adam Lifshey.
        pages   cm
    Includes bibliographical references and index.
        ISBN 978-0-472-07293-4 (hardcover : acid-free paper) — ISBN 978-0-472-05293-6
(pbk. : acid-free paper) — ISBN 978-0-472-12152-6 (ebook)
        1. Philippine literature (Spanish)—History and criticism.   2. American
literature—Filipino American authors—History and criticism.   I. Title.
    PQ8711.L54   2016
    899'.21—dc23

                                                                        2015020150

For Landon

Contents

✿

Acknowledgments

In the last stages of revising this manuscript, I accidently came across a curious monument to Filipino freedom in my hometown, a New Jersey suburb of Philadelphia. This was pretty much the last place I would have anticipated finding such a thing. My dad had suggested that we meet at a nearby restaurant for lunch, and when I looked up the address online, a map popped up indicating that a statue of José Rizal stood on the banks of a river across the street. I knew that river from early on in my life, even went to nursery school not far from it, and my dad still walked alongside it several times a week for exercise. We had never noticed the statue before. The odds of there being an homage to the Filipino national hero in my own random suburb, not to mention my learning of it at the moment I was finishing up another book on freedom and Filipino literature, seemed pretty astonishing.

After lunch, I went across the street to take a closer look. It turned out that the statue, according to an inscription below the figure of Rizal, had been erected in 1998 "as part of the Philippine independence centennial celebration." Moreover, the monument actually consisted of two parts that faced each other in a kind of barbell shape. At one end stood the grim but resolute Rizal, his arms bent over his chest as if guarding it, a book grasped in his left hand, a quill gripped in his right hand at level with his neck and parallel to the sky. He was executed for that book at an age ten years younger than I am now.

At the other end of the memorial, linked to the statue of Rizal by an open pathway of some fifty feet, a dark and inclined slab honored Filipino and American "joint forces" who fought, suffered, and died together in the Bataan Death March and related ravages of World War II in the Philippines. The Death March was a horrible experience for humanity and, like the life and death of Rizal, more than merits its remembrance.

And yet, for me, the most vocal part of the twin memorial was the silence in between: the rolling, empty air above the open pathway in the middle. For no mention was made of what happened in the decades after Rizal and before the Bataan Death March, or why it was that American soldiers were in the Philippines in the 1940s in the first place. No indication was given that the inscription under Rizal about "the Philippine independence centennial" was a sleight of hand, that 1998 did not mark a century of Philippine liberty at all. Instead, the pathway, composed of a matrix of black squares, carried no verbal text, just images of the Philippine flag at the Rizal end and the American flag at the Bataan end, meeting each other in sinuous orange lines in the middle.

The something that happened in the unspoken half-century that is represented by the pathway was the American colonization of the Philippines. But anyone who visits my hometown monument to Filipino freedom will come away with the clear misunderstanding that the Philippines became independent in 1898 and that American and Filipino forces united to preserve that freedom in the 1940s. The open space above the pathway tells nothing of what happened in between. This book, in large part, seeks to remember that space differently and to act on it accordingly.

I would like to thank all those who have supported this endeavor one way or another. Tom Dwyer at the University of Michigan Press encouraged its consolidation by asking me when I might have a new project available and putting my proposal under review when I did. Aaron McCollough gave it a green light at a critical juncture as well. Two anonymous reviewers worked hard to read the manuscript closely for the Press and offer valuable feedback to me. Organizers of various academic gatherings gave me opportunities to share subsections of my work in progress and improve them as a result. So too did fellow members of the Americas Initiative and the Comparative Literature program at Georgetown University. Colleagues in the Philippines, the United States, and elsewhere, in sundry university departments and libraries, helped out by sending me copies of rare texts and by lending expertise here and there on specific doubts of mine regarding one matter or another. My thanks go out to all of you for your time, labor, and thoughtfulness.

Everything in this book was assisted by all those who taught and helped and supported me in the past. For the particularities of this project, I would like to thank especially my research assistants who contributed directly to it. In various visits to the Library of Congress, Porter O'Neill located most of the newspaper reports that appear in the first two chapters of this book. Yoel Castillo Botello and Jafte Dilean Robles Lomeli also found many useful documents in their sustained searches. Larissa Ong and Gabriela DeRobles read the second-to-last manuscript version and offered valuable criticism and proofreading. Felipe Toro gave very helpful proofreading advice on the last version. Jemm Excelle S. Dela Cruz did wonderful work in producing the first translation of a Pedro Paterno opera in over a century by rendering the ornate Tagalog of his *Gayuma* into English so that I could understand it.

I would also like to thank Jen for her encouragement and readings of this project and for all the laughter along the way. A long endeavor like this was more fun to carry to a conclusion because we could laugh about some of its sillinesses together.

Chapters 4 and 5 of this book include new versions of previously published material. Those earlier publications are "América Is in the Archipelago: Mariano De la Rosa's *Fíame* and the Filipino (American) Novel in Spanish of World War II," *Kritika Kultura* 18 (2012): 5–24; and "Allegory and Archipelago: Jesús Balmori's *Los pájaros de fuego* and the Global Vantages of Filipino Literature in Spanish," *Kritika Kultura* 17 (2011): 5–22.

As a great poet once sang, I have tried, in my way, to be free. This book stands as one more attempt in that direction, one more gesture at *kalayaan* for the world, for myself. Where the manuscript fails, where I fail, is not from lack of hope. As another great poet sang, there is, yet, a time of peace. It's not too late. So at the end of the day, despite the many darknesses, I will still pick up my folk guitar and sing something from the Sixties for you, Landon, and then at your request, bang out an endless rendition of Chumbawamba as you jump up and down on our bed amid the thousand multicolored pom-poms and grin and shout and sing along. My son, as you grow up and seek out your own, other kinds of *kalayaan*, may peace and love and happiness fill your life. Your mom and I will always be there for you. We love you with all our heart. When you get knocked down, however far away we may be, our love is helping you rise.

Introduction

To be American is to be defined by American hegemony and to define it in turn. The story of the American century is the story of American power wherever and however it prevailed, but also wherever and however it failed in the attempt. For where there is empire, there is sedition. And so to leave out of the narrative of America the narratives of those gripped in its talons, struggling for freedom, is to misunderstand both America and the century. And that is to misunderstand the world.

The mark, recognized or otherwise, accepted or otherwise, of American forces of might, is the mark of American identity, regardless of where an individual or society may be. This identity is not exclusive and is not static. It does not preclude other identities, including the aboriginal or local or national, and it does not admit an essence. Geography does not limit it, for whether the experience of American power is located within the formal borders of the United States is irrelevant: America in the 20th century proved global. Today still, American identity is forged not only at home but also on the other side of the world, which in fact is home, for since 1898 there has been no other side of the world for America.

If modernity, a polyvalent and protean phenomenon, is premised upon the planetary rise and reach of the United States, then Filipinos are the first moderns because they were the first to revise that rise and redefine that reach. Correspondingly, 20th-century literature from the Philippines in Spanish is the leading indicator of the long American century of globalization that begins in 1898 with victorious invasions in the Caribbean and Southeast Asia and ends in the early 2000s with failed invasions in Central Asia. Yet the Philippine literary tradition remains in oblivion, particularly in the United

States. Although a scattering of Americans who read fiction in Spanish may be vaguely aware of two novels by José Rizal, a Filipino intellectual who was executed by Spain in 1896, the same cannot be said of the literature that succeeded him. And the 1898 war, in which the United States took Cuba, Puerto Rico, Guam, and the Philippines from Spain, barely registers among Americans today, if at all.

But that depends on how "Americans" is defined. The governments of Puerto Rico and Guam are still directly controlled by the United States, while that of the Philippines is indirectly controlled. These realities result from the stamp of a globalized American empire that impressed the world in its image from its ascent at the end of the 19th century to its descent at the start of the 21st century. Such are the parameters of this latest version of modernity. And it is a cohort of Filipino authors who first established the subversions and sub-versions (that is, alternative, less visible versions) that are the antipodal responses to an America no longer antipodal to anything at all. That is why Filipinos are the first moderns. They were the first people to experience and respond to American occupation on the other side of the world. In so doing, they acted upon the American century and enacted anew America itself.

Put another way, the moment the United States gained overseas colonies, it gained overseas colonial writers. The tensions that arose at that instant necessarily redefined the United States across a global matrix. Suddenly at stake were the most fundamental questions of American identity, for the distance between home and abroad had dissolved. The Philippines, an archipelago that the United States wrested from independence-seeking revolutionaries after wresting it from Spain, is the birthplace of a new kind of America, one with a planetary reach that was met with resistance by local peoples. This is not the story of America once upon a time, once upon a place. This is our world, the one we all inhabit today. This is our time. And it begins in the Philippines, in a war that, chances are, you have never heard of, a war in which the United States killed directly and indirectly an estimated quarter of a million people, if not hundreds of thousands more (Kramer 157; Campomanes 138). A war fought explicitly by the United States in the name of crushing freedom, not supporting it. A war in which the United States decided, as it would in Guantanamo a century later, that it was a good idea to torture perceived enemies with water. This is our world, our time. On whose hands is the blood?

It is the truly global scope of American empire, not expansion per se, that arises in 1898. The American process of seizing lands and peoples, of course, starts not in Manila but in Jamestown. As a site of invasion and resistance at such an immense distance from Washington, however, the Philippines marks the start of what the United States would become in Vietnam, Iraq, Afghanistan, and elsewhere. That is, the attempted dominance of America over the archipelago would reappear in other theaters in the decades to follow, whether via overt military operations in Latin America and Southeast Asia and Central Asia, or via covert actions around the world that toppled one popular government or populist leader after another. And it is 20th-century Filipino literature in Spanish that testifies crucially to the global push of American power, for it is the first creative reaction whose language reveals the reality that this new global empire seized land from an old global empire and now stood in its stead. Yet Filipino literature in Spanish produced under American hegemony is invisible in American studies programs, Asian studies programs, English departments, Spanish departments, and everywhere else. This book aims to change all that.

A reasonable objection to this effort is that it sidelines the Philippines too much by swerving across the Pacific, that it ignores the critical importance of indigenous Filipino languages in multiple insurgent arenas, including the arts. Nearly all anticolonial archipelagic theater at the start of the 20th century appeared in Tagalog, for instance, not Spanish and certainly not English. But that vernacular dramatic tradition is virtually absent in the forthcoming pages. And an acute accusation could be advanced that the ostensibly anti-imperial argument of this book is actually insidiously neoimperial in its claiming of Filipino resources as American. Perhaps this is just one more act of transpacific theft, passed off as benevolent assimilation yet again, purported by another American at that. The anticolonial intent of considering Filipino authors as American is perhaps just intellectual neocolonialism at its nefarious heart. Well . . . yes. This would seem to be true, at some level. Unavoidably and embarrassingly so. We all are condemned by History the moment we speak, particularly those of us who strike out from rich and powerful countries to consider places that our predecessors struck out for and conquered.

And yet . . . no. At least, also no. For one, nothing is exclusive here: this book assesses Filipino writers amid an American admixture, but there are, of course, other frames, other filters, and other formats to be formulated, all of them fair game to be forwarded as fundamental. Furthermore, there are certain advantages to be gained by taking, in this particular project, the American angle and the Spanish specialization. For one, appositions of America rather than absolute oppositions to America make the subject more complicated and contradictory. And that is more compelling than some banal binarism in which the good guys are easily distinguishable from the bad guys, ideologies are immaculate, texts are teleological, writers mean what they say, and so on. The authors featured in this book lived in the age of Freud; we live in the age of Derrida; surely all the traditional questions of intent are just water cooler idlings by this point?

Besides, Filipino literature in Spanish written under the American regime currently has a quantifiable readership in the United States approaching zero. Also, for that matter, in the Philippines. The attempt of this book to demonstrate the fundamental importance of the tradition to America, to show that America was remade in its image, hopefully will lead people of diverse backgrounds to the Philippines, to Filipino studies, people who have never before seen the archipelago as relevant to their lives or work at all. And that is a worthy goal. After all, there is reality to deal with: like it or not, these Filipino authors were American subjects, American nationals, and American thinkers. The America that exists today does not exist without them. But audiences of all kinds across the United States do not know this. This book will reverse that. But of course, the arguments herein do not constitute an exclusive endeavor. Of course, other individuals can approach this tradition differently! If others want to draw the lines elsewhere, if others want to read 20th-century Filipino literature in Spanish, for example, only within the contexts of other Filipino literatures in other tongues, well, of course! Such projects are worth undertaking, of course! But so is this one.

As for the emphasis on Spanish, a focus on revolutionary Filipino arts in languages indigenous to the Philippines would highlight the dialectic of colonized versus colonizer. To stress the struggle in Spanish, however, constantly keeps in the foreground the larger imperial background, the foundational but oft-forgotten fact that the United States gained global power via great power gameplay. But even within a more narrowly archipelagic context, how Filipino fictions in Spanish developed in the 20th century is important because Spanish was the common language of the elites who had taken over the independence movement initiated by lower urban and countryside classes. The subversions that this book studies are all by upper-class Filipinos born in the waning years of the Spanish empire who, in their texts and their persons, sought to succeed amid the 20th-century actualities of American power in the islands. Spanish for them was a native and living language, yet also one acquired amid a now defunct regime. This put them in a permanently paradoxical position as individuals with strong ties to an old context but just as strong desires to triumph in a new one.

These authors were Filipino nationalists with little interest in national upheaval, for any true inversions in the social order of the archipelago would jeopardize their own class position. They wanted a very different status quo for the islands without any profound changes to, well, the status quo. All these contradictions would yield simultaneous seditions and sycophancies in their creative work. Insurrection and assimilation in this literature, in other words, are ultimately inseparable. As Resil Mojares argues in his own study of Filipino intellectuals of the early American colonial period, "The binaries of collaboration and resistance, acceptance and rejection, are reductive polarities that flatten out historical reality" (*Brains* 499). This held true even after enough decades of American colonialism had passed for English to become a new native tongue and lingua franca among Filipino elites.

Despite the long period of American occupation, the Philippines today is pretty much absent among the same American media that once took it as a primary subject. Save for when natural disasters befall the archipelago and so make for marketably maudlin video for armchair pathos (or the correlate, sadistic comfort), the country is pervasively ignored by American news operations. This is notwithstanding the enduring relevance of the Philippines to American concerns, starting with its enormous population of one hundred million people, its status as the country of origin of the second largest Asian American community, and its position as perhaps the third most numerous English-speaking country in the world. The Philippines also retains a crucial presence in sectors of major American interest such as the military, health care, international shipping, and prostitution.

Things were different at the start of the 20th century, though, when matters involving the Philippines were widely reported across the forty-five states of the Union. Everyone knew the archipelago was why the sun would no longer set on American rule. Many people in the United States, not to mention in the Philippines, voiced sharp opposition to the imperial grab and subsequent purchase of the islands from Spain for twenty million dollars. Among them was Mark Twain, who told the *Baltimore Sun*, "There were the Filipinos fighting like blazes for their liberty. Spain would not hear to it. The United States stepped in, and after they had licked the enemy to a standstill, instead of freeing the Filipinos they paid that enormous amount for an island which is of no earthly account to us; just wanted to be like the aristocratic countries of Europe which have possessions in foreign waters" (Twain 184).[1] Authority over the archipelago, by virtue of its location on the other side of the world, implied a manifest destiny much more expansive than control of the nearby islands of Cuba and Puerto Rico, which also had been taken by the United States from Spain and local independence movements in 1898.

Far less incorporated into the nation than other nonstates of the era such as Oklahoma, New Mexico, and Arizona, far more distant than the territories of Hawaii and Alaska, the Philippines was important precisely because it was the most outlying of outliers. Elites of all kinds in the islands knew that as a result they were contesting for global stakes. That contest would have repercussions in continental America too, for surveillance and punishment in the antipodes would transit across the Pacific and permanently reorder the United States. According to Alfred McCoy, "The pacification of the Philippines served as both blueprint and bellwether for Washington's nascent national security state. In its search for security in the midst of revolution, the U.S. colonial regime at Manila drew untested technologies from the United States, perfected their practice, and then transmitted those refined repressive mechanisms back to the metropole, contributing to the formation of a federal internal security apparatus" (346). It is true that the Philippines, a formally independent nation since 1946, is no longer part of America. But that truism is also profoundly false.

An early case of Filipino literature in Spanish that reveals how authors and authorities in the archipelago altered America altogether is that of *La alianza soñada* (*The Dreamed Alliance*), a 1902 opera that is the focus of the opening chapter of this book. The librettist was Pedro Paterno, a wealthy intellectual who had written the first Filipino novel nearly two decades earlier and who had played important political roles since. The guest of honor at the gala performance of the opera was colonial governor William Taft, who later would become president and then chief justice of the United States. And on the surface, *The Dreamed Alliance* seems to propose harmony between the American regime and its Filipino subjects. In opaquely overt ways, however, the opera promotes the opposite. The conflicting messages of this apparently collaborationist opera arise from the duress under which it was produced. The previous year, Taft had prohibited opposition to American rule and legalized the death penalty for those who defied that decree. He directed his draconian diktat to dissident dramatists in particular. This is not how the American century is usually characterized, but this is how it began. As a result, *The Dreamed Alliance* had to articulate its anticolonial aims via allusion and allegory and all the ambiguities that those modes automatically assume.

How Paterno staged his drama within and against colonial power suggests how he and his guest of honor jointly authored a globalized America that would dominate the world for a century to come. This is to say that *The Dreamed Alliance*, from positions of apparent weakness—its colonial context then and its evaporation into oblivion since—demands basic rethinkings of such seemingly self-evident rubrics as "the United States" and "American literature." For to be an American is not to be a U.S. citizen but to be interdefinitive of American authority, regardless of where that interdefining may take place. Such an American identity does not alienate other identities, including the local: Filipino and Afghan writers who wrestle with America in their work are still Filipino and Afghan. But the power of texts such as *The Dreamed Alliance* to force new conceptions of the United States and American literature is great. Once Paterno is seen to join Taft on an American stage in Southeast Asia, once this is viewed as a pivotal and predictive moment of the 20th and 21st centuries, then everything is suddenly up for redefinition. Textbooks, disciplines, nations, national senses of self—all are bound to change. At stake is not a forgotten opera in the Philippines so much as the world we know today.

This argument is counterintuitive. Therein lies its potential. Arriving at unexpected angles into assorted fields and institutions, it can provoke questions of acute kinds across all areas. *Subversions of the American Century* therefore aims to impact anyone interested in America or Asia or world literature or, for that matter, the world. Hopefully, many narratives presently told in history, literature, and language books and classes will be revamped in order to account for the centrally important fact of Filipino literature in Spanish. For at this moment, very few people are aware that Filipino literature in Spanish was produced under and against American power for more than half a century. And no one seems to have adjudged that this tradition redefined the scope of American literature itself. Even a wonderfully innovative recent book such as *A New Literary History of America*, edited by Greil Marcus and Werner Sollors, for all its creative and inclusive takes on America and American literature, mentions the Philippines but a few times in passing and, in terms of the literary import of the archipelago, only as a kind of background space that inspired the colonial propaganda of men such as Theodore Roosevelt and Rudyard Kipling (444). Not once do Filipino writers emerge as creating their own subjective takes on the United States or, more fundamentally, creating modern America per se. *Subversions of the American Century* demonstrates the need for Filipino literature in Spanish to appear in future editions of the Marcus/Sollors book and others influenced by it.

The borders, explicit and otherwise, of many academic fields are rendered unrealistic the moment Filipino literature in Spanish is featured. There is probably not an Asian studies program in the world that trains its students in Spanish. This needs to change. Contemporary Asia is incomprehensible without considering the full and formal thrust of American power across the Pacific, the consequences of which are first evident in post-1898 Filipino literature. In the United States, however, introductory courses on Asian cultures and histories, whether at the high school or college level, routinely emphasize China and Japan and, during war reviews, Korea and Vietnam. The Philippines usually disappears off the scholastic map despite having set its very contours. So it seems likely that the interrelations today of the West in general with the peoples of Southeast Asia and East Asia will take on a new look once the concerns of Filipino literature in Spanish are recognized as a vital precursor.

Revisions will be requisite too by people interested in Latin American and Iberian literatures who, almost uniformly, are unaware that Asian traditions exist in Spanish as well. Twentieth-century Filipino literature in Spanish presents a cultural geography unrecognized by nearly all scholars in Spanish departments, so up for redefinition are underlying notions and narratives about the scope of the Spanish-speaking world and its divergent identities. On an adjacent track, within the more specific context of Philippine studies, the parameters of cultural investigations of the archipelago need to be overhauled to account for the relevance of literature produced in Spanish after 1898. Currently, the only Filipino fiction or poetry originally composed in Spanish that is read by more than a handful of people in the islands is the translated work of Rizal, who wrote primarily in Europe and who died before the U.S. colonization began.

On a rather more narrow scale, this book functions as a kind of sequel to its predecessor, *The Magellan Fallacy: Globalization and the Emergence of Asian and African Literature in Spanish*. However, *Subversions of the American Century* moves in a new direction by interacting continuously with the United States and focusing directly on questions of American power. The hope here is to offer alternative approaches in order to recast the issues in play and to reach new audiences in so doing. Creating a field anew on a constant basis makes for a more compelling endeavor for everyone, author and readers alike. It is good to have the ground shift again and again because it forces us all to keep in mind that wherever we stand is always conditional and so could be otherwise. Staying too long in one place not only takes away some of the potential, fleeting joy of this bleak, blood-strewn world, but also tends to make us forget the invisible coordinates that set our positions in the first place. And if we forget that everything that we take for granted arises from usually tragic contingencies, then we are likely to learn nothing at all. We may claim to see the bodies piling up before us, yet their number is few compared to the bodies that have piled up below us.

Amid that gruesome count, amid the horror that is the history of humanity, there is laughter to be had within the accounting. It helps get through the horror if nothing else. Academic books are so often so dour. So much sobriety, so little fun. So boring, so dutiful, so indebted to conventions that cotton to no one. No wonder no one reads them. This book too follows what it is supposed to even as it proclaims that nobody should follow what they are supposed to. The contradiction there is unfortunate. But there is some laughter here to leaven the load, at least. Why not chuckle at Paterno at the start of this book? He was the most unintentionally hilarious revolutionary of the 20th century. The man has been dead now for a hundred years and is unlikely to object. And why not giggle at the novel that ends this book, a fantastic tale that claims, more sincerely than can be imagined, that Africans come from the sun and that Mongolians come from Pluto. Such laughter does not mean that these writers are not worth taking seriously at the same time. This book, in fact, is in most cases the only one to *ever* take them seriously. So, amid the ongoing tragedy that is the post-1898 Philippines and, by extrapolation in all directions, humanity, it seems okay to grin when the urge comes. As Sheryl Crow once said, if it makes you happy, it can't be that bad.

There are probably a lot of errors in this book, unintentional all of them. Every effort has been made to ensure that they do not exist, but so it goes. At least, as Billy Joel once said, your mistakes are the only things that you can truly call your own. Hopefully, other folks will come along and figure out what the unfortunate moments in this narrative are and tell a better tale as a result. Hopefully, they will locate all sorts of absent texts that will inform and produce fuller and richer interpretations, such as the many months of many Filipino newspapers that cannot be consulted because they are not known to be held by any library and yet may survive somewhere, in offline or private collections or in dusty attics. And hopefully too, even without the surfacing of additional sources, the main texts under discussion here will receive all sorts of other readings by scholars working from different vantages and inspired by different isms (or non-isms, as the case may be) and by other folks just looking for some new old narratives worth checking out.

Whoever does decide to spend some time on these stories would ideally be in a position to read them in the original Spanish or, next best thing, a top-notch translation. Much of the existing scholarly commentary, such as it is, on the primary texts under consideration in this book seems to be based not on the actual material but on earlier commentary by authors who also could not read Spanish and who depended on still earlier commentary by people also apparently unfamiliar with the original texts. A lot gets lost or mixed up along the way. Once the original sources are consulted, declarative statements by multiple individuals about seemingly incontrovertible facts routinely turn out to be inaccurate. Billy Joel may not have said anything pithy about that, though. Somehow it seems more like a Bon Jovi narrative.

The following, however, is a reasonably accurate sketch of what is in this book . . .

Chapter 1 interprets the first Asian opera in Spanish, *La alianza soñada* (*The Dreamed Alliance*) by Pedro Paterno, as an allegorical promotion of Filipino independence from the United States. Ostensibly set in the 16th century, the plot tells of an alliance of Filipino villages that arises to repulse an invading Islamic army that has demanded the most beautiful local virgins as booty. Symbolically, this reads as a call for Filipinos to join together to repulse not a 16th- but a 20th-century army that has invaded Manila, that of the United States. The libretto is therefore insurrectionary when interpreted in its contemporary sociopolitical context. The story line sounds even more daring given that William Taft, the head of the American colonial regime, was the star guest at the most heralded performance of the opera. Nevertheless, *The Dreamed Alliance* was not received by Taft or the other Americans in the audience as radical at all. This was in part because literally they could not understand it. The show was staged not in English but in a Tagalog translation of the original script by Paterno in Spanish. The figure of Paterno himself also tended to distort the seemingly transparent politics of his own production. In many ways, he was more of an elite reactionary than an avant-garde revolutionary. He was a Filipino so ensconced in the social stratosphere that he was capable of composing only in Spanish, not in any language indigenous to the archipelago. He was a preening plutocrat, an inveterate narcissist, and a committed sycophant to boot. At the gala performance, he staged an elaborate honoring of Taft in between acts even though the plot on stage was calling for a unified stance against the occupation that Taft led. Twentieth-century American literature as well as 20th-century Filipino literature begins amid these paradoxes and tensions.

Chapter 2 analyzes a variety of subsequent theatrics by Paterno on- and off-stage as the Taft regime segued into its successors. The second opera by Paterno, the 1903 extravaganza *Magdapio*, was performed for the latest American ruler of the Philippines, the new colonial governor Luke E. Wright on the night of his inauguration. Although seemingly ridiculous in every way imaginable (and then some), *Magdapio* offers a critique of American imperialism just as obliquely and, simultaneously, just as acutely, as *The Dreamed Alliance*. As with its predecessor, *Magdapio* is set in a remote archipelagic past while hailing as heroes an array of Filipinos who resist an invasion by foreigners. The title character is a young Filipina maiden who represents the Philippines as a land whose fate hangs in the balance between two destinies: the body of the virgin (land) either will be united in love with a local boy (society) or ravished by usurpers from abroad. In *Magdapio*, as in *The Dreamed Alliance*, Paterno clearly favors the former option despite the massive power and presence of the invaders. And once again, he staged this patently anticolonial plot directly in the face of colonial leadership. How could he get away with such chutzpah? Clues abound in the reviews and reception of the show that the import of *Magdapio* was actually quite fluid, that the opera meant rather different things to different people, and that *Magdapio* itself circulated in a variety of incommensurate versions. This multiplicity of meaning is manifest in the American periodicals that covered the show, such as the *Manila Cablenews* and the *Manila Times*, which ought to be considered just as constitutive of the turn-of-the-century United States as leading newspapers of the era such as the *New York Times* and the *San Francisco Chronicle*. The global reach of America begins in the Philippines, so investigations of American media in Manila and of Filipino productions for American audiences are of utmost importance to understanding the birth of the new planetary empire. And Paterno did not end his paradoxical push for liberty with *Magdapio*. A year and a half later, when William Taft made a return visit to the archipelago in his capacity as U.S. secretary of war, Paterno prepared for him still another homage, this time the opera *On the Arrival of Taft*. Yet here too Paterno explicitly advocated for Philippine independence. And sometime before or after that in the opera *Gayuma*, Paterno offered a narrative of tragic love and rival Filipino villages in order to urge archipelagic societies to come together in the cause of freedom. The theatrics of all these musical dramas, along with those of other highly stylized performances by Paterno on paper and in person in those same years, determine American power and American identity in the early 20th century as much as the fictions of the most resonant American writers who were his immediate contemporaries, Upton Sinclair and Jack London.

Chapter 3 advances the argument to the midpoint of the American colonization of the Philippines and the eclectic oeuvre of Guillermo Gómez Windham, author of the anthology *La carrera de Cándida* (*Cándida's Career*) and other prose in the first half of the 1920s. *Cándida's Career* won the first Zóbel award for the best Filipino literature in Spanish. This annual writing competition would become the most famous in the archipelago despite rewarding cultural production in an old imperial language, Spanish, that was increasingly being sidelined by a new imperial language, English. The anthology by Gómez Windham consists of two novellas, four short stories that resemble character studies of real people, a theatrical dialogue, a Socratic-style dialogue, a fairy tale, and two short essays of personal reflection. These narratives are all interdefinitive of America, most obviously the title story about Cándida. She is a provincial Filipina girl who is inspired by her suffragette teacher from the United States to learn English, go to business school in the nearest city, and put professional success above everything else. At business school, however, she falls in love with Bert, a rich boy whose parents are so horrified that he has a girlfriend of peasant origins and modern ways that they send him to Boston to study at MIT. This most American of tales takes place in a seemingly least American of locales, a small city on a small island on the other side of the world from Washington. Yet the story of Cándida is American not merely because American characters, forces, and places appear in it, and not due to some kind of imprecise metonymic extrapolation. Rather, everything written by every Filipino at the time was, de facto, American literature, for all Filipinos were considered by the United States to be American nationals. And literature by American nationals is American literature, whatever its authors or audiences might think. It is not exclusively American, of course, but it is American regardless. America, therefore, is also constituted and reconstituted by other narratives by Gómez Windham, including "La odisea de Sing-A" ("The Odyssey of Sing-A"), the rise and fall narrative of a Chinese immigrant to the central Philippines that at first glance seems to have nothing to do with the United States; and the ghost story "Tia Pasia" ("Aunt Pasia"), which gains its dramatic energy via the specter of a Filipino rebel who was executed by the United States in the early years of colonization.

Chapter 4 moves forward chronologically to the cataclysm that was World War II in the Philippines. When Japan bombed the American air fleet in the Philippines ten hours after bombing Pearl Harbor, the archipelago was already on a path to independence under a transitional government known as the Commonwealth. Douglas MacArthur, who commanded American forces in the Philippines at the time of the attack, was the son of Arthur MacArthur, an early military governor of the archipelago who forty years previously had helped prevent Pedro Paterno from delivering a proindependence speech. The story of Douglas MacArthur is a quintessential narrative of 20th-century America and yet is indissoluble from the Philippines, where he made an incredibly narcissistic decision to wage culminating land battles with Japan. He ignored his advisors on this count because he felt his personal reputation was at stake. The cost of that feeling was probably a million dead Filipinos.[2] Nevertheless, MacArthur and American actions in the war are hailed by the novel analyzed in this chapter, *Fíame (Filipinas-América)* (*Trust in Me (Philippines-America)*) by Mariano de la Rosa. Yet *Trust in Me* also offers a subtly subversive plot in which two couples, each composed of a Filipino and an American, develop romantic relationships before, during, and immediately after the war. The symbolisms of these relationships can be connected to questions of Filipino American identity that are implicit in the National World War II Memorial in Washington, D.C., where the Philippines is the only (presently) foreign nation honored alongside current American states and territories. *Trust in Me* can also be read alongside the coeval narrative *America Is in the Heart* by Carlos Bulosan, a Filipino laborer in the continental United States. Interpreting these three texts together bolsters the argument that the concept of "Filipino American" is redundant, for all Filipinos during the American colonial period were Americans by definition, irrespective of whether they left the archipelago for the continent or not. The life story of de la Rosa, along with the readership and paratexts of his novel, underlines this conclusion.

Chapter 5 investigates wartime Filipino literature in Spanish as well. It extends further the question of whether all literature written by Filipinos in the Philippines after 1898 can be considered American literature. An affirmative answer is more complicated in this case because the novel under consideration, *Los pájaros de fuego* (*The Birds of Fire*) by Jesús Balmori, relegates to deep background the long-standing American presence in the archipelago. The text focuses instead on a Spanish-speaking family of rural oligarchs as they are destroyed during the Japanese colonization of the Philippines. In contrast to *Trust in Me*, there are no primary or even secondary American characters in *The Birds of Fire*. Plus, the presence of English is just about nil. The only substantive representations of the United States involve its armed forces, most notably a joint prewar military parade that features American and Filipino troops, and, at the end of the novel, the return in 1945 of American pilots over Manila as they pursue the Japanese. Otherwise, Balmori writes a half century of American occupation of the Philippines out of existence. He recognizes virtually no American cultural, linguistic, or social influences on the archipelago. And this nearly wholesale refusal to acknowledge the mammoth effects of American colonization on just about every facet of archipelagic culture amounts to an intense rejection of the same. In place of any embrace of modernity is an obvious sympathy for a bygone and rather imaginary order of a hispanized Philippines in which Filipino elites and their hyperconservative value systems were untrammeled in any way. *The Birds of Fire* is therefore a radically reactionary take on the American century.

Chapter 6 travels past the World War II years to study *La creación* (*The Creation*) by Mariano de la Rosa, the only known Asian science fiction novel in Spanish. In this endlessly surprising text, a multiethnic group of world-famous intellectuals gathers in Manila and comes up with the startling theory that different races on Earth are descended from different planets. The young adult children of the intellectuals then build a spaceship and venture into the solar system to test the theory. In the course of their voyage, they prove that East Asians are descended from a royal society on Pluto and that white people are derived from interbred aliens from Mercury and Mars. The strangenesses of *The Creation* revise in remarkable ways the nature and scope of both American and Filipino literature. As a saga of space travel finished just two years after *Sputnik* but in a dead imperial language, *The Creation* appears at the cutting edge of modernity and, at once, quite behind it. In addition, the novel is anachronistic with respect to the American empire that formally had ceded independence to the Philippines in 1946. The use of American toponyms in *The Creation* and the fact that all the protagonists talk to each other in English suggest that the legal decolonization of the archipelago was one thing and ongoing cultural and sociopolitical realities another. The most important characteristic of this persisting, deformalized American occupation of the Philippines is its tacit integration into a neocolonial afterlife. Yet such integration is also pervasively countered in the novel in ways far more nuanced than its outlandish plot. Implicitly, for instance, de la Rosa positions the Philippines at the intellectual and political center of the world. This stands as a sharp rebuttal to the American dominance that pervaded so many aspects of the postindependence Philippines. And de la Rosa, like Balmori in *The Birds of Fire* and unlike himself in his earlier *Trust in Me*, abstains from obvious opportunities to cast an American among his lead characters. *The Creation*, therefore, amid its mixtures of assimilation and resistance, offers a test case for American literature that emerges from nations that are technically independent but still deeply affected by American cultural, political, and economic power. The counternarratives of the novel can be viewed as part of the burgeoning American counterculture of the late 1950s and early 1960s that rewrote the stories that canonical America always had told about itself.

The epilogue of this book recasts all the above arguments as a mystery with a buried body that needs to be exhumed and interrogated. That body is the corpus of Filipino literature in Spanish produced under American hegemony. What scars does it bear? What tales of crime and passion does it tell?

How do new understandings of the past and present come to the fore once it is unearthed? Hardboiled fiction in continental America was a popular genre during the second half of the main run of Filipino literature in Spanish. It seems fitting to end this book with a pivot in that direction. Academic work of this kind is forensic foraging, among other things. You who read this book stand as witness, judge, and jury to evidence concerning a dead body. It is evidence that, surely to your surprise and probably to your dismay, condemns you as defendant too. As Bob Dylan asks, how do you plead?

Regarding citations in the pages ahead, any perceived irregularities in spelling or punctuation, including accent marks or the lack thereof, reflect exactly the source documents. Most of those documents can be found via on-line searches of library catalogs such as WorldCat and those of the Library of Congress, the National Library of the Philippines, and the major university libraries of the Philippines. The locations of most source documents that are indexed and held in less-known places are indicated after their entry in the list of works cited. All translations are original and by the author of this book unless otherwise stated. The page numbers given after translations therefore refer back to the original source and not any published translations by other parties, again unless qualified otherwise.

So, that is what lies ahead. The goal is that the world, wherever you stand in it at this moment, will appear differently to you as the pages turn. In need of revision. Dylan also once said that the only thing we knew for sure about Henry Porter was that his name wasn't Henry Porter. The world you know at this moment is Henry Porter. If you do not realize that even just one paragraph from now, then this book has failed.

one

The Seditious Sycophant

Pedro Paterno's *La alianza soñada* (1902)

The global reach of the United States in the 20th century, a regime referred to by its supporters as the American century, began with the persecution of dissident playwrights. On November 4, 1901, Act 292 of the Taft Commission, a governing body charged with stabilizing the new American colony of the Philippines, went into effect with an intent evident in its title: "AN ACT DEFINING THE CRIMES OF TREASON, INSURRECTION, SEDITION, CONSPIRACIES TO COMMIT SUCH CRIMES, SEDITIOUS UTTERANCES WHETHER WRITTEN OR SPOKEN, THE FORMATION OF SECRET POLITICAL SOCIETIES . . ." (*Public* 346). The first section of Act 292 threatened the death penalty to any Filipino convicted of treason against the United States.[1]

The eighth section honed in on rebellious writers, that is, "Every person who shall utter seditious words or speeches, write, publish, or circulate, scurrilous libels against the Government of the United States or the Insular Government of the Philippine Islands . . . which tend to stir up the people against the lawful authorities or to disturb the peace of the community, the safety and order of the Government" (*Public* 348). Act 292, known as the Sedition Law, was decreed in Spanish as well as English but not in any vernacular Filipino language. This constituted de facto acknowledgment of the lingua franca of the archipelagic elite who had risen under the Spanish colonial regime that fell to American and Filipino firepower in 1898.

Nine months after the proclamation of Act 292, with the Taft Commission still ruling over the islands and Taft himself sitting in the audience in a Manila theater, Pedro Paterno staged *La alianza soñada* (*The Dreamed Alli-*

ance), the first Filipino opera, whose plot called for a united stand by Filipinos to expel foreign invaders. This patently seditious drama was, remarkably, presented as an homage to the American occupation. Taft did not understand the subterfuge and did not arrest Paterno afterward. Paterno probably did not understand much about his own production either. It was a moment of foundational blindnesses of many kinds. What took place on that stage on the other side of the world from Washington, what was seen and what was not, and why the Sedition Law and *The Dreamed Alliance* were issued in Spanish in the first place, is seminal to the global disciplines and discontents of the 20th century itself.

In Spain, the loss of colonies in 1898 is considered significant in literary and academic circles for having launched reflections on the allegedly post-imperial, parochial nature of Spanish identity.[2] Renowned Spanish writers of the early 20th century focused their attentions inward on a national landscape no longer defined, as they saw it, by overseas expansion. Meanwhile, the literary consequences of 1898 in the Philippines, the archipelago that marked the truly global reach of the Spanish empire, tended to be as ignored by them then as it is by scholars now. In fact, few people today in any of the world regions involved—western Europe, North America, Southeast Asia—have the faintest idea that a 20th-century Asian literary tradition in Spanish exists, much less that it was a subversive one whose early creators, particularly in theatrical genres, produced their art at the risk of being severely punished by the United States.

Yet the protagonists in the theater that night in August 1902 at the gala performance of *The Dreamed Alliance* were hardly minor characters. Pedro Paterno, its librettist and impresario, had published years earlier the first Filipino book of poetry in Spanish and the first Filipino novel in any language. He also had played significant political roles during both the end of the Spanish colonization and the start of the American colonization. William Taft, whose commission legalized death for any Filipino convicted of disloyalty to the American regime, would use his position in the Philippines to become the only individual ever to serve as president of the United States and, later, chief justice of its Supreme Court. Both men, whose historical reputations oscillate darkly between disdain and dust, spotlighted together a new global theater. In so doing, they proved far more important to the world of today than many of their more famous contemporaries. Yet scholarship on both Paterno and Taft is scant.[3]

The years leading up to the debut of *The Dreamed Alliance* are complicated. The short version is that José Rizal, a Filipino who wrote two Spanish-language novels in Europe that were critical of the way Spain and priestly orders ran the archipelago, was executed for subversion in December 1896. He was mistakenly associated by Spain with the far more radical Katipunan, a Filipino revolutionary organization of lower urban class and peasant origins whose armed uprising earlier that year was led by the charismatic Andrés Bonifacio. In December 1897, Pedro Paterno, who had preceded Rizal as a novelist during their many years in Europe, helped negotiate an infamous truce between Spain and the Katipunan upon which the leaders of the latter went into exile in Hong Kong. The rebels at that point were led by Emilio Aguinaldo, a more conservative and contradictory figure whose factional victory had led to the execution of Bonifacio in May 1897 and an ascending co-optation of the independence movement by Filipino elites. In April 1898, the United States declared war on Spain; on May 1, the American navy destroyed the Spanish navy offshore Manila; on May 19, Aguinaldo returned from Hong Kong. Allied American and Katipunan forces began defeating what remained of Spanish military might in the islands. On June 12, the rebels declared independence for the archipelago. Spain, eager to save face by surrendering to Americans rather than Filipinos, then arranged for a theatrical performance far more preposterous than anything Paterno would later come up with: a staged battle that both Western parties agreed to wage without informing the Katipunan of its fakery. After that performance, the American flag duly rose over Manila on August 13. In September, Aguinaldo established the Malolos Congress, the constitutional convention of a nominally free Philippines. Paterno, though known for his love of European culture and his two decades of strutting around Madrid, was named its president. In December, the United States paid twenty million dollars to Spain for the Philippines and declared the archipelago to be an American possession. By early 1899, the Katipunan and the United States were fighting each other.

In June 1900, Taft landed in the Philippines. He had been assigned by President William McKinley to impose a legislative regime on the archipelago while the American military worked at crushing the Katipunan. Technically, Taft was not appointed governor until the Fourth of July, 1901, but extremely broad powers were available to him the moment he arrived in Manila. The Philippine-American War that continued during his reign does not register in most U.S. history classes, yet the brutality and scale of American violence is mindboggling. Through a combination of outright slaughter, obliteration of villages, deliberately induced famine, and the inadvertent introduction of foreign diseases, Americans savaged the population of the islands. In assessing the casualties, Oscar Campomanes writes, "I have seen a more consensual figure of 250,000 Filipino deaths but those who cite it do not explain the basis for their common agreement. Indeed estimates have ranged from a low one hundred thousand to a high of one million, which at its worst would have meant the depopulation, by one-sixth, of the turn-of-the-century Philippines" (138). Paul Kramer concludes that "the estimate of 250,000 Filipino war deaths appears conservative" (157). Rural Filipinos may have had little immunity to pestilences brought accidentally from America, but, as Kramer points out, they died in the numbers they did due to American policies such as "'reconcentration,' which brought together malnutrition, overcrowding, unsanitary conditions, and social dislocation in a formula for mass disease and mortality" (157). Reconcentration, meanwhile, turned out to be a very successful military approach. The strategy, as Kramer notes, "aimed at the isolation and starvation of guerrillas through the deliberate annihilation of the rural economy: peasants in resistant areas were ordered to relocate to garrisoned towns by a given date, leaving behind all but the most basic provisions. Outside of the policed, fenced-in perimeters of these 'reconcentration camps,' troops would then undertake a scorched-earth policy, burning residences and rice stores, destroying or capturing livestock, and killing every person they encountered" (152–53).

Torture too was a technique used by Americans in the field, often via the medium of water. The United States also would torture prisoners with water a century later in the Guantanamo prisons in Cuba, another island taken from Spain in 1898. Gregg Jones writes of how one Filipino mayor, accused of siding with the Filipino struggle for freedom, was treated by American interrogators:

> Two soldiers forced Ealdama's mouth open, positioned his head beneath the tank's faucet and turned the spigot. When his stomach filled with water and became hard as a drum, the soldiers pounded his midsection with their fists. Ealdama screamed in agony, and water and gastric juices erupted from his mouth and nose. His stomach now empty, the torture began anew.
>
> As the water did its cruel work, the American officers watched casually. Past experience left little doubt how this would end . . .
>
> Filipino collaborators had taught Americans the technique, but its origins resided in Spain. The "strangling torments" of torture by water had been perfected during the Spanish Inquisition . . . it inflicted

excruciating pain and terror. Victims experienced the simultaneous sensations of drowning and of being burned or cut as internal organs stretched and convulsed. (2)

This particular nadir of American rule in the Philippines took place in November 1900, less than half a year after Taft had set foot in Manila. Measuring precisely the total carnage of the occupation over which he presided as top civil authority is impossible. But there is no question about its hyperbolic awfulness.

The summer of the arrival of Taft, Pedro Paterno found himself under arrest by colonial authorities, but he was released on July 2 after having sworn loyalty to the United States (Medrano 562). Arthur MacArthur, the American military governor of the Philippines and father of a future destroyer of Spanish-speaking Manila, Douglas MacArthur, later testified to the U.S. Senate that he had let Paterno go in order to gain his cooperation "to bring about a peace . . . at one time I had occasion to suspect Paterno, but on the whole I concluded that he was a useful man" (*Affairs* 1964–65). When Paterno proposed for the end of July a "banquet and public fiesta, to last two days" to celebrate a general amnesty proclamation, MacArthur "consented to it with the distinct understanding that it should be simply what he suggested, that there should be no effort to bring in any recognition of Filipino national independence; and he readily consented" (*Affairs* 1965–66).[4] Nevertheless, Paterno prepared to proclaim a speech before Taft at the banquet that would promote the idea of Philippine independence under an American protectorate.[5] The oration would feature the applause line, "Brindo por la unión fraternal de alianza eterna de los pueblos filipino y americano, ambos libres" ["I toast to the fraternal union of eternal alliance of the Filipino and American peoples, both free"] (Medrano 570). However, Taft learned of the speech a short while earlier that day, thanks to a Spaniard who had gone to him and informed him of both its existence and the sizable print run that Paterno already had initiated (*Affairs* 1966).

Any public proposal for Filipino freedom was a serious manifestation of subversion, regardless of whether the independence suggested would take place under an official American aegis. Taft requested a transcript of the address and a translation from the Spanish, and then took out a red pencil and marked all passages to be eliminated (Medrano 568). In addition, both Taft and MacArthur sent personal letters to Paterno that same day admonishing him.[6] According to Antonio Medrano, a Spanish reporter who eventually possessed and published the copy personally expurgated by Taft, Paterno "no quiso resignarse á la mutilación y prefirió guardarse el discurso" ["did not want to resign himself to the mutilation and preferred to keep the speech to himself"] (Medrano 568).[7] MacArthur, who as a military authority resented the civil power of Taft, did not mention in his Senate testimony the censorship by his rival. Instead, MacArthur represented himself as the primary agent involved: "So after the people got to the tables there was no banquet, because Paterno was with me trying to reach a modus vivendi upon which we could stand. And finally I told him that this speech must not be delivered" (*Affairs* 1966). But regardless of which American ruler played the principal role, Paterno decided to declaim nothing. And probably the saddest part of the evening for him was not being able to deliver the following lines:

> Nada temas, pueblo querido, que yo te he consagrado toda mi existencia. He defendido y defenderé tus ideales en los campos, en las montañas, en las ciudades, en todas partes. No importa que yo sucumba y muera, pues, como sucumbe y muere el sol al declinar la tarde, levantándose con nuevo calor, nuevos resplandores, á la mañana siguiente, me levantaré también para darte todo el fuego de mi nueva vida, todas las energías de mi nueva existencia. . . . Nada temas, pueblo amado y sígueme.[8] (Medrano 569)

> [Fear nothing, my beloved people, for I have consecrated to you all my existence. I have defended and I will defend your ideals in the fields, in the mountains, in the cities, everywhere. It is not important if I succumb and die, for as the sun succumbs and dies as the afternoon wanes, rising up with new heat, new splendors, the following morning, I will rise up too to give you all the fire of my new life, all the energies of my new existence. . . . Fear nothing, my beloved people, and follow me.]

Indeed. The only person who ever followed Paterno, however, was Paterno.

Other Filipinos, however, did follow other writers. Popular dramas began appearing on stage that promoted the efforts of the Katipunan against the United States via transparently allegorical plots. These anti-American plays, which came to be known as the sedition dramas, developed organically from preceding anti-Spanish plays. These were flexible productions, capable of mutating in a moment through script and acting from seemingly harmless melodramas to energetic agitprop. Some of the anti-American dramas, which Amelia Lapeña-Bonifacio denotes as "Chameleon Plays," even could instantly turn all the fictional antagonists from Americans into Spaniards if it were known that American policemen, gumshoes, or surveillants were in the audience at a particular performance (30–35). The crowd would recognize the maneuver and still understand the political message, while the American colonial agents would be unable to prosecute based on Act 292. Tomás Hernández thus suggests that "little essential difference exists between the anti-Spanish plays and the anti-American seditious dramas. The main characters and symbolic referents are ultimately the same or similar: the oppressed = the Filipinos–good men; the oppressor-Spaniards = Americans = evil men" (112). In broad, structural strokes, this may have been true for most of the plots. Yet if the sociopolitical environment of a performance changes, so too does the import of even its most familiar tropes. Spain and the United States were imperial siblings but not imperial twins. And the death penalty for insurrectionary drama rather changes the stakes of subversion on stage.

The Show Goes On

When the Sedition Law was issued in November 1901, one of its principal goals was to crush the revolutionary playwrights. Eight months thereafter, on the Fourth of July, 1902, Theodore Roosevelt, then president of the United States and a veteran of the Cuban theater of the 1898 war, declared the end of hostilities in the Philippines. A month after that, on August 2, *The Dreamed Alliance* premiered on a Saturday night ("La ópera" 3).[9] According to Resil Mojares, the opera "had a modest run of at least eight performances" (*Brains* 38). All of the shows were apparently performed in Tagalog, not the original Spanish of the libretto. Paterno, though born and raised in the Philippines, hailed from such an elite background that the only language that he knew well enough to write in was Spanish. Putting on his shows in Tagalog therefore always required a translator for the scripts as well as thespians more versed than he in the language of his own theater. Among the consequences of this disjunction is that the actually performed words and paratext of *The Dreamed Alliance* and his later operas could greatly exceed in content and connotation whatever he might otherwise have been able to control in his overlapping roles as writer, director, and promoter. Subversively minded actors, for example, had opportunities to imbue his allegories with allusions that could have escaped Paterno altogether. Whether this happened is difficult to determine with certainty, but the possibilities were certainly there. The rest of Manila theater performed in Tagalog in that era was the most ferociously political and anticolonial in the history of the archipelago. It was also highly symbolic in nature. The Tagalog-speaking Filipinos who acted in *The Dreamed Alliance* were surely well aware of that dramatic context. Some of them perhaps took up roles in those other plays too. And more than a few of the Filipinos in the audience for Paterno productions must have seen other seditious shows in Tagalog as well.

Meanwhile, the intended American audience of Paterno knew neither Spanish nor Tagalog and so was linguistically twice removed from the opera ostensibly created for them. Nevertheless, they received *The Dreamed Alliance* positively. Mojares writes that "this unabashed endorsement of U.S. rule was financed by Paterno. Its gala performance on August 27 was attended by 'some 1500 people,' including many Americans led by Taft. It was 'well-applauded,' so reported Manila's American press" (*Brains* 39). E. Arsenio Manuel concludes that the opera "reflects the thinking of Paterno and the attitude of collaboration with the Americans, that is, Filipino acceptance of American sovereignty and cooperation with the new rulers" ("Bonus" 60). The website of the Filipinas Heritage Library in Manila states that "this opera symbolizes acceptance of American rule in the country" ("Sangdugong Panaguinip: The First"). The assimilation of Paterno to the new order would seem complete. Yet the underlying argument of *The Dreamed Alliance* runs contrary to that conclusion. The opera, in its depths, is the speech to Taft that Paterno never gave, only far more radical. It is once more with feeling.

The superficial plot of the opera is easy to summarize. The first of the five acts features an indigenous seer named Lapu who dreams of "un cometa convertido en un grupo de estrellas, semejante al de la bandera de E.U. de América" ["a comet converted into a group of stars, similar to that of the flag of the U.S. of America"] (9; all translations herein are original and made from the Spanish, not reproduced from the English version of the libretto by W. H. Loving). Lapu interprets the image of the comet as that of "un pueblo nuevo y poderoso de allende los mares, que nos tiende sus manos en muestra de alianza fraternal" ["a new and powerful people from beyond the seas who extends its hands to us in a show of fraternal alliance"] (9). Lapu is surrounded by various dancing and singing spirits, the *anitos*, who perform "actos mitológicos conforme á las tradiciones populares" ["mythological acts in accordance with popular traditions"] (5). The second act shifts to a nonsupernatural setting in which Filipinos from three Tagalog villages are desperate because Moors (that is, Muslims from the south) who have invaded are demanding a tribute of the prettiest local virgins. Filipino men in the villages bemoan their fate and call upon Lapu for aid and inspiration. The guru advises them to unite and guides them through a mysterious blood pact to that end. In the third act, the men drink to the beauty of the virgins and swear together their belief in Bathala, a precolonial Filipino god. They also commit to a unified stand against the Moors. The fourth act switches to the despairing virgins, who are now captives of the rapacious Moors, and to a leader of one of the Filipino villages who has been defeated on the battlefield. The act ends, however, with the triumphant arrival of the rest of the Filipino alliance.

As far as dramatic action goes, that is pretty much it. The narrative is generally reminiscent of the *moro-moro*, a Filipino stage genre developed during the 19th century in which Christian characters battled against Muslim counterparts amid lots of spectacle and special effects. The broad dialectic of the *moro-moro* was lifted from the struggle in Iberia in which Christians tried to put an end to centuries of Islamic power in the peninsula. The eventual victors referred to this effort as the Reconquest, which was finally achieved in 1492 with the defeat of Granada, the last Moorish kingdom in Spain. In line with the over-the-top theatricality of the *moro-moro*, the fifth and final act of *The Dreamed Alliance* ends with all the Filipino characters, dead and alive, chorusing, "Brille eterna nuestra alianza fraternal con la gran República democrática. Brille sin nube alguna en nuestro cielo la gran constelación de las estrellas americanas" ["May our fraternal alliance with the great democratic Republic shine eternal. May the great constellation of American stars shine without a single cloud in our heavens"] (28). This desire is represented literally, as the dead characters are chiming in from high above in a rainbow, "formando un grupo de estrellas semejante al que se ve en la bandera de E.U. de América" ["forming a group of stars similar to that which is seen in the flag of the U.S. of America"] (27). According to the stage directions, the drama then concludes with the music of "los sones del *Himno nacional americano* en combinación con la *Marcha filipina*" ["the sounds of the *American national anthem* in combination with the *Filipino March*"] (28).[10]

The lack of any clear connection, however, between the first and last acts of the opera and its *moro-moro* middle indicates that the plot at hand is not really the plot at hand. A lot more must be going on to explain the leap from the reconquest of the Moors at the end of the fourth act to the exaltation of the United States in the fifth act. And central to any such explanation must be that the alliance hailed by the plot is manifestly that of the three Tagalog villages. It is only through the union advised by Lapu, the coming together as a single people, that Filipinos are able to regain their endangered land and their endangered virgins. This is the true dreamed alliance. The titular alliance with the United States that is dreamed by Lapu in the beginning and celebrated by all the Filipinos at the end is irrelevant to the plot in between. There are no American characters anywhere in the opera and certainly none who intervenes, anachronistically, to assist the Filipinos in defeating the Moors in a long-ago historical moment. According to the libretto, Filipinos solve their problems by drawing on their own forces of will and culture, not those of any outsiders. The title of the opera is therefore a ruse.

The temporal context of the action is also not as straightforward as appears. Paterno notes in his synopsis of the play, which appears before the script in all published editions, that the plot takes place in the 16th century. However, the first act is flush with indigenous traditions that suggest a much more remote era. The brief fifth act, in contrast, featuring the apotheosis of the martyrs and a full cast adulation of America, emphasizes instead a post-1898 setting. Temporality is further complicated by the figure of Lapu. His name evokes the indigenous leader Lapu Lapu, whose forces in 1521 killed Ferdinand Magellan, leader of the first fleet of Europeans to reach the archipelago. This iconic inaugural repulsion of invaders in the islands resonates with the Filipinos in the play who unite to repulse later invaders. The Lapu of *The Dreamed Alliance* therefore straddles multiple eras. His words that launch the opera invoke Bathala, a god whom Paterno often claimed to be the focus of Filipino monotheism from prehistory onward. The *anitos* who then dance and sing throughout the first act while chanting praises of Bathala also embody indigenous narratives and religious concepts. This precolonial spectacle, nonetheless, takes place simultaneously in the 16th-century moments of the Muslim invasion (the *anitos* sing of it too) and of the Magellanic invasion that is metonymic with Lapu Lapu. Yet it also unfolds in the post-1898 world, given that Lapu's dream of an alliance with the United States culminates the act. Put another way, the role of Lapu in the opera is to project an alliance of Filipinos against both Moors and Europeans in the 16th century and, at once, an alliance of Filipinos both with and against the United States in the 20th century. In his own person, he evokes an era of prehistoric traditions that Paterno denominates as "lo mitológico" ["the mythological"], two 16th-century episodes (the Magellanic attack outside the text, the Moorish attack inside it), the arrival of the United States in 1898, and, as the fifth act implies, a future in which alliance will lead Filipinos to entrance into heaven and union with Bathala (10, 27). In short, Lapu is eternal, and all temporalities in *The Dreamed Alliance* are one and the same.[11]

At stake, therefore, is not a theatricalized conflict with Moors in a particular time and place but a transhistorical metanarrative of invasion and resistance that now is staged amid its latest incarnation, that of the United States versus the Katipunan. The opera is thus seditious, notwithstanding the reputation of its librettist as a procolonial paramour of the previous empire in the Philippines, as the negotiator of an armistice with Spain that put an end to an earlier phase of the Katipunan revolt, and as just about the last man likely to be interested in upturning social orders. Throughout his life, Paterno enjoyed partying with the rich and the famous, the powerful and the popular. To conclude that he was a toady would malign only the toads. Yet *The Dreamed Alliance* is rebellious at its roots, proclaiming that Filipinos should unite and rise up against outsiders who occupy the archipelago. They also, in this case, occupy the seats in the literal theater of its staging.

The timing of the run of *The Dreamed Alliance* furthers its political charge. Just days after enacting the Sedition Law in November 1901, Taft went back to the United States for a leave that lasted until August 1902 (Cullinane 73–74). In other words, he did not return until after Roosevelt had declared the archipelagic war over in July 1902 and right before *The Dreamed Alliance* premiered. The opera was probably the first frontal challenge to the Sedition Law that Taft witnessed in person. Moreover, with Taft in the audience, Paterno was able to give, transposed into opera and this time entirely uncensored, the proindependence speech that he did not deliver to the colonial governor at the banquet two years earlier. Taft may not have recognized *The Dreamed Alliance* for what it was, taken in by the opening and closing hailings of the American flag, and Paterno seems to have been rather blinded too, taken in, as usual, by himself, so the opera is deceptively insurrectionary. It is also deceptively American.

The Dreamed Alliance is American because it is by an American colonial subject against an American colonial occupation in a theater that America claimed as its own for half a century and in many ways still does. The story of turn-of-the-century America should not only include Paterno, it should *spotlight* him. The round-the-world reach of the United States, and therefore the 20th century onward, is incomprehensible without considering Paterno. The Philippines is where the United States joined the historical ranks of global imperial powers. The Philippines is where the United States wrested land at the greatest geographic distance from another global power. The fact that Paterno could compose only in Spanish, despite being a native of Manila, testifies to these chilling facts. The American invasion and occupation of the Philippines is demonstrably what led to the American invasions and occupations of Vietnam and Iraq. Pedro Paterno is the clue to those Afghans authoring dramas of one kind or another today. And the Philippines, as Alfred McCoy notes, is where modern statehood itself was reformulated: "As the first civil governor of the Philippines, William Howard Taft was constructing a new kind of state based not on physical coercion but on control over information" (95). The national security state that vigils and punishes today, both the domestic version within the formal borders of the United States and the borderless one extrapolated around the earth, launched its judicial and extrajudicial life in the Philippines. As McCoy writes, Taft "erected a comprehensive apparatus for colonial repression, with harsh laws and an efficient police network that gave him the means to suppress both armed resistance and political dissent" (60). The short run of the first Filipino opera is not a footnote to history, literary or national or otherwise, not if it speaks truth to power at a determining moment of global narrative. This is certain even though so many of Paterno's claims to truth were apocryphal. The subversions that he staged, knowingly or not, foreshadow those to come elsewhere. Paterno is not irrelevant to the story of the Philippines because he wrote in a language few Filipinos today call their own. And he is not irrelevant to the story of the United States because he wrote in a land few Americans today call their own. His relevance, precisely, is his repression. Much would be revealed by its representation.

At first glance, the narrative of the middle three acts of *The Dreamed Alliance* is melodramatic and, therefore, mundane. The second act opens with Filipinos from the three villages on stage with torches and a chorus crying out, "¡lamentos y gemidos de las dalagas arrancadas de sus hogares como tributo al moro! Busquemos una idea salvadora. Busquemos á Lapu para que nos inspire esa idea redentora" ["laments and moans of the maidens dragged from their homes as a tribute to the Moor! Let us search for a salvational idea. Let us search for Lapu so that he inspires in us that redemptive idea"] (11). Salvation and redemption are here looked for not from Christ, as might be expected from a pro-Christian writer such as Paterno, but from the namesake of the indigenous leader whose army killed Magellan and repulsed a European armada.[12] Salvation, that is, will come from turning to a foundational blow for indigenous autonomy; redemption will come from turning to indigenous solidarity against foreign aggressors. The resonances of such a call by Paterno on a stage in 1902 with the head of the American colonial regime sitting in the audience seem rather obvious. *The Dreamed Alliance* is evidently not about the Moors at all. Yet the play does not catch the conscience of the colonizer. The plot does not reveal truth by allegory to the illegitimate powers that be. Instead, that truth filters through only to some Filipinos on stage and in the audience amid the florid entertainment of lusting Moors and weeping virgins and all the thrills of battlefield bloodshed.

The second act lays out all the main elements of the plot. Distraught youths from the three villages call out to Lapu and bewail the imminent fate of their damsels. The maidens themselves do the same. The chorus announces that "si mañana no se entrega al moro el tributo de doncellas; si no satisfacemos esa órden absoluta y cruel, pasado mañana quemarán nuestros Barangaes [pueblos]; el juez de cuchillo no dejará cabeza de hombre, ni de mujer en todos los pueblos" ["if tomorrow the tribute of the maidens is not turned in to the Moor; if we do not satisfy that absolute and cruel order, the day after tomorrow they will burn our villages; the judge with the knife will not leave a head upon man or woman in all of the villages"] (12–13). To this Grecian lament, Lapu steps forward and urges the three villages to unite against the enemy. When the chorus asks how such an alliance be formed, Lapu tells the townsfolk to read a secret document he has prepared, memorize it, and never speak of it to anyone (14). He adds that he has invented a talisman that "cambiará el curso de las cosas" ["will change the course of things"] and which turns out to be a magic potion (14). All the Filipinos then draw blood from their arms and mix it with the elixir. The men drink the brew while delivering Romantic lines about sacrificing themselves for their beloved country and their beloved virgins. Paterno describes the elixir as a "filtro" or philter, rather than with a more general term such as "potion" (15, 16). This implies that love, namely the synonymous love of Filipino land and Filipina lasses, is fundamental to the cause of the villagers. The articulated vows of the young people reinforce the equivalency of the beautiful resources in peril. The lad Tarik, for instance, speaks of "morir por ti, querida Tining [su novia], y morir por ti, pueblo amado" ["dying for you, my beloved Tining [his girlfriend], and dying for you, my beloved people"] (16).[13] His peer Limbás tells his girlfriend Uray, "Es un filtro que me inspira un amor inmenso; que abarca á ti y al pueblo querido" ["It is a philter that inspires in me an immense love that embraces you and the beloved people"] (16).

All of this may seem stock rhetoric and stereotypical exposition from any number of Western and Filipino traditions: a bit of Romantic tragedy here, some *moro-moro* there, a classical Greek chorus for emphasis, a classic Filipino figure to anchor it all. The blood pact of the protagonists resonates with other such accords in the history, literature, and lore of both the Philippines and the West. And so it is difficult not to groan inwardly at hackneyed lines such as those by Limbás. The most familiar narratives, however, can set forth seditious sentiment when resignified in new contexts. This is notwithstanding the lifelong elitism of Paterno and his even longer posthumous reputation as a bootlicker to whichever bevy of brahmins he was bounding about with in a given time and place. The fact remains that the opening act of what is essentially a three-act play—the first and fifth acts of the opera amount to a prologue and epilogue that are dramatically irrelevant to the action in between—proposes a secretive alliance of Filipinos inspired by a seer who is homonymous with the leader of the foundational Filipino victory against foreign aggressors. And the entire cast concludes the second act with the following rousing chorus:

> La alianza aumenta el valor y las fuerzas para defender lo bien
> amado.
> Nuestra alianza brille en el *Balañgao* (1);
> Abra las puertas del Kalualhatian; (2) y nos una con *Bathala*. (3) (16)

> [The alliance increases the courage and the forces to defend the
> well-loved.
> May our alliance shine in the *Balañgao* (1);
> Open the doors of the Kalualhatian; (2) and unite us with *Bathala*.
> (3)]

Paterno was a great fan of glossing himself and the parenthetical single digits correlate in the libretto to these footnotes:

> (1) *Balañgao*. Arco-iris, camino del cielo.
> (2) *Kalualhatian* la gloria
> (3) *Bathala*. Dios (16)

> [(1) *Balañgao*. Rainbow, path of heaven
> (2) *Kalualhatian* glory
> (3) *Bathala*. God]

In this triumphal ending to the second act, the alliance that is celebrated is clearly the one just sworn to via a blood pact among Filipinos. It is not a transpacific arrangement with the unmentioned American arrivistes. It is an alliance based on ancient indigenous ideas and articulated in a local language, not on novel concepts imported from abroad and expressed in English. The defense of "the well-loved" is a defense of the Philippines and of Filipinas, which/who are symbolically the same. Superficially, the title of the opera and the dream of Lapu suggest an embrace of a new foreign power and thus style Paterno as the sycophant he serially strived to be. The actual play, however, presented within and against that new foreign power, is nothing short of revolutionary. It is not the Moors who have occupied Manila the night *The Dreamed Alliance* premiered. It is the Americans.

Significantly, various concepts associated with the Katipunan appear in the opera. Raymond Ileto notes that veterans of the Katipunan were "sometimes referred to as 'men of anting-anting'"; he defines "anting-anting" as an "Amulet or potion that gives special powers, such as protection from injury and ability to pass through walls" (23, 269). The philter that Lapu invents and that the heroes drink evokes a larger worldview permeated with anting-anting. In addition, the theme of a fragmented Filipino populace fusing into a single force flows readily with "the meaning of 'wholeness' or 'becoming one' implied by the term *katipunan*" (Ileto 87). Ileto points out too that the Katipunan was a fraternal organization that emerged within a broader archipelagic tradition of brotherhoods that brought diverse Filipinos together in common cause (78). The unification through a blood ritual in the opera plays into this sense of a purposeful fraternity comprising Filipino men of different provenances. These Katipunan subtexts of *The Dreamed Alliance*, whether consciously inserted by Paterno or not, would have been read as such by anyone not obtuse or ignorant in the audience. And it is a measure of the purblind propensities of potentates everywhere, not just the American overlords in the archipelago, that Paterno was acclaimed rather than arrested after the show. *The Dreamed Alliance* debuted only a month after the official defeat of the Katipunan as proclaimed by President Roosevelt. On stage, the opera proclaimed the opposite. After all, *The Dreamed Alliance* announces the triumph over foreign forces by a fraternity of Filipinos inspired by a blood pact and motivated by a potion of special powers.

The third and fourth acts of the opera fill in further the definitive frames established in the second act. In the third act, Lapu reappears and announces, "Seríamos mayor en número y en armas, si tuviésemos unión, un pueblo bien unido siempre es fuerte, y nadie puede con un pueblo unido" ["We would be greater in number and in arms if we had a union; a well-united people is always strong, and no one can defeat a united people"] (19). Again, Lapu pronounces these lines directly in front of Taft, the head of the American occupation, who is sitting in the audience. The seer cannot possibly be talking only about the Moors. The same holds when the third act climaxes with all the Filipino men chorusing an oath to Bathala that concludes, "Juramos poner término á la invasión de los moros de Borney. Por nuestra unión; por nuestra alianza, muramos todos. Muerte al que retroceda ¡muera el traidor! Marchemos, pues, ó triunfar ó morir" ["We swear to put an end to the invasion of the Moors of Borney. For our union; for our alliance, let us all die.

Death to he who goes backward, death to the traitor! Let us march, thus, and triumph or die"] (21). This is a patent defiance by Paterno of the American interdiction against insurrectionary theater. A collective of armed Filipinos avows here to terminate a foreign occupation or die trying. They pledge as well to mete out death to any turncoat among them. This is no light evening entertainment.

How Taft could fail to comprehend the cast before him suggests the exorbitant degree of his hubris and that of all the subsequent Americans rulers in Asian countries (Korea, Vietnam, Iraq, Afghanistan, and the list goes on) who likewise believed they understood the dramas before them. As for Paterno, always preoccupied more with himself than anything else, he may have wanted for personal more than sociopolitical reasons to appeal to Filipinos who favored freedom. Five years previously, he had negotiated the truce that had halted the revolution against Spain. Since then, he had been considered by many Filipinos to be an unreliable patriot at best. Having his characters shout "death to the traitor!" may have been a way of trying to resituate himself on the right side of History. Of course, he musters this shout quite belatedly. Paterno was the sort of man who always sought to make a mark and somehow always missed it.

His protagonists also tended to time their passions ineptly. That is, Paterno, throughout his authorial career, delighted in sexual surgings that, inopportune, verged tantalizingly short of consummation. Nothing quite rings of Paterno like a scene in which a busty Filipina virgin is being dragged toward deflowerment. A threatened or incomplete penetration of the Philippines by foreigners is the national extrapolation of this motif. The fourth act of *The Dreamed Alliance* thus opens with the Moors lusting after the young Filipinas, who sing and dance for them while lamenting. The dialogue here includes, for example, "Doncellas tagalas ¡cuán hermosas són! ¡cuánta voluptuosidad encierran! estas doncellas no han tenido lugar, ni tiempo, ni tentador, gocemos de sus primicias" ["Tagalog maidens, how beautiful they are! How much voluptuousness they enclose! These maidens have not had the place nor time nor tempter; let us enjoy their first experiences"] (23). Meanwhile, the virgins secretly put poison in the Moors' cups before drinking the toxin themselves in despair.[14] Somehow, one of them manages to do this even though a split second earlier a Moorish general had been (as is inevitable in Paterno) dragging her "hacia dentro del escenario" ["toward the rear of the stage"] (24). Tarik, one of the Filipino leaders, then shows up as a prisoner of war and, mistaken in the belief that the revolutionary alliance has lost, asks his beloved Tining to kill him with a knife. She eventually obliges and then kills herself with the same knife, which is among the least necessary Romeo and Juliet moments ever to grace global theater due to, among other considerations, the fact that she had already poisoned herself. An instant after the lovers expire, the victorious Filipino brotherhood arrives, liberates the remaining virgins, and choruses a huzzah to the Filipino alliance, to Filipinas, and to the Philippines, all of which are the same thing: "!Viva la alianza! ¡La unión ha triunfado! ¡Vivan nuestras mujeres! ¡Viva nuestra Libertad!" ["Long live the alliance! The union has triumphed! Long live our women! Long live our Liberty!"] (26). This jubilant cry is then quickly veiled by the absurdity of the fifth act in which the protagonists form the star-spangled banner in the rainbow and all the players sing praise of the United States.

Despite that acclamation, rebellion against an occupying force is far more central to *The Dreamed Alliance* than alliance with it. This is made evident by the hollow frame that is constructed by the opening and closing acts. If *The Dreamed Alliance* had any actual connection to a transpacific pact, it would have at least hinted something to that effect in acts 2, 3, and 4. Moreover, the plot does not ride on the plight of the women, whose rendition to the Moors happens offstage in between acts. If *The Dreamed Alliance* were primarily the sexualized melodrama it appears to be, then the actual taking of the women would provide the foregrounded foreplay, and the taking of them back would produce the climax. Clearly, however, the fundamental issue established in the first act of the inset three-act play (technically, acts 2–4) is the absence of union among Filipinos, the lack of intercourse on a national scale. The next act correspondingly focuses on the resolution of that issue as a Katipunan-style brotherhood is consolidated. The final act of the inset play then naturally entails a triumphant domination by that brotherhood over the foreign aggressors. Now the invaders are dancing to a Filipino tune and not vice versa. Consequently, this opera set in the 16th century is not set in the 16th century and those Moors are not Moors. Steeped in the allegorical traditions of Filipino literature and in the oeuvre of Paterno in particular, *The Dreamed Alliance* is a 20th-century drama about Americans and a fraternal movement to overthrow them, routed through a 19th-century war against Spaniards and a blood pact designed to overthrow them, and also through a fight against Magellan *and* Moors in the 16th century *and* against Moors during the centuries of the Reconquest in Iberia. These multiple and multilayered maneuverings are all mutinous despite the fact that Paterno promoted Spanish control over the Philippines until the last possible moment and despite the fact that his irrepressible sense of elitism made him an unlikely champion of any cause against standing orders.

For all the tired lines, *The Dreamed Alliance* is hardly a tired narrative. Or, rather, it is an old story with new meaning, thanks to the struggle of the Katipunan against Spain and then the United States. After all, the play proposes a secret alliance among Filipinos against a foreign occupation, which is exactly what the Sedition Law intended to punish. And the overseer of that edict, Taft, was the guest of honor at the gala performance, which makes the opera even more contestatory. Taft did not apprehend the treason before him and so did not apprehend Paterno. Yet it appears that Paterno too did not quite grasp the extent of his subversion. Certainly, he had a long track record of misreading himself, not to mention the world. He was a historian who consistently misjudged History, always arriving late to a context that already had changed or to one that never had existed in the first place. His reputation in the Philippines, then and now, is largely that of a pretentious pretender to whatever pomposities populated his presence, whether in Madrid or Manila, whether among Spaniards or Filipinos or Americans. This is a man, after all, who dedicated the English translation of his lone novel to the wife of William Taft.[15]

Shifting Alliances

There is no indication that Paterno purposefully styled *The Dreamed Alliance* as seditious. On the contrary, the night of the gala performance he adhered to a gold standard of groveling. Or at least a golden vessel. As the *Manila Cablenews* put it in its lead the next day, "Little Señor Paterno and big Governor Taft stood in a starred and stripey box at the Zorrilla Theatre last night and exchanged box office receipts, a gold vase and compliments" ("Governor" 1). This exchange took place between the third and fourth acts when Paterno went to the "box of honor" with the entire take of the gala performance and

> told Governor Taft that the money was to be applied to any charity the executive chose to name. This the señor said in Spanish. Governor Taft smiled and smiled and looked as if he understood, but it was Secretary Fergusson who interpreted the speech into excellent English. Governor Taft, addressing Señor Paterno, said that he would be glad if the author would convert the money to the use of a conservatory of music for the benefit of the Filipinos. Mr. Fergusson obligingly translated this into Spanish, whereupon Señor Paterno clasped the Governor earnestly by the sleeve and begged that he be allowed to record the gift as coming from Governor Taft. ("Governor" 1)

After he "begged," Paterno turned up his performance a notch by giving Taft a "handsomely carved golden vase" inscribed in Spanish and, following "a little speech of thanks" by Taft, "smiling left the box, and with him a number of native gentlemen who had followed to witness the presentation. The Governor glanced appreciatively at the golden gift, which was allowed to rest on the corner of the box. The large audience looked up and cheered for Governor Taft, Señor Paterno, and 'A Dreamed Alliance'" ("Governor" 1).

The whole scene is enough to make a theater critic rush to look up the spelling of *obsequious*. Doing so, however, might result in missing the start of the fourth act and, more importantly, overlooking the climax of the third act that directly preceded the extratextual scene of Paterno and the golden vase. That is the act that ends with a united Filipino (male) populace swearing to a precolonial Filipino god, "For our union; for our alliance, let us all die. Death to he who goes backward, death to the traitor!" (21). The text condemns its writer. The alliance contemns its assimilation. The oath of loyalty is pledged to a power of the indigenous past, not of the foreign present. The gelt exchanged and the praises traded may have left Paterno and Taft smiling, but at least some of the natives in the audience, if not the "native gentlemen," surely remained restless ("Governor" 1).

For despite the myopias of author and authoritarian alike, the subversions of *The Dreamed Alliance* seem to have been sensed and sustained among those in attendance who saw themselves on stage. Filipinos in the theater who favored the Katipunan would have understood the underlying codes even if the official coders and decoders did not. This was grasped by Arthur Stanley Riggs, an American who appeared in Manila amid the wave of seditious plays and was so exasperated by what he witnessed that he wrote a massive book indicting them.[16] Riggs was that rare kind of American racist who moonlighted as a hilarious (at least in retrospect) theater critic. For example, on seeing *Magdapio*, a sequel of sorts to *The Dreamed Alliance* that appeared in late 1903 and early 1904, Riggs described Paterno as "a wildly ebullient half-caste *farceur* who [engages in] the systematic cozening of the poor and deception of the rich" (*Filipino* 8). Despite this assessment, Riggs saw *Magdapio* as a subversive drama and concluded that *The Dreamed Alliance*, whose run had ended shortly after he arrived in the Philippines but which he never saw, was so too: "Other plays of a seditious charater [*sic*] than the ones already named, included . . . *Sang Dugong Paniguinip* [this is the Tagalog title of *The Dreamed Alliance*], attributed to Pedro Paterno and directed against the Spanish government. This play is declared to have been written and produced secretly, because of the rigorous behavior of the governor-general" (*Filipino*

55). Riggs is wrong on his facts. The opera is only obliquely directed against a Spanish regime (one that no longer existed in any case), and it certainly was not written or produced secretly. Yet Riggs gleaned his impression of the opera as seditious from sources who definitely were not the Americans who applauded it.[17] Some Filipinos, it would seem, had taken *The Dreamed Alliance* as an anticolonial production, and Riggs had picked up on that.

And perhaps Paterno did know what he was doing, deep in his subconscious or, perhaps, not so deep after all. Perhaps he was not so much a fawn as a fox, or perhaps he felt flattered by himself to figure as both. Although historians, like many of his contemporaries, cast him as somewhere between irrelevant and, in all senses, incredible, it is hard to ignore his post-1898 political postures. In the range of Filipino elites, he did not rank among the most conservative elements despite his immense wealth and education and his (somewhat invented) patrician lineage. He stood elsewhere. In 1900, he signed a platform that "stated that the territory of the Philippine Islands might be considered as one of the states of the Union" (Kalaw, *Development* 281). Though hardly revolutionary, this was a significant move to empower the Philippines given other options in the air such as continued colonization or formal annexation. Supporting a push to make the Philippines equal in law to continental American states can be appreciated today as a fairly bold gesture, particularly given the recoil even now among the American public to the idea of granting statehood to Puerto Rico, another island colony from 1898. And in November 1901, the same month in which Act 292 (the Sedition Law) was decreed, Paterno formally went on record as opposing annexation for the lack of self-government it would grant the archipelago (Kalaw, *Development* 281). The following October, in a moment of political liberalization by the colonial regime just a couple months or so after Taft had seen *The Dreamed Alliance*, "Among the first ones to move was Paterno, who tried to organize his Liberal Party" as an organization dedicated to "self-government," albeit without invoking the word "independence" explicitly (Kalaw, *Development* 285). And but two months after that, "Paterno changed the name of his party to *Partido Independista*, probably because he believed that the feeling for independence was growing. The program of the party was also changed, and this time it frankly advocated the independence of the Philippines as the aspiration of the people" (Kalaw, *Development* 286). On the literary rather than historical scholarship side, Daisy Hontiveros-Avellana includes Paterno without qualification in an account of the most prominent "propaganda playwrights" because he "wrote *Sandugong Panaginip* (The Dream Pact) and *Magdapio* (Fidelity Rewarded)" (671). Amelia Lapeña-Bonifacio, who published the principal study of the seditious plays, does not mention *The Dreamed Alliance* but does treat Paterno matter-of-factly as a writer of other rebellious operas.

American media also could style Paterno as a substantive if slippery subversive. The fine office workers of a classic American city such as Scranton, Pennsylvania, read coverage in their hometown newspaper of the banquet in July 1900 at which Paterno intended to deliver his proindependence speech. An article in the *Scranton Tribune*, written by an Associated Press correspondent in Manila, was headlined "Pedro Paterno's Peace Festival: Details of the Much-Discussed Fiasco at Manila: Amusing Efforts of the Tricky Tagal to Entrap the American Commission and Military Authorities into Recognition of the Aguinaldo Republic" (4). The reporter pointed out that the lavish festivities prepared by Paterno leading up to the banquet were rife with insurrection. Amid such touches as "horse races and regattas, parades by day and night, dancing, illuminations and fireworks. . . . Paterno caused to be erected on Manila's main street ten triumphal arches. . . . portraits of Aguinaldo were given prominent places on some of the arches . . . in one instance pictures of President McKinley and Aguinaldo were placed side by side under the same big wreath, and . . . the inscribed sentences declared for Filipino independence" (4). The article even characterizes the banquet speech as "the coup contemplated by Paterno" (4). This is hardly the profile of a serial sycophant, which is how Paterno is usually represented and how, for that matter, he liked to represent himself. The *Scranton Tribune* rightly concludes in its final subheading that "Paterno Deceived Everybody" (4). This is more accurate than the reporter suspects, for Paterno routinely deceived himself too: he is fully part of that "Everybody." He may have been the klutziest revolutionary of all time, fully capable of risking everything while trying to ensure the opposite. Not without reason does the *Scranton Tribune* note that "it may be decided that in the deception he attempted, and, in a measure, did practice, he has violated his oath of allegiance to the United States, in which case his punishment could be severe" (4).

Nevertheless, Manila press reports on the opera that he staged two years later tended to take its blarney at face value. The coverage in the *Manila Freedom* of the performance for Taft featured the front-page headline "'The Dreamed Alliance' A Brilliant Success" and a lead paragraph that announced that the opera "which has been given to the world by Pedro A. Paterno . . . will undoubtedly go down into history as one of the best ever written by a Filipino" (1). This is something of a misrepresentation, as at that moment it was the only opera ever written by a Filipino. The reviewer also gushed that "the music of the opera is inspiring and created much favorable comment among the brilliant throng of American men and women who were present" (1). This would seem to speak very well of Paterno, who is foregrounded in the article. However, the composer of the music was actually Ladislao Bonus, a fact not tacked on until the last paragraph. With regard to the people in attendance, the journalist added that "there was a very distinguished audience present, among whom were observed the Civil Commissioners and the Executive Secretary and ladies and a great number of Army officers. The comments, as the audience left the house, were most favorable and Senor Paterno is to be congratulated on writing an opera which promises to live for ever among the Filipino people" (7). The prediction proved wrong.

A front-page review of the gala performance in the *Manila Times* was also positive, albeit not hyperbolically so, commenting that "the theatre was well filled, both with Americans and Filipinos, the occasion evidently being regarded as of unusual interest . . . The Dreamed Alliance, taken as a whole, may be considered a very good production for these islands" ("The Play" 1). An assessment in *La democracia*, a pro-American Filipino newspaper, was critical about certain elements of the premiere several weeks earlier but concluded, "En resumen, la ópera resultó bastante aceptable. Por tal motivo felicitamos á los autores . . . el paso que han dado estimulará seguramente á genios musicales inactivos hasta hoy. Con doble motivo, pues, hemos de enviar nuestra felicitación á los Sres. Bonus y Paterno. Que sigan adelante" ["In summary, the opera ended up being sufficiently acceptable. For that reason we congratulate the authors . . . the step that they have taken will surely stimulate musical tempers that have been inactive until now. For a doubled reason, therefore, we have to send our congratulations to Messrs. Bonus and Paterno. May they continue forward"] ("La Opera" 3).

In all these praises are holes of a most gaping kind. It is not a coincidence that both of the Americans who wrote the above reviews remarked that they and their compatriots in the audience had no idea what was actually being proclaimed on stage. The Filipinos who issued the Spanish-language paper said nothing of the sort. Thus the reporter for the *Manila Freedom*, right after hailing "the brilliant throng of American men and women who were present," cheerfully observed that "it is an opera, that even if many who listened to it did not understand, would be enjoyed on account of the rhyme and the beautiful voices composing the chorus" ("The Dreamed Alliance' a Brilliant Success" 1). That chorus, however, might not have sounded so "beautiful" had the reviewer known it was shouting "Long live our Liberty!" in Tagalog (26). The journalist of the *Manila Times*, a bit more self-aware, admitted that "a knowledge of Tagalog would doubtless give a better appreciation to Americans of some parts of the extravaganza, which of course appears meaningless to those ignorant of that language" ("The Play" 1). The ironic spaces in which Paterno was working were uncommonly large. At a linguistic level, the distinguished colonial crowd that enjoyed and acclaimed the night of theater had little or no idea what they had just heard. Culturally too they were clueless or next to it, out of touch with the acute attention to allegory of so many Filipino plays of the time. But the opposite was true of the Filipinos in the crowd, whether elite collaborationists or petit bourgeois ticketholders or poor Katipunan sympathizers sweeping the aisles and selling foodstuffs. All of them understood the Tagalog, and all of them knew the theatrical environment of the era in ways that Taft and the other Americans did not. The dissonance among potential interpretations of the play was therefore profound. Merely presenting *The Dreamed Alliance* in a local language when an English translation was available for performing was an unrecognized statement in itself. It was a deliberate nod by Paterno toward indigenous autonomy and a direct rejection of the need to be comprehended by colonialists. The staged Tagalog version was a translation too, after all, so the decision by Paterno to put on the opera in an island idiom rather than in the Spanish of his original script or the English of the occupiers, that is, either imperial tongue, was a calculated one.

The aggregate presence of multiple printed versions of *The Dreamed Alliance* in Spanish, English, and Tagalog confounds any attempt to arrive at conclusions about the opera as an organic text with a definitive ideology. Although all the librettos were published in 1902, it is unclear whether one or more of them appeared prior to the August performances and therefore could have framed the show for theatergoers ahead of time. No known press reports indicate that any of the librettos were circulated publicly beforehand, but this does not settle the question one way or another. The Spanish version was surely the one overseen most closely by Paterno—he did not speak English, after all, nor Tagalog well enough to translate his own writings—and in fact was printed by an entity, "Estab. Tipográfico de M. Paterno y Comp." ["Typographical Estab. of M. Paterno and Co."] named after his own father or brother.[18] Paterno could have cranked out (perhaps literally) this publication at any point, just by, say, going downstairs. Throughout his life, he certainly leaped at every opportunity to publicize himself. And some script in Spanish, if not the final published one, had to exist before the August performances, because that was the language in which Paterno composed the opera.

A Tagalog version also had to exist prior to August 1902, though again, not necessarily the published one, since that was the language in which the opera was staged. And once a script in Tagalog circulated among the actors, the barrier to bringing it to print would have been small. A desire by Paterno to bolster his own refurbished Filipino identifications, which were always suspect, likely explains as well why a Tagalog libretto was published. Paterno had not arranged for his many pre-1898 works in Spanish to be translated into Tagalog, but back then he was intent on being a Spaniard as well as a Filipino. Back then, moreover, his audience was men in Madrid more than men in Manila. Things, as Dylan points out, have changed. Paterno found a Tagalog translator for the published version of *The Dreamed Alliance*, Roman Reyes, who later would do the same job for various other Paterno texts in the next half dozen years.[19]

As for the English translation, the most likely reason for its creation would have been for vetting by the vigorous American censorship apparatus before the opera premiere, or at the very least before the gala performance for Taft. The translator of the English version, W. H. [Walter Howard] Loving, was a complex figure in his own right as an African American son of former slaves who had risen to become director of the band of the Philippines Constabulary, a police and surveillance force run by the United States. Loving would later lead that band at the 1904 St. Louis Exposition, a world's fair at which Paterno's subsequent opera *Magdapio* was slated to be performed. Eventually, Loving would also play important roles in domestic American intelligence operations as the "leading expert on 'Negro subversion'" (McCoy 313).[20] Once Paterno made it known that he was putting on an opera, the normal functioning of the colonial authorities would have been to respond quickly by arranging an English translation of its libretto for the purposes of sniffing out any subversion. Paterno, of course, had already had a rather dramatic speech of his translated into English by the regime so that Taft could personally censor it before the July 1900 banquet. Paterno was a marked man in more ways than one.

Nevertheless, the various differences among the published versions of *The Dreamed Alliance* in Spanish, Tagalog, and English do not square with the supposition of an English version that was ordered and approved before the August run. Surprisingly, it is the English text that is the most revolutionary, the most likely to raise concern among colonial officials ahead of time. It achieves this distinction by excluding the references to a dreamed alliance that, in the Spanish original, indicate that the eponymous union is between Americans and Filipinos, not just among the latter. In other words, there is no confusion in the English translation about the fact that the alliance entails an entirely Filipino pact. To wit, in the plot synopsis that precedes the main text in the Spanish libretto, Paterno refers to "la nueva constelación de las estrellas americanas, mostrando *alianza fraternal* de E. U. de A. guiada por las deidades hacia Filipinas" ["the new constellation of American stars, showing *fraternal alliance* with the U. S. of A. guided by the deities toward the Philippines"] (unnumbered page). The italics stress that this transpacific alliance is the union to which the title of the opera alludes. In the English version by Loving, however, the italicized phrase and its explicit signaling of the United States disappears altogether. The synopsis now speaks only of "the new constellation of American stars steered by the goddesses toward the Philippines"] (unnumbered page). A comparable cut is made after Lapu wakes up from a dream sequence that ends, in the Spanish version, with the Statue of Liberty appearing onstage while the orchestra strikes up the national anthem of the United States and a comet transforms into a field of stars like that on the American flag (9). In the Spanish text, this is when Lapu interprets his dream as revealing the presence of "un pueblo nuevo y poderoso de allende los mares, que nos tiende sus manos en muestra de alianza fraternal" ["a new and powerful people from beyond the seas who extends its hands to us in a show of fraternal alliance"] (9). In the English translation by Loving, however, this sentence is absent. The omission again of the key phrase "fraternal alliance" shifts the interpretive possibilities of the opera title away from union with the United States and toward the union of Filipinos that is emphasized in the plot itself. In the English libretto, the newly arrived foreigners still appear as benevolent patrons of the Philippines, but that appearance is now deeply backgrounded. From the synopsis and the title page onward, the focus is much more clearly on the locals who take power into their own hands.

The Spanish version, consequently, pushes more the idea that the alliance dreamed by Lapu is with the Americans. It also culminates with Filipinos hugging the Statue of Liberty (28). This would have comforted Taft and the colonial regime, but of course Spanish was not their lingua franca any more than Tagalog. In the English translation by Loving, there are no final stage directions that indicate a literal embrace by Filipinos of the Statue of Liberty. It is not until the brief final act, subtitled as an epilogue, that the phrase "fraternal alliance" surfaces in the English libretto to refer to a union of Filipinos with Americans (22). Given this extremely belated appearance and its organic irrelevance to the preceding plot, the multiple mentions of "alliance" in the final act as a transpacific bond feel like a fig leaf. Indeed, in that same epilogue, the words "alliance" and "allies" refer more often to the newly formed ties among the Filipino villagers (21–22).[21] And in the final passages of the just concluded fourth act, "alliance" and "allied" and "allies" appear seven times in the English translation and in all cases refer exclusively to the union of Filipinos (19–20).

The question of who is allying with whom is less clear in the misreadable subtleties of the Tagalog translation by Reyes. Its startlingly different title, *Sangdugong Panaguinip*, that is, *The Dreamed Blood Compact*, points purposefully to a storied historical episode that is otherwise not explicitly alluded to in the play. The episode features Miguel López de Legazpi, who commanded the transpacific fleet in 1564–65 that established continuous Spanish settlement in the archipelago, and Sikatuna, an indigenous leader on the central Philippine island of Bohol. The foundational narrative here is that after meeting, Legazpi and Sikatuna pledged mutual allegiance by drawing blood from their respective arms, mixing it with each other's libations, and drinking up. This is a famous moment in archipelagic lore that signifies solidarity, even friendship, between Filipinos and foreigners. It would seem to correlate well to the fact that the Tagalog libretto does include the two passages about a fraternal alliance with the United States that appear in the Spanish version but disappear in the English version. At the same time, though, the titular blood compact of the Tagalog translation is not so easy to interpret at all. For one, it seems unlikely that Taft or most other Americans in the audience, given their deep ignorance of Filipino languages and culture and history, would have caught the allusion to the Legazpi/Sikatuna accord. But even if they did recognize it, they would have rejected any implication that Americans now played the role of Spaniards in the islands. The whole premise of the American presence was that it was entirely the opposite of that. And most importantly, while the title of the Tagalog text refers to an alliance between Filipinos and foreigners, the narrative of the opera still does not. The characters who cut their arms, merge their blood with an elixir, and drink it in the name of union are all Filipinos. The title leads the Americans toward pretensions of solidarity. The text leads Filipinos toward intentions of subversion.

It is difficult to reconcile the contrary tendencies of the published librettos and argue convincingly for their order of appearance and the consequent causalities of their contents. Perhaps the most likely conjecture is that, whether before or during or soon after the August performances of *The Dreamed Alliance*, Paterno released the Spanish version first—it was the one whose composition and publication he most controlled—and shortly thereafter the Tagalog translation; and that the English translation was not made, for whatever the reason, before the run; but that after the successful reception of the opera, Paterno was emboldened enough to give a Spanish version to Loving for a translation that left out some of the early sycophantic framings while retaining, as a rear-guard defense, the final hailings of a fraternal alliance with the United States. Regardless, it seems certain, the lines that were actually uttered in the Tagalog performance for Taft will remain impossible to determine. The same goes for the body language of the actors, the manipulation of any lighting, the spatial arrangement of particular props, and other potentially signifying paratext.

But of course, no one understood much about *The Dreamed Alliance* the night of its gala performance either. As the Americans filed happily out to their after-show parties and palaver, they had no idea that America itself had just been redefined in the most revolutionary of ways. And that was true not only of America but of the century. The opera by Paterno is critical to comprehending the overseas rise of the United States and the globalization to which it predominantly is tantamount. The play would not have existed without the advent of American imperialism across the world, and it is meaningful beyond melodrama only within the context of an oppressive American administration. The man who led that administration and legalized death for those who opposed it would use the Philippines as his stepping stone to becoming secretary of war of the United States, then president, then chief justice of the Supreme Court. Pedro Paterno wrote within and against the Taft regime and so is part of the history of America as well as of the Philippines. He is a founding father of the modern United States even though his position as such is complicated due to his elite Europhile education, his unstable relationships to successive stages of indigenous revolt, and his long-standing dedication to the previous empire to run the archipelago and execute local dissidents. Paterno authored America after the turn of the century as much as Taft, both of them rewriting the United States in the Philippines in mutually definitive productions of invasion and resistance that resonate still a century and counting later. The crowd who watched the dramas playing out in the theater, the actors who waged those dramas on stage and in the box of honor, would all appear around the world in other moments, in other scenes, in other theaters, but in the same long-running show. And that show goes on still.

No audience for *The Dreamed Alliance* exists today. The opera is never staged, and few copies of the librettos are known to exist. Two pages of its arias were once published in an entry for the composer Ladislao Bonus in a biographical dictionary ("Bonus," pages inset between 60–61). The rest of the score, if extant, is held offline somewhere; as of 1970, it was reported to survive with the heirs of one of Paterno's sisters ("Bonus" 59). Scholarship on the opera and on other post-1898 creative writings by Paterno is next to nil, notwithstanding a range of good books on the Philippines of the era and the common assumption of academics today of the value and political relevance of cultural studies investigations.[22] But even if *The Dreamed Alliance* were readily available, few in the Philippines could read the original Spanish of this exemplar of what Lapeña-Bonifacio calls "our bravest chapter of Philippine theatre" (vi). The anglicization of the archipelago by the United States in the first half of the 20th century, along with the apocalyptic Japanese takeover of the islands during World War II, eliminated Spanish as a lingua franca among most Filipinos whose families once spoke it.

The opera, nevertheless, remains relevant both to the Philippines and to the century at large. And so its languages should no more restrict its circulation in Manila than in Manhattan. *The Dreamed Alliance* should be put on stage once more, this time in front of coastal American power as well as overseas American power. Perhaps this time the gala performance would ring closer to home. Perhaps this time the subversions of a sub-version would be understood. There are still American troops in the Philippines, operating there with the explicit aim of crushing Muslim forces in a battle against what Washington today refers to as terrorism and what Washington yesterday referred to as sedition. Taft still watches an opera rendered in various codes that he does not comprehend. Paterno still interrupts a revolution bearing gifts of gold, ascending to the box of honor, trailed by a native retinue. Filipinos, filtering the dramas before them, still fidget below. Foreign powers still arrive at distant capitals, and local people still kneel in homage and rise in response. Teddy Roosevelt, pumping his chest about the Philippines in 1899, still harangues, "Resistance must be stamped out" (188). The story of the United States is a global one and the dream of Lapu Lapu, if not that of Lapu, presents an alternate narrative in its stead. There are times to navigate a nightmare that has descended, times to negotiate through it, but there are also times, at once subtle and resounding, to dramatize a dream in its place.

two

Theatrics of Resistance

Pedro Paterno's *Magdapio* and Other
Performances (1903–1905)

The second American colonial governor of the Philippines topped off his first
day in office by attending an anti-American opera. On February 1, 1904, as his
predecessor William Taft assumed his new posting as U.S. secretary of war
on the other side of the world, Luke E. Wright sat down at 8:30 p.m. as the
guest of honor at a special showing of *Magdapio*, the latest composition by
Pedro Paterno. As with the gala performance of *The Dreamed Alliance* for Taft
nearly a year and a half earlier, Paterno presented an opus written in Spanish
but performed in Tagalog as an ostensible homage to the leader of the American occupation. Once again Paterno fawned over the star guest. Once again
that guest understood few if any of the words in the play. And once again the
stage offered a spectacular melodrama about virginal bodies long ago.

This time, though, the allegory was more apparent to both the Americans
and Filipinos in the audience. Most significantly, a patriarch strode about
stage in a robe emblazoned with the insignia of the Katipunan, the militant
Filipino organization that had burst into revolution against Spain in 1896
and subsequently against the United States. And the heroine of the opera,
a maiden who symbolized the Philippines, threw herself into the sea rather
than be ravished by the head of a foreign occupying force. The message to the
American colonial regime could not have been clearer. Yet this was not the
first performance of *Magdapio*, and so Wright, like Taft, was aware to some
extent of what he was going to see. He crowned his rise to power with the
opera anyway. Perhaps, then, the message was not clear at all. And Paterno,

as usual with him, probably misunderstood much of it too. This was likely the case as well with the next two operas he produced, *On the Arrival of Taft* and *Gayuma*. In all three shows, and in all the offstage performances of Paterno in person and in print during those years, the visions of colonizers and colonized alike blurred with blindnesses of eye-opening kinds.

What Paterno discerned and what he did not in any given moment or text is never possible to determine. He could not have figured himself out had he tried, which, being an individual prone to the opposite of introspection, he probably did not. He was so dextrous at doublespeak that he surely believed half of it and then some. All the time, he honeyfuggled himself as much as anyone else. Thus in August 1903, barely a year after *The Dreamed Alliance* premiered and just a few months before *Magdapio* appeared, he signed an editorial in his journalistic organ, *La patria* (*The Fatherland*), that at once conceded power and did nothing of the sort:

> Nuestra política obedece á la realidad. La realidad nos muestra que la soberania americana se halla establecida en el Archipiélago, abriendo nueva era en el desenvolvimiento del pueblo filipino. El Gobernador Taft inaugura esa nueva era.
>
> Nuestra publicación genuinamente filipina, por nativas y valiosas que sean sus propias convicciones se supedita á la *suprema ratio Taft* que impera y se traduce en ley, y siendo ley, fuerza es acatarla.
>
> LA PATRIA desea vivamente ayudar al Gobierno Taft, á fin de que, con el órden, la concordia y armonía de paz completa, se establezca cuanto ántes la *Asamblea filipina*, fundamento del *Gobierno propio y responsable.*
>
> Hay que confesar desde luego, que como hombres y hombres nuevos en la Administración, hija de la mayor República democrática y descentralizadora, jamás enseñada en el país, hemos de caer en faltas; pero, sin duda, involuntarias, pues en sirviéndose advertirnos el Gobierno Taft, ya que tan amante de los filipinos y tan humanitario procede, veráse en nosotros la rectificación, la enmienda inmediata, con que demostraremos la buena fé y la lealtad de nuesros [*sic*] actos." ("La nueva" 1)

[Our politics obey reality. Reality shows us that American sovereignty finds itself established in the Archipelago, opening a new era in the development of the Filipino people. Governor Taft inaugurates that new era.

Our genuinely Filipino publication, native and valuable as its own convictions may be, is subject to the *supreme reasoning of Taft*, which prevails and is translated into law, and being law, it is necessary (forced) to obey it.

THE FATHERLAND desires intensely to help Governor Taft so that with the order, concord, and harmony of complete peace, the *Filipino Assembly* be established as soon as possible, the foundation of the *Government that is our own and in charge*.

One must confess of course that as men and new men in the Administration, daughter of the oldest democratic and decentralizing Republic, never trained in the country, we will necessarily commit slipups, but, without a doubt, involuntary ones, and since the Taft Government will be so kind as to inform us, since it is so loving of Filipinos and proceeds in such a humanitarian fashion, it will see in us rectification, immediate correction, with which we will demonstrate good faith and the loyalty of our acts.]

For a figure regarded by contemporaries and historians alike as a bloviator and betrayer—Paterno is often dismissed as a hoity-toity hispanophile who sold out the earlier uprising against Spain—he seems instead here remarkably rebellious in his obeisance. Unctuous and uxorious as ever, kneeling before his Zod in hopes of "the order, concord, and harmony of complete peace," he brandishes even as he blandishes. He pushes for self-government for his land while pushing himself into the ground. He recognizes American rule only because it is reality. He pledges to be an extremely dutiful subject of a regime to which he clearly does not wish to be dutiful. This is a tractable and traitorous stance. His treachery now is not to the pre-1898 Filipino revolution against Spain but to the post-1898 rule of the United States. But at the same time, there is enough cloying cant in his capitulations to keep an insular colonialist content. There are enough pretensions to good faith and loyalty. It is, indeed, quite a show. So too are his operas. And Paterno loved being the star of a show. He especially loved being its creator, impresario, and shill as well. And he seems to have bought everything that he sold.

Saddling Up

Magdapio was probably written and translated not long after this conciliatory and combative August 1903 editorial, since its first public showing took place the subsequent January. The official broadsheet program for the second public showing, the one for Wright in February, nevertheless stressed that deference, continuity, and comprehension were going to be the markers of the evening. Four photos border the left and bottom margins of the program, with the topmost and largest headshot being that of Wright. The caption proclaims him to be the civil governor of the Philippines, a title he had held for less than a day (Riggs, *Filipino* 338). A nearby subheading announces that he would attend the show along with Mrs. Luke E. Wright (Riggs, *Filipino* 338). The photo below that of Wright features Ladislao Bonus, the composer of *The Dreamed Alliance* but not of *Magdapio*. The decision by Paterno to publicize an upcoming opera by highlighting the composer of a previous opera appears illogical only initially. The caption below the photo of Bonus clarifies the matter by noting that the musical talent behind *The Dreamed Alliance* has penned a new *Magdapio* song especially for the gala performance for Wright.[1] In short, the civil governor is gone, long live the new civil governor. The same composer who had written music for Taft now has returned to write music for his successor.

Seamless political and cultural transitions are suggested throughout the rest of the broadsheet as well. A photo of Alejo Carluen, the composer of the rest of *Magdapio*, appears below the image of Bonus. Carluen also had ties to *The Dreamed Alliance* as "the musical director of the orchestra" for its performances ("Molina" 285). And the last photo on the program is that of Paterno himself, bow-tied and debonair, gazing suavely at the onlooker. These visual and verbal codings collectively reassure readers that harmonious order reigns despite the change in reins from Taft to Wright. The broadsheet also points out that *Magdapio* has been translated into English by "General Henry T. Allen" and into Tagalog by Roman Reyes, who also had translated *The Dreamed Alliance* into Tagalog (Riggs, *Filipino* 338). In other words, the whole gang is back in the saddle: Paterno, Bonus, Carluen, and Reyes. The only thing is, of all these usual suspects, none of them was suspect. The translation of General Allen and the presence of Governor Wright confirmed it. The official program of the show assuages any assumptions of authorial unrest. And yet allegorical agitprop is about to arrive onstage.

The plot of *Magdapio* at first seems fairly straightforward and apolitical. The opera opens with a chorus announcing that, on Mount Magdapio, "los árboles crecen con toda libertad; nadie impide su frondosidad y desarrollo. Mirad sus anchas hojas y sus flores que pregonan la riqueza de su savia, jamas ceñida á otras leyes que á las de la naturaleza" ["the trees grow in all liberty; nobody impedes their abundance and development. Look at their wide leaves and their flowers that proclaim the richness of their sap, never adhering to laws other than those of nature"] (7; all translations herein are original and made from the Spanish, not reproduced from the Allen libretto).[2] The trees are not alone in their richness of sap, for that is an apt description as well of the maiden Magdapio who lives inside the mountain. She is akin to plants who "al llegar a su perfecto desarrollo lo demuestran con su florecimiento y con sus frutos" ["upon arriving at their perfect development show it with their flowering and with their fruits"] (8). Her time has come to "respirar esa libertad de que goza el pajaro . . . poder disfrutar de la dicha de vivir" ["breathe that liberty which the bird enjoys . . . to be able to enjoy the happiness of living"] (8). This happiness of living turns out to involve being deflowered by Mapalad, chief of the indigenous Aetas (8). Mapalad has never met Magdapio, but the youths are destined to be together. The earthquake god Lindol parts Mount Magdapio in two and reveals to Mapalad its beautiful resources of precious metals and a precious virgin. The Aetan lad then declares, "Como primeros ocupantes de esta abertura de monte á nadie mas que á nosotros pertenecen esas riquezas" ["Since we are the first occupants of this mountain opening, these riches belong to no one more than to us"] (9). This exciting scene is then suddenly interrupted by war cries from an invading army of Malays and their god Baguio. They declare that Mount Magdapio belongs to them. The Aetas and their god Arao announce that they shall defeat the Malays.[3] So ends the first act.

The second act leaves the impending battle behind to foreground the encounter of Mapalad with Magdapio beneath the benevolent well-wishes of Botokan, her father. The lovers are overjoyed with each other. In ecstasy, "MAPALAD coje la mano de MAGDAPIO y le invita pasar el riachuelo para dirijirse al lecho nupcial y cuando los amantes dan el primer paso, una lluvia de flechas tiradas por enemigos ocultos cae" ["MAPALAD takes the hand of MAGDAPIO and invites her to cross the stream in order to head to the nuptial bed, and when the lovers take the first step, a rain of arrows shot by hidden enemies falls"] (13). Sex in Paterno, as usual, is rapturously unconsummated at the last possible moment. A wounded Mapalad falls into the arms of Magdapio, who promptly faints. Botokan also falls wounded, and Magdapio is seized by the arriving Malay archers. As the scene concludes, according to Paterno in his stage directions, "Tratese de imitar en todo el rapto de las Sabinas" ["Everything tries to imitate the rape of the Sabines"] (13). Actually, there is only one pseudo Sabine here, Magdapio, and there is no Romulus figure apparent. But Paterno was never a stickler for detail or, for that matter, accuracy or coherence, so a rape of the Sabines it is.

The third act of the opera begins with King Bay of the Malays "recibiendo a varios pueblos que le rinden tributo y dan gracias al Dios Tempestad [Baguio]" ["receiving various villages that pay tribute to him and give thanks to the God Tempest [Baguio]"] (14). All the Malays in court are thrilled because Magdapio is en route, slated to become their queen. To their dismay, when she arrives and awakens from her faint and learns of this plan, she rejects King Bay and declares eternal love for Mapalad.[4] The foreign monarch, outraged, orders the body of the Aetan swain to be thrown "al mar para ser pasto de los caimanes" ["to the sea to be food for the alligators"] and "como tributo rendido al Dios Baguio, la Tespestad [*sic*]" ["as a tribute paid to the God Baguio, the Tempest"] (16). Magdapio, distraught, hurls herself into the depths after him. The fourth and very brief final act consequently takes place at the bottom of a large lake, Laguna de Bay. This underwater environment neatly complements the rainbow in which the protagonists perch in the last act of *The Dreamed Alliance*. Baguio, now referred to as the "Dios del mar" ["God of the sea"] sits in his throne as "un Caiman arroja el cuerpo de MAG-DAPIO" ["an Alligator hurls the body of MAGDAPIO"] at his feet (16). Baguio admires the beauty of the dead virgin and asks her why she has come hither. She explains. This would seem to be information that he likely already knew, but so it goes. Baguio listens with unexpected thoughtfulness and promises to reward her fidelity to Mapalad by making her "la Reina del Mar de Oriente" ["the Queen of the Oriental Sea"] (16).[5] And . . . curtain.

In place in *Magdapio* are therefore many of the same elements as in *The Dreamed Alliance*. Here again, for example, is a military contest over a beautiful land and beautiful virginal bodies. *Magdapio*, though, seems more removed from contemporary concerns than the previous opera. The plot is set much further back in history, and there are no explicit references to the United States at all. And yet Arthur Stanley Riggs, an American who saw the performance for Wright, asserts that "almost every one of the more important characters was nearly enough seditious to make the Americans in the audience restless and decidedly uneasy, for the governor himself was present" (*Filipino* 336). How could this seemingly silly opera be so taken, particularly when it was performed in Tagalog? It is hard to imagine that Governor Wright or many of his colonial cronies in the theater had become fluent enough in that language to follow any subtleties on stage. And had they sensed subversion ahead of time from reading the English translation by Allen, the performance never would have been allowed to proceed in the first place. Wright certainly would not have allowed himself to be publicized ahead of time as the featured guest. Furthermore, the opera had been staged once already, and the known media reviews of that premiere do not speak of its sedition at all. All its American observers, in other words, apparently observed nothing. Yet Teofilo del Castillo y Tuazon, writing three decades later, states without reserve that "an excellent illustration of the way in which the later dramatists preached the doctrine of revolution is to be found in the play *Magdapio* by Pedro A. Paterno. Although the characters have mythical names, this play was so revolutionary in content that it was supressed [*sic*] by the American Government" (197). Castillo y Tuazon may be inaccurate on the last point, as no known documents indicate that the reason *Magdapio* was not performed after the show for Wright is because the regime shut it down for subversion. But how could his conclusion that *Magdapio* "preached the doctrine of revolution" square with the melodramatic malarkey of its plot and the willingness of Wright to watch it in the first place?

Bad Reviews

For starters, the media reception of *Magdapio* reveals that the meaning of the opera was deduced differently depending on where its audiences, actors, and author stood. Since those standings themselves could be internally inconsistent and, moreover, adjust as the show underwent all sorts of alterations, the range of interpretive possibilities is represented more by the panorama of press reports than the literal tale told by any of the librettos. For instance, the day after Wright saw the opera, a scathing review appeared in the *Manila Cablenews* by the dubiously monikered Jack O'Lantern.[6] The subheadline referred to *Magdapio* as the "Queerest Operetta Ever Perpetrated" and O'Lantern opined that "the acting was almost as bad as has ever been seen in Providence . . . some of the costumes were remarkable. Not for their beauty was this the case, but because they were, to be truthful, ugly" (5). He specified, however, that "the one objectionable feature of the piece" was "the turning of a stiff and ungainly ballet of six in the third act into a disgusting and silly hoochee-hoochee, done by young women" (5). An anonymous blurb in the *Manila Cablenews* the next day judged that "Pedro Paterno's opera was not a success. The Filipino is possessed of great musical gifts but they seem to be those of imitation and not originality. Pedro's operas will never set the world on fire" ("Pedro Paterno's opera" 4]. Riggs, writing with a bit more élan, averred that *Magdapio* offers "the spectacle of the noble art of the drama fallen to its lowest ebb of meaningless words, banal effects, and total weakness, without a single feature to redeem it from utter flaccidness and intellectual senility . . . if it may be judged from the dramatic standards the Filipinos themselves have set in their plays during the past three or four years, this latest work of any importance may safely be declared the worst of all, and representative of nothing more substantial than the egregious vanity of the men responsible for it" (*Filipino* 334). He added that the dancing interlude was "revolting . . . wild and disgusting" (*Filipino* 336). Based on such verdicts, Resil Mojares concludes that *Magdapio* "was a pathetic coda to Paterno's career" and "bizarre" (*Brains* 40, 41).[7] He also writes that the play "was badly mangled by the Manila press and failed to draw much of an audience" (*Brains* 39).

None of this is true. Or, rather, it is all half true, and it is the other half that counts more toward any nuanced understanding of how global American power played out in the 20th century and why Filipino literature in Spanish redefines the United States. To begin with, the O'Lantern and Riggs reviews are far more complicated in import than their own authors recognize. Despite himself, O'Lantern acknowledges in his lead paragraph that the hoochee-hoochee, which he took to be horribly lurid, was in fact "twice encored, the plaudits fairly drowning out all of the hissing and opposition" (5). So who was applauding and who was catcalling? It turns out that the young women doing the hoochee-hoochee "were egged on by the frantic howls and hoots of the crowd, many of whom seemed thoroughly to appreciate the exhibition, and which brought back the 'dancers,' or rather wooden contortionists, to answer two calls. A deadly silence pervaded one or two of the boxes during this episode, and a good many hisses were heard as the crowd woke up to the fact that the governor and his lady were displeased with what was evidently intended to be a star feature" (5). The dance, in other words, created a space of open challenge to authority. The Filipino audience, whom O'Lantern animalizes with his depiction of "frantic howls and hoots," takes a stand against the disciplinary silencings of Wright and, well, his lady.

The Filipinos are literally pitted against the colonial governor here, for O'Lantern notes that "the pit was filled solidly, where it was full at all, with natives. None of the richer or more prominent of the native element were out either" (5). In other words, as the American colonial governor watched a play put on specifically for him on the day of his inauguration, a moment appeared when the show itself repelled him. The nonelite Filipinos who were in attendance celebrated that same moment, their endorsement rising from below to the displeased powers in the box of honor. The politics of these nonelites may have aligned closely with those of the Katipunan, the revolutionary movement that drew its supporters from the lower urban classes as well as the peasantry. After all, the seditious plays in Tagalog that were staged at the start of the American colonial era were primarily an urban phenomenon. Some of the Filipinos in the pit at the *Magdapio* showing for Wright probably had attended anti-American dramas in Manila already and knew how to interpret this one. The primary differences here were of setting and occasion more than content, for those other plays usually took place in clandestine, relatively informal stages as far away as possible from the eyes of the American security apparatus. In *Magdapio*, however, the show went on before the head apparatchik himself and in a prominent, formal Manila theater. Meanwhile, the elite Filipinos who had chummed up to the colonial administration were absent in the audience. This meant that their possible interventions as assimilationist middlemen were not part of the dynamics that night. The fissures between the locals and their overlord were wide. So too were their reactions. Whatever Wright expected to see by way of entertainment the evening of his inauguration, it was certainly not, as Castillo y Tuazon would describe *Magdapio* and other plays in 1937, an opera "written for the specific purpose of arousing the revolutionary spirit" (210).

On the contrary, Paterno and Carluen came on stage halfway through the show in order to venerate the American colonial governor. According to Jack O'Lantern, Paterno appeared "scraping and smirking" and waved his arm at the troupe and proclaimed, "I thank you. All the applause and thanks we have received, tonight, we lay at the feet of that most estimable lady, Mrs. Wright'" (5). His eager adherence to newly enthroned order, however, runs counter to the many elements of the opera that made it a rather unstable presentation before Wright and his consort. For instance, the play was performed in Tagalog, not in its English translation or, for that matter, its original Spanish, which meant that neither Wright nor Paterno could follow exactly what was going on. Paterno, though a Filipino raised in the Philippines, did not know the local language well enough to write in it or to translate his own texts into it. And Wright certainly could not understand Tagalog. As O'Lantern notes, "The words were, of course, unintelligible to the white men present" (5). Any direct voicings from colonized subjects to their colonial rulers are always bound to appear in an opaque space in which anticolonial sentiment can be at once partially transmitted and partially obscured. In the case of the *Magdapio* performance for Wright, however, the ironic potentials of ambiguity were especially great because the colonial ruler could not even comprehend the literal words spoken to him. And whatever the governor might glean from acting and intonation, blocking and orchestration, would surely be insufficient to inferring the extent of any insurrection under way. Wright must have been familiar with American press reports about the premiere of *Magdapio* several weeks earlier, but those reviews display no grasp of the allegorical politics of the play. He also must have read the English translation of

Magdapio prepared by General Allen. But that text did not contain costume notes or stage directions that implied rebellion to the colonial order that Wright now personified. It did contain symbolic contestations in abundance, but such subtleties are rarely sensed by censors, wherever and whenever they set their sights.

O'Lantern notes that since the January 8 premiere of *Magdapio*, which took place nearly a month before the performance for Wright, the costumes of various cast members "had been changed somewhat and some of the characters set down in the program failed to appear, while several details of 'business' and by-play were altered, cut out entirely or changed so completely as to make it impossible to recognize them for the same" (5).[8] Since it is a costume, the patriarchal robe in revolutionary Katipunan colors, that is the primary political sign that Wright would have been able to recognize, the wardrobe metamorphoses in between the two *Magdapio* performances seem particularly meaningful. Wright attended the opera as a way of sealing his new status as the American ruler of the Philippines. He could not have anticipated that the clothing of a character would communicate a message opposite to that of the official opera program. Nor could he have foreseen the hoochee-hoochee. And his tightlipped disapproval of the Filipino dancers was certain to be observed by media in attendance. Yet it was those same dancers who garnered the most favorable response from the lower-class locals in the audience. O'Lantern and Riggs dismiss the crowd reaction as crass, but that is a prudish construal laced with the inherent racism of assuming tropical peoples to be lewd brutes. Perhaps the dancers actually signified to the Filipino crowd something rather different, such as freedom of movement in an unfree land. The hoochee-hoochee obviously unsettled the Americans in attendance for its liberated content and its liberal audience. The new governor could not govern any of this.

In a larger sense, Wright could not govern *Magdapio* because the opera as a single coherent text did not exist. There were at least five versions of *Magdapio*—three written, two performed—competing in the space before Wright that night, all of them crashing against his ken. There was the original version in Spanish, published in (presumably late) 1903. The Tagalog translation of *Magdapio* by Reyes was directly made from the Spanish and also was published in 1903 (Riggs, *Filipino* 337). The English translation by Allen was produced straight from the Spanish too and "privately printed" by him, in 1903 as well (Riggs, *Filipino* 337; Castillo y Tuazon 238).[9] Allen was head of the Philippines Constabulary, which Alfred McCoy describes as "an almost accidental creation born of a brutal colonial pacification that could not succeed without an adaptable force of Filipino soldiers under American leadership . . . the constabulary's mission was twofold: first, disarm the countryside using paramilitary patrols to capture both guerrillas and their rifles strewn by the revolution; and, second, secure the capital using intelligence operatives to round up subversives and monitor radical nationalists" (82).[10] Troop leader and translator were parallel roles in service of this same American colonial repression. As Paul Rodell notes, "The military government assumed the duty of suppressing seditious drama as part of its campaign of 'pacification.' Brigadier General Henry T. Allen as the Chief of the Constabulary, was put in charge of this activity" (103). Riggs recalls with admiration that "General Henry T. Allen's task as Chief of Constabulary was exceedingly difficult. To raid, suppress the plays, and jail the participants, he had to move with unusual speed" ("Seditious" 204).

Allen, who is buried in Arlington National Cemetery for a globalized military career that would peak with high command in World War I, was closely attuned to possible subversion from his position in the Constabulary. According to McCoy, "The real achievements of its founder and first chief, Henry Allen, lay not in his storied combat operations but in the less visible realm of political intelligence. From his years of prior service in the Military Information Division and as a military attaché in czarist Russia, Allen had gained the experience needed to make the constabulary's Information Section an effective secret police" (104). In fact, this was the second time in a row that an English translation of a Paterno opera had emerged from that policing force. Walter Loving, leader of the Constabulary band, had produced the English version of *The Dreamed Alliance*. The primary intended reader of both opera translations was almost certainly the highest American authority in the islands, that is, first Taft and then Wright. The American century thus starts with the surveillance of plays and playwrights. But scanning a script for subversion is one thing. Seeing it is another.

Given the circulations of the various librettos of *Magdapio* in late 1903, just about everyone in Manila who was literate in any of the three languages then dominant among power brokers in the capital could have been exposed to the opera before its debut on January 8, 1904. This was a drama that everyone saw coming. At the same time, *Magdapio* was evidently in constant flux. To that degree, no one saw it coming at all. There are notable differences among the versions in Spanish, English, and Tagalog, such as swaths of dialogue that are present or absent depending on the text. Plus, there is no reason to think that the premiere hewed particularly close to any of the published scripts, including the Tagalog version by Reyes. The second show, the one for Wright, was definitely dissimilar to its predecessor in its text, paratext, and score. All the published versions of *Magdapio*, including those translations from Spanish created for this book, cannot help but misrepresent the unrecuperable texts of what was actually spoken on stage in either of the two performances. Indeed, many of the most significant elements of one or both shows, such as the appearance of actual villagers meant to represent tribal culture, are never mentioned in the librettos in any of the languages. None of the librettos indicates the revolutionary robe of Botokan either. The night of the gala performance, myriad versions of *Magdapio* swirled around discordant with each other. The order of the overseers was opposed by constant escape from the same.

Proof of the ungraspability of *Magdapio* is that the degree to which the press panned the opera correlated inversely to their degree of interpretive insight. An article in the *Manila Cablenews* on January 27, for example, carried the gleefully sarcastic headline "See Magdapio Monday Night: Wonderful Production Will Be Given Then in Honor of Governor Wright" and chortled, "Any American who wants to have an evening of fun would do well to go and see this indescribable hodgepodge, which is far and away funnier in its arch-solemness than than [*sic*] anything George Ade or Peter Finlay Dunne ever turned out by the yard, had set to alleged music and reeled off at a dollar-fifty a seat to a Broadway audience" (3). The reporter guffawed because he could make no sense of the "indescribable hodgepodge." Surely, Jack O'Lantern was grinning devilishly as he read that. Yet both reviewers had eyes and saw nothing. By contrast, the day after the *Magdapio* premiere, the *Manila Times* pilloried the score by Carluen but did not question the coherence of the show ("Filipino" 2). The subtitle of the article announced that the opera would be presented at the forthcoming St. Louis Exposition, that is, world's fair. A neutral plot summary followed, culminating with the observation that "an interesting feature is the performance of the ancient tribal dances of the Aetas, a troop of seventeen of those primitive savages having been brought from the mountains of Bataan, for the purpose" ("Filipino" 2).[11] The awfulness to 21st-century eyes of presumptive "savages" being inserted into *Magdapio* should not obscure the fact that the *Manila Times* was impressed by such pseudorealism and raised no issue with the plan for the opera to represent Filipino culture in mid-America.

Antipodal America

In fact, Manila was *already* in mid-America, fully in the mainstream of the westering mission of conquest and uplift that the United States long had assigned itself and that had produced parallel cities such as St. Louis as a result. As Victor Bascara writes, "The 1904 fair in St. Louis . . . was for many Americans an introduction to the country's new possessions in the South Pacific. The Philippine Islands had recently been mapped into America" (97). The leap from fighting indigenous people in the West to fighting indigenous people in the Philippines was nothing of the sort; in fact, the warring was often done by the same soldiers. The world's fair, which opened in May 1904 and which has received substantial attention from scholars, aimed to celebrate the centennial of the Lewis and Clark expedition. The intent of those explorers had been to survey lands of the United States that had been newly acquired via the 1803 Louisiana Purchase; the goal was to map the people and resources of those lands and indicate the way for the Americanization and exploitation of both. The extension of that narrative to the freshly obtained lands of the Philippines was self-evident to organizers and attendees of the St. Louis Exposition a century later. After all, the archipelago also lay to the west and also had been won in war against natives. And it too had been bought from a European power, since after triumphing militarily Washington had made the gesture of purchasing the Philippines from Spain for twenty million dollars.

The Philippine exhibit, the largest of any at the world's fair, therefore appeared as a natural complement to the American Indian exhibit. At hand, evidently, were parallel occupations and civilizing missions. It was not a coincidence that the Philippine exhibit in St. Louis was known as the "Reservation." And the seventeen Aetas whom Paterno stuffed into the *Magdapio* premiere a few months previously were no outlier. Similarly, "nearly thirteen hundred natives" were put in the Reservation in St. Louis as living artifacts, including some Aetas (*Report of the Philippine Exposition* 41). William E. Curtis, an American correspondent in Manila at the time, enthused for newspapers in Washington and Chicago that "the most interesting part of the exhibit will be the human documents that have been sent over, the colonies of the semi-savage tribes who have constructed miniature villages on the grounds and will there exhibit the native habits, industries and amusements as at home" (3).

Some of those "human documents" were perhaps the same Aetas who were uploaded into *Magdapio*, for Pedro Paterno was the only Filipino appointed to the original three-member board that prepared the St. Louis exhibition ("Philippine" 519).[12] The "official staff of the board" eventually grew to include twenty-six individuals, all but one of whom had an official title and official responsibilities. The lone exception was Paterno, who was listed merely as a "member" (*Report of the Philippine Exposition* 7–8). His only duty, essentially, was to be Pedro Paterno. In the capacity of himself, he was slated to make the trip to St. Louis, which was legally required of all board members. Yet for unknown reasons, as a St. Louis newspaper reported, "Mr. Paterno was unable to come," and so Abram W. Lawshe, auditor of the Philippine government, was chosen to take his place on the board and at the world's fair ("Lawshe" 5). Had Paterno arrived in St. Louis, he would have been associated there with "a delegation of from 30 to 50 prominent Filipino gentlemen of education and culture" ("Philippine" 520).[13] And had Paterno made the trip, *Magdapio* probably would have been performed at the Exposition, not for the first time in America but, given its premiere in Manila and the performance for Wright, the third.[14]

A blurb that appeared in the *Manila Times* on January 15 did announce that a second performance of *Magdapio* would take place on January 17 and concluded, "The opera made a big hit at its first production and the outlook for Sunday night indicates an immense audience" ("Opera" 4). This brief article amounts to a rave review and counters all conclusions elsewhere about the original reception of *Magdapio* as thoroughly negative. *La democracia*, a pro-American Filipino newspaper, declared that the premiere drew a crowd, as "acudiendo á la función bastante público" ["attending the performance was a substantial audience "] ("Espectáculos" 4). There is no reason to think that the reviewer for *La democracia* inflated the size of the audience in a general attempt to promote the production. On the contrary, he ripped both Paterno and Carluen as barefaced plagiarists and slammed the singing talent of the actors. In fact, he judged that the tenor was so bad as to be "fusilable" ["deserving of being shot"] ("Espectáculos" 4). Amid such excoriations, however, the reviewer did compliment the actors on their effort, if not their aptitude. Furthermore, he added, "la *miss* [*sic*] *en escena* hay que confesar que estuvo bien, haciendo la Sra. Juana Molina elegantes trajes, sobre todo en el acto tercero" ["the mise-en-scène, it must be confessed, was done well, with Mrs. Juana Molina wearing elegant costumes, above all in the third act"] ("Espectáculos" 4).[15] And, significantly, he described the hoochee-hoochee dancers as "superiores, demostrando que saben *jalearse* por lo que el público pidió la repetición de sus danzas, que, despues de todo, fué lo más atractivo de la noche" ["superior, demonstrating that they know how to *dance with enthusiasm*, for which the public asked for a repeat of their dances, which, given everything else, were the most attractive element of the night"] ("Espectáculos" 4). It is difficult to know whether to take this assessment at face value, due to the unclear intonation of the italicized *jalearse* (perhaps it was Manila slang for shaking their thing) and given the comparison to the rest of the show, which the reviewer ridiculed for the most part. Nevertheless, the immediate context of the *jalearse* passage is unironically positive about the efforts of the actors, the mise-en-scène, and the wardrobe, so it seems probable that the reviewer genuinely did think that the hoochee-hoochee dancers were "superior" and that the public was justified in asking for an encore.

The repeat performance of *Magdapio* planned for January 17 never did take place, as Paterno explained later to *La democracia*, "por hallarse ligeramente indispuestos varios de las artistas" ["because various actors found themselves lightly indisposed"] ("'Magdapio'" 4).[16] The reporter who quoted him, however, seems to suggest that the real reason for the cancellation was that the opera was undergoing modifications after being sharply criticized in the media for having stolen much of its score. Although *La democracia* mentions that revisions were apparently being made by Paterno to the script as well, the main problem with the opera noted in its reviews and those of others involved the music by, or purportedly by, Carluen ("'Magdapio'" 4). Riggs, in his book manuscript, describes the score as "musical contortions suggesting haphazard stealings from *Gismonda*, *Faust*, and other world-known operas, combined with barbarous original themes, motives and lyrics with the accompaniment of vociferous brass and wind in the pit which half the time was flat and beyond control" (*Filipino* 337). Elsewhere, he sniggers that "the music, declared to be 'strictly Filipino,' is strangely reminiscent of 'La Giaconda,' [*sic*] 'Faust,' and other well-known operas, with preludes and intermezzos really original" ("Drama" 282). Most sources concur, usually in a tone of hilarity mixed with horror, that the music was both egregious and egregiously plagiarized. Jack O'Lantern opined that "the music was easily intelligible. At the beginning of the second act there was a duet which might have been taken almost note for note from Aida . . . other equally famous operas all contributed their fair share to the honors of the evening, though the music was said to be entirely original. It certainly was—as it was rendered. But most of it was very, very reminiscent" (5).[17] The *Manila Times* likewise reported that "the music, by Senor Carluen, was bad, being a rehash of airs from popular operas of great composers, worked over in a way to make them turn over in their graves" ("Filipino" 2). Even *La democracia*, in its initial report on the premiere, observed that "como el *Sandugong Panaguinip* [*La alianza soñada*], la música de *Magdapio* es una hermosa recopilacion de operas conocidas, escuchando nosotros anoche el 4° acto completo de *Il Trovatore*" ["Like the *Sandugong Panaguinip* [*The Dreamed Alliance*], the music of *Magdapio* is a beautiful compilation of familiar operas, for we listened last night to the complete fourth act of *The Troubadour*"] ("Espectáculos" 4). Not only Carluen but Paterno too could be charged with plagiarism. The reviewer for *La democracia* noted drily that "que para ciertas cosas tiene habilidad el autor del libreto se demostró bien claro anoche, en que el público pudo apreciar escenas parecidas á otras de varias óperas y zarzuelas" ["it was demonstrated quite clearly last night that the author of the libretto has an ability for certain things, for the public could appreciate scenes that resembled others from various operas and zarzuelas"] ("Espectáculos" 4).

These are, it must be emphasized, American reviews. This is the American media. The *Manila Cablenews* and the *Manila Times* were American newspapers as much as the *San Francisco Chronicle* and the *New York Times* and everything in between. Wright was an American autocrat, and the Philippines was an American colony. *La democracia* was an American publication too, a direct product of American colonial rule issued by American colonial subjects. The journal of the collaborationist Federalista Party, *La democracia* had been founded by T. H. Pardo de Tavera, the most prominent pro-American Filipino and, among local elites, the key point man of Taft (Mojares, *Brains* 145–49). There is, in fact, nothing "strictly Filipino" about anything involving *Magdapio* (Riggs, "Drama" 282). The opera exists only because of American empire. It signifies only in that context, at least originally. The distance from a theater in Manila to a theater in Missouri is therefore insignificant. The "primitive savages" transported from their homes into *Magdapio* would also be transported to St. Louis and into the Reservation there ("Filipino" 2). In parallel movement, William N. Swarthout, an editor of the *Manila Times*, transported himself "on special duty" onto the official staff of the Reservation board and probably over to St. Louis as well (*Report of the Philippine Exposition* 7). The American heartland *is* the Philippines. There may be multiple *Magdapios* with multiple meanings, but the matrix in which they merge and diverge is that of America. *Magdapio* is not some parochial play by a backwater twit, no matter how it appeared to some Americans, but a profoundly conflicted staging of tumultuous transpacific import. The Philippines is where the United States launched its global regime of surveillance and punishment that would dominate the 20th and 21st centuries. The frowns of Wright at the uncontrolled movements of natives before him is the framework for fistfuls of decades to come. And as Alfred McCoy argues, the regimes of Taft and Wright and the governors who followed them would remake continental America itself: "Colonial rule had a profound influence on metropolitan society, introducing an imperial mentality of coercive governance into U.S.

domestic politics. Inspired by an expansive sense of dominion over colonized peoples abroad, Americans would apply similarly coercive methods to the reformation of their own society" (346).

The American national security state that today unstoppingly surveils whomever it deems suspicious emerged first at a global level in the Philippines. Then as now, the attempt was to arrest assertively antagonistic actors of all kinds, on all stages. When *Magdapio* appeared in early 1904, the Sedition Law that Taft had decreed in November 1901 with an eye to crushing anti-American plays was still in effect. This was the case even though its tenth section indicated that the official end of war hostilities, which U.S. president Theodore Roosevelt had declared on the Fourth of July, 1902, would eliminate the prohibition "for any person to advocate orally or by writing or printing or like methods, the independence of the Philippines Islands or their separation from the United States" (348–49).[18] Although in the moment of *Magdapio* the war was no longer considered by America to exist, the drones of the regime still kept hitting their marks. American authorities still meted out jail and fines to dramatists who offended it, including in the months surrounding the *Magdapio* performances. For example, as Michael Cullinane observes, the anticolonial Filipino playwrights Mariano Martinez and Maximo de los Reyes were "arrested after performances of their plays in early 1904"; and Juan Abad, a Filipino dramatist who had "developed working relationships among most of the prominent oppositionists, including Pedro Paterno," put on a play in May 1904 that resulted in his "arrest, trial, and eventual imprisonment" (117–19). Yet Paterno, operating before the gaze of a newly inaugurated American colonial governor, remained free the next day and thereafter. And this is despite producing a play whose stagecraft was, as Riggs would figure out, "a deal more seditious than it was admitted to be by the government" (*Filipino* 61).

The continuing liberty of Paterno was not due to leniency from Wright, who was no benevolent patron of the Philippines or Filipino arts. On the contrary, he was substantially more ill-spirited than Taft. That took some doing, given that Taft had legalized the death penalty for Filipinos convicted of agitating for independence. Compared to Taft, as Cullinane notes, Wright's "more outwardly racist views alienated him from Filipinos" (102–3). How Paterno managed to pull off his play before that panoptic putz therefore points to praxes of resistance that can inform others that have been enacted around the world ever since. The pivotal ploy would seem to be the paradoxical ambiguities that left all his texts so easily read in contrary ways by distinct publics. As Paul Rodell writes of *Magdapio* and other seditious dramas, "In all of these plays the real situation was never directly dealt with and America was never named outright because arrest would have been immediately forthcoming. The strategy was to use a presumably innocuous sounding plot but to fill the production with a number of double meanings, revolutionary symbols, and allegorical situations rendering the real purpose of the play explicit to only the native audience" (111). This inherently deconstructive strategy surely could escape the control of its author as well. With the hoochee-hoochee dancers, for example, Paterno may not have intended either offense or official misreadings but rather simply aimed to impress the Americans in his audience by incorporating a popular fad in the West with roots in a previous world's fair, the 1893 extravaganza in Chicago. The Filipina dancers themselves, taking advantage of the openness of opera as a live genre and of the potential politics of the *Magdapio* plot, might have chosen to play particularly provocatively to their own peers in the crowd and so improvised a performance far more powerful than anything Paterno himself would have planned.

It seems that no one in authority quite saw how *Magdapio* played out differentially, not Wright, not Paterno, not anyone in the press. Riggs was completely bewildered by the opera he loathed so energetically: "The array of the opening chorus-ballet was fantastic and freakish, but the climax of absurdity was reached when *Mapalad*, the hero and victim appeared" (*Filipino* 335). The illogic he admonishes is a direct challenge to the logic everyone tried to impose on the play. In reality, everything that happened on stage was beyond the ken of everyone. Whichever authority attempted to authorize it, failed. In this lay the potency and prolific counterpunching of the opera. Its polyphony and pluralities allowed for both an incitement to revolution and a plausible plea before those charged with censoring the same. John Foreman, a contemporary of Riggs who likewise felt inspired to compose a tome about the new American archipelago, wrote in 1906 that "SEDITION, in its more virulent and active forms, having been frustrated by the authorities since the conclusion of the war, the Irreconcilables conceived the idea of inflaming the passions of the people through the medium of the native drama. How the seditious dramatists could have ever hoped to succeed in the capital itself, in public theatres, before the eyes of the Americans, is one of those mysteries which the closest student of native philosophy must fail to solve" (553–54). Foreman, indeed, failed to solve it so much that he proceeded to name "Don Pedro A. Paterno" as a nonseditious playwright and in fact "one of the best native dramatists" (554).

But the leading misinterpreter of a Paterno performance of any kind was surely Paterno himself. Always out of step with History, he was one of the

last major Filipino figures to favor national freedom. His earlier decades hob-
nobbing in Madrid with the Spanish elite scarcely styled him a revolutionary
of any kind. Paterno was far more conservative than Rizal, who himself had
favored only peaceful attempts to convince Spain to change its behavior toward the Philippines. Neither armed insurgency nor Filipino independence
was the solution of Rizal—he rejected a fictional uprising in his 1891 novel
El filibusterismo (Subversion) as well as the actual revolt of the Katipunan in
1896—and certainly those were not viable options either to a backslapping
toff such as Paterno. Andrés Bonifacio, the original and charismatic leader
of the Katipunan, was the opposite of an armchair intellectual and primp-
ing aristocrat such as Paterno. Paterno was criticized in his time, and has
been reviled often since, for negotiating a December 1897 armistice in which
he arranged for the Filipino revolutionaries of the day to leave for Hong
Kong. This allowed Spanish colonialism to reconsolidate, albeit temporarily,
in the islands. At that point, Paterno was helping to suppress an independence movement that was already more conservative than its 1896 version.
As the rebels eventually returned, revived, and as Spanish power evaporated
in the archipelago, Paterno raced to catch up with reality. As Mojares writes,
"Paterno was forced to cast his lot with the revolutionaries. He had little
choice. The Spanish government to which he had sworn allegiance had been
terminated and Paterno was not one who would stay outside the center of
events" (*Brains* 23–24). His protean persona, however, preserved its propensity
for paradox. T. H. Pardo de Tavera, the founder of *La democracia* and a fellow
elite Filipino with long experience in Europe, noted that at the start of the
Malolos Congress in the autumn of 1898, that is, after the definitive fall of
Spain in the islands, "Paterno always had the idea of again restoring the sovereignty of Spain" (*Report of the Philippine Commission* 391). This would not be
so striking had it not been for the fact that Paterno actually was president of
that Congress, a body that had convened to ratify archipelagic independence
and draft a national constitution. Consistent in his complexities, he used his
position as president of the newly declared state to crush the ideas of more
militant and less monied men at Malolos while seeking surrender (or something akin to it) to the surging imperial power in the archipelago, the United
States (Mojares, *Brains* 24–25).

Nevertheless, as a librettist a few years later, Paterno openly offered operas
far more oppositional than anything he had written in the past. In doing so,
he added a strident voice to what was left of the revolutionary chorus. Given
his tendency to dissonant timing, this probably indicated the end of viability
of the chorus itself. After the performance for Wright, *Magdapio* would never

be staged again. Riggs therefore concludes that *Magdapio* was the last major anticolonial play put on by Filipinos before "America firmly and, it is to be hoped, forever quashed their theatrical propensities for inciting treasonable acts and utterances among the mass of the people" (*Filipino* 335). Riggs also describes *Magdapio* as "the last dramatic composition of any importance by a Filipino" (*Filipino* 37). These assessments are inaccurate, as significant anti-American plays in Tagalog and perhaps other Filipino languages continued to appear for some time thereafter (Lapeña-Bonifacio 49). That *Magdapio* was penned in Spanish, however, by a Filipino so impacted by a previous conquest that he could not write or speak comfortably a Filipino language, lends the opera special resonance as a reminder that the United States did wrest its colony from a previous colonizer as well as from locals, that the dramatic space of the play was not just national or binational but global. In *Magdapio*, the usurpations uttered and upbraided were of a theater as large as the planet.

Staging Rebellion: *Magdapio* and Modernity

The scale of that theater is the reason why the gala performance of *Magdapio* constitutes a pivotal moment in the history of modernity. The occupation of the Philippines marks the global turn of American empire, a round-the-world reach that would know no end in the century ahead. And *Magdapio* provided the first boards on which antipodal anticolonialism asserted itself so aggressively against American authority. The subversive plays in Tagalog were often more direct than *Magdapio* but they were staged as secretly as possible, away from the officers of the occupation. Paterno put on his anti-American performances in front of the highest-ranking American authorities. This took an extraordinary amount of chutzpah. True, Botokan, the father of Magdapio, has no spoken lines of political import. His verbal voicings are restricted to trite comments about his daughter and her beau, while Mapalad and the Aetas get all the lines about autonomy. But the robe of Botokan bespeaks plenty. It offers a sartorial counterargument to the presumably official outfit of Wright. The design of the costume is not mentioned in the published versions of the play, but Riggs notes that "his robe was of pale blue silk or satin, bearing embroidered upon both back and front the dreaded symbol of the Katipunan, the blood-red rising sun and rays" (*Filipino* 336).[19] Draping the land and its resources in that insignia, on the inauguration day of a new colonial governor no less, is as treasonous a symbolism as imaginable from the perspective of American occupiers.

It is probably not a coincidence that the first syllable of "Botokan" is also that of "Bonafacio." Paterno always favored this type of pseudolinguistic association in his historical writings. There is no way that Wright would have picked up on such a metonymic connection, but any Filipino familiar with the Paterno oeuvre might very well have ascertained in the alliteration a pledge of nonallegiance. And it is probably not an accident that Botokan falls wounded in the play but is not heard from again. His death is therefore not confirmed. Offstage for the moment, perhaps he shall recover from his wounds and then stride forth anew, Katipunan symbolism ablaze, to the center of the story, the center of History. Bonifacio may be dead—his rival Emilio Aguinaldo had arranged for his execution—but his spirit survives in some form. He may well come back, this revenant of revolution. A patriarch can be killed but not his ghost. And haunting is a power unto itself.

The robe of Botokan alone would have been enough to unsettle the Americans in the audience who, as in *The Dreamed Alliance*, saw themselves metaphorically condemned on stage. It is not the only clue in the play, however, that would have unnerved any card-carrying colonialist in the crowd who was paying attention to its allegorical possibilities or who suspected that something lay beyond the nearly rumpled nuptial bed and the vanquished yet victorious virgin. Baguio, for example, is a particularly evocative name for the god of the invaders, as it is also the name of a mountain town built up by American troops after Taft had decided, barely after having first set foot in the Philippines, that a refreshing retreat from the tropical heat of Manila was sorely needed. As a military project imposed on the Filipino highlands, the Baguio of Taft contrasts to the entirely natural beauty and richness of Mount Magdapio. When the Baguio of the Malays issues lines like "Yo soy la fuerza . . . no permitire que sean de otros las montañas de Magdapio; de nadie mas que de los Malayos" ["I am the strength . . . I will not permit that the mountains of Magdapio belong to others; they will belong to no one else but the Malays"], the allegorical meaning is transparent: those Malays are Americans (9).[20] "Baguio" meant one thing to everyone in the Philippines in 1904, and it was not a Malay deity. And like the United States, the Baguio of the opera turns out to be a naval power of great reach, a sea god who wreaks tempests on Filipino soil. When King Bay of the victorious Malays apostrophizes, "Oh MAGDAPIO mia, objeto de mis amores, ven a mis brazos" ["Oh, my MAGDAPIO, object of my love, come to my arms!"] upon seeing her sentient for the first time, he is using the language of affection to veil a vicious conquest (15). There are echoes here of the infamous American catchphrases of goodwill toward the Philippines: the policy of "benevolent assimilation" declared in 1898 by President William McKinley, the references to "little brown brothers" by Taft. Both men, like King Bay, expressed dedication and promised exaltation to what they were setting up for penetration. They too wanted to win hearts and minds. Baguio is a most brutal god of love.

As for the Aetas, the native defendants, they evidently stand for both the Katipunan in particular and for the larger mass struggle of Filipinos against the American occupation. That context is inextricable from the cry of the Aetas to the Malays: "No os conocemos; ya podeis abandonar nuestra montaña" ["We do not know you; you can abandon already our mountain"] (9). Imperial attitudes are equally inseparable from the reply of the Malays: "Sois unos debiles y miserables" ["You are weaklings and wretches"] (9). Plus, the Aetas are ur-Filipinos who personify the most ancient source of archipelagic autonomy. Alternatively known as Negritos or Itas, the Aetas are the Filipino people long assumed to be the first humans to arrive on the islands in prehistoric times. They are the same aborigines about whom Paterno published a 440-page account in 1890 entitled *Los itas* and declared, "Impórtanos que Filipinas no se excluya del Universo. Para el progreso de Filipinas es necesario el conocimiento de sus tradiciones; en [*sic*] respetarlas" ["It is important to us that the Philippines is not excluded from the Universe. For the progress of the Philippines, knowledge of their [the Itas'] traditions is necessary; so is respecting them"] (3). The Reservation at the St. Louis world's fair also focused on the enduring existence of Aetas by featuring them in a special area, as it did individuals from other purportedly representative Filipino societies. As the *Report of the Philippine Exposition Board* explained, "The Negrito Village contains the lowest type of inhabitants of the archipelago. They are the most primitive, and are regarded as the true aborigines" (37).

Paterno believed that the Aetas/Itas/Negritos of his day continued to lead a "vida salvaje" ["savage life"] like other "civilizaciones inferiores" ["inferior civilizations"] but insisted that "las estudiamos con amor" ["we study them with love"] because they were the primordial society at the roots of archipelagic culture (*Los itas* 4). Indeed, he argued, "Las Islas Filipinas llamadas están á un brillante porvenir glorioso . . . si saben adaptar al Progreso sus antiguas tradiciones. De éstas no se puede presentar un estudio exacto y completo sin conocer el pueblo *Ita*, de donde dimanan gran parte de ellas" ["The Philippine Islands are called to a brilliant and glorious future . . . if they know how to adapt their ancient traditions to Progress. A precise and complete study of these traditions cannot be presented without being familiar with the *Ita* society, from which a great part of those traditions arise"] (*Los itas* 4). To protagonize the defense of the homeland in *Magdapio* with this society is therefore not merely to stake a contemporary Katipunan claim against the newly arrived forces of Baguio. It is also to stake that claim in the most ancient of Filipino peoples and the most foundational of land and cultural rights, those of original inhabitants. Paterno always lent his ear to the eternal, seeking to connect the prehistory and earliest mythologies of the islands (including those he made up) to Filipino identity in his era and beyond. Drawing the Aetas into battle against the hordes of Baguio was a way of rooting the events in *Magdapio* at once in the early 20th century and in a timeline (even if invented) as long as Filipino civilization itself.

Magdapio might be jagged in its structure and ragged in its staging, but it is not inexplicable. The apparent absurdities of the opera, from the voluptuous mountain virgin in the beginning to the astonishingly adroit alligator at the end, along with a set deemed ludicrous and a score deemed lifted, is why *Magdapio* is savaged by Riggs and others. It is easy to see why the whole thing seems jury-rigged at best. And of course the jury was rigged, yes. But there was a lot more than one jury and one rig in every Paterno performance. *Magdapio* was no pointless product of a plutocrat with a printing press who potchked around one day and patched together some preposterous pastiche. There is instead much purposeful consistency in *Magdapio* within the overall literary output of Paterno. For instance, fidelity to the cause of union, both romantic and geopolitical, marks its heroine in death just as it did protagonists of *The Dreamed Alliance* previously. Once again, the melodrama of heterosexual couples who never quite get to couple is the vehicle through which Paterno relays an anticolonial critique. And as in the rest of his fiction dating backward to his 1885 novel *Nínay* and forward to his 1910–11 short stories, the principal symbolic tension revolves around who gets to have sex with a virgin who represents a virginal Philippines. The tantalizing options in *Magdapio*, as customary for Paterno, range from sweet, celebratory deflowerment to violent, lusty deflowerment to awkward combinations of the two. And as in most Paterno plots, all these outcomes remain unrealized. At the last moment, a petal or more stays unplucked. In contrast to a later American musical, every mountain is not quite climbed. The stream leading to the nuptial bed does not quite get forded. The Philippines stays virgin. But penetration happens repeatedly in *Magdapio* and Magdapio and Mount Magdapio anyway. The earthquake god does part the mountain. Mapalad and his men do claim its treasures as "primeros ocupantes de esta abertura de monte" ["the first occupants of this mountain opening"] (9). And the Malays and their allegorical American counterparts do invade the fertile land. These are ways of avoiding intercourse while having it all the time. Or, as Riggs complained about the bathos of *Magdapio* and the allegedly less frontal Filipino plays that followed it, "Sturdiness became flabby" (*Filipino* 349). This is the age when Roosevelt was talking about his big stick, of course. Freud really would have enjoyed reading his contemporaries in the Philippines.

Riggs found the opera to be ghastly art but coherent at least in its political cowardice. He concluded that *Magdapio* was a timorous attempt at treason by a talentless taleteller and that the Filipino audience disliked it because it was not sufficiently insurrectionary. *Magdapio*, he wrote, "fell flat; the natives realized exactly what was wanting, and the piece proved very tame and stale to them, for though much of the sinister suggestion of other plays was there, the artificial mask of the deeper villainies, the smooth skin of sultry words, was entirely missing, and the very innocence of the piece killed it in native esteem" (*Filipino* 61).[21] There is no reason to believe, however, that this appraisal of the audience was accurate. It is highly improbable that Riggs could follow the Tagalog in which Filipino theatergoers were conversing with each other, or that he was adept at reading the cultural nuances of their gestures, tones, and other nonverbal responses to the action on stage. He was a sojourner in the Philippines, after all. Riggs may have misunderstood completely what was going on among the groundlings when he notes that, throughout the opera, "the native part of the house commented aloud and talked freely, showing plainly its lack of interest in the proceedings. Even while the author himself was addressing them the conversation did not cease, nor was it greatly modulated. The truth was that the natives found the production as dull and commonplace as the eager Americans found it exasperating. The natives saw how very close the author had sailed to the skirts of sedition, but since he saw fit to keep his pen out of the gall they imbibed with such relish, they would have none of him nor of his work" (*Filipino* 337). Yet in many cultures, chatter in the house can convey enthusiastic engagement with a show, not detachment. This is the case in many Manila stage and film audiences today. Riggs, like Wright, may have misread what was happening right before him.

Staging Submission: "The Hon. Taft and His Successor, Governor Wright"

The creative output of Paterno after the *Magdapio* performance for Wright, along with the ideological contortions of the author himself, remains for the moment unclear. A full year and a half would pass before the presumed debut of his next known musical drama, *On the Arrival of Taft*, in early August 1905. In the meanwhile, Paterno likely continued to write fiction of one kind or another, yet the extensive bibliography of his work compiled by Resil Mojares shows a blank for all of 1904 (*Brains* 533). The only original composition of any kind that Mojares assigns Paterno after *Magdapio* and before *On the Arrival of Taft* is a zarzuela with the Tagalog title *Ang Buhay ni Rizal* (*The Life of Rizal*) that supposedly was "staged in Manila on January 14, 1905" (*Brains* 533).[22] Neither the original Spanish version of this zarzuela nor the Tagalog translation is known to be extant. Future research may turn up either text and perhaps press coverage of the staging as well. For the production of *The Life of Rizal*, Paterno enlisted his frequent Tagalog translator Roman Reyes and *Magdapio* composer Alejo Carluen (*Brains* 533; "Carluen" 107). It seems unlikely, though, that this zarzuela was the only creative writing that Paterno produced in the year and a half between *Magdapio* and *On the Arrival of Taft*. He had easy access to both stage and print media and loved to wax rhetorical whenever possible, so there is reason to hope that unknown texts from this chronological gap will surface eventually.

A major issue in researching Filipino literature in Spanish is always the extensive range of seemingly lost texts. For instance, no archive seems to retain anything close to the full run of the morning newspaper *La patria* (*The Fatherland*), which functioned as a kind of mouthpiece for Paterno during that era. Only the Library of Congress seems to hold any copies of the periodical, and yet its microfilms are missing various issues, including all those from 1904. Thanks to the American surveillance network in the Philippines, however, a clipping from *La patria* that year ended up in a collection of William Taft papers that is also held by the Library of Congress. The survival of this clipping and its official English translation suggests that Paterno inserted new, charged stories into the newspaper with some regularity and that the Wright regime, like its Taft predecessor, kept a wary eye on the man and his prose. Eternal vigilance was the price of denying Filipino liberty.

The clipping in the Taft papers includes two texts that parallel each other as the lead narratives on the left and right front-page columns of the August 13, 1904, issue of *La patria*. The American intelligence operation saw fit to translate for Wright the signed story by Paterno on the right, which carries the title "El Hon. Taft, y su sucesor el Gobernador Wright" ["The Hon. Taft and His Successor, Governor Wright"] (1). Just as significant, however, is the anonymous and untranslated article on the left that notes with resignation that six years earlier to the day, the American flag had replaced the Spanish standard above the walls of Manila ("El trece" 1). The anniversary of that event was apparently quite important to Paterno. The previous August 13, he had issued the editorial in *La patria* that requested "as soon as possible, the foundation of the *Government that is our own and in charge*" ("La nueva" 1).

His opinions of August 13, 1904, however, were conveyed not via an editorial but as a short story. "The Hon. Taft and His Successor, Governor Wright" opens by declaring that the time was propitious to "consultar á nuestro amigo el gran Profeta Lapu" ["consult with our friend the great Prophet Lapu"] about the future of the Philippines ("El Hon." 1). This seer lives in a cave filled with the "espíritus inmortales de la Historia filipina" ["immortal spirits of Filipino History"] ("El Hon." 1). Lapu is a resonant name for Paterno. Another wise Lapu had cued his opera *The Dreamed Alliance* two years earlier and urged a Filipino alliance against invaders. And that plot in turn recalled the indigenous leader Lapu Lapu, whose forces killed Magellan and repulsed his attempted conquest in 1521.

In the latest incarnation of Lapu, nevertheless, the tide seems to have turned: the Lapu of "The Hon. Taft" issues "amonestaciones porque nos hemos atrevido á mirar en sentido contrario ó mejor dicho, bajo varios puntos de vista, la obra gubernamental del sabio Mr. Taft" ["rebukes because we have dared to look at in a contrary way or, better said, from various points of view, the governmental work of the wise Mr. Taft"] ("El Hon." 1). Paterno, having scolded himself for thinking differently than Taft, then decides (as usual for him) that full-on prostration is really the way to go: "Taft es un genio," explains Lapu, "cuyo elevado criterio de gobernante no podeis alcanzar; básteos decir que ese hombre si vá á Roma es Papa; si á Rusia, Czar; si á Francia, Presidente; conforme vino á Filipinas de Comisionado se hizo gobernador y gobernador excelente. Su obra artística no la mireis mas que como se juzga un cuadro al óleo monumental, que solo tiene un punto de vista" ["Taft is a genius whose lofty judgment of governing none of you can attain; it is enough to tell you that that man, if he goes to Rome he is Pope; if to Russia, Czar; if to France, President; correspondingly, he came to the Philippines as Commissioner and he became governor and an excellent governor. Do not look at his artistic work but as one judges a monumental oil painting, which only has one point of view"] ("El Hon." 1). Paterno giftwraps this gibberish with a final smarmy moral: "Así querido lector, confiemos en nuestros actuales gobernantes y sin volver la vista atras caminemos siempre adelante" ["So dear reader, let us trust in those who currently govern us and without looking back let us walk always forward"] ("El Hon." 1).

This claptrap convinced the colonialists. On the clipping, between the headline and the lead paragraph, some high-ranking American scrawled, "Don Pedro again in the fold" ("El Hon." 1). "Don" is a Spanish honorific that implies the elite status of Paterno; "Don Pedro," without the surname given, reveals how familiar the writer was with Paterno; and "in the fold" indicates that the kowtowing was taken as sincere. It also confirms that Paterno was often considered to be *not* in the fold, an assessment that does not square with his historiographical reputation as a recidivist betrayer of Filipino independence. The typed English translation of the story, which is preserved along with the Spanish original in the Taft papers, was made precisely because the issue of whether Paterno was or was not allied at that point with the American regime needed to be clarified. Two distinct handwritten notations appear atop the translation, neither of which resembles the handwriting about "Don Pedro" on the clipping in Spanish. This implies that at least three different American officials actively processed the surveilled story. One of the scribbles on the English typescript seems to read "Translation. B[e?]all" ("The Honorable" 1). The reference is likely to M. E. Beall, who is described in the 1903 *Official Handbook of the Philippines and Catalogue of the Philippine Exhibit*— the exhibit being the Philippine Reservation at the St. Louis world's fair—as "chief of the compilation and translating division" of the Bureau of Insular Affairs in Washington (13).[23] The Bureau was the section of the U.S. Department of War charged with overseeing American island possessions such as the Philippines and Puerto Rico.

The second handwritten comment on the typed translation appears in a different font and reads, "This was sent by Allen" ("The Honorable" 1). The reference here is surely to Brigadier General Henry T. Allen, the intelligence and military chief of the Philippines Constabulary who, less than a year earlier, had doubled as the English translator of *Magdapio*. And it seems quite possible, therefore, that the remark "This was sent by Allen" was penned by Wright himself. The colonial governor, after all, was almost certainly the intended reader of the translation. Similarly, four years earlier, an English translation of a suspicious Paterno banquet speech had been made for Taft, who proceeded to take out a red pencil and personally censor it. In other words, in the case of the Prophet Lapu parable in *La patria*, the machinery of American surveillance went through its well-oiled motions. But at the end of the day, Paterno proved more oleaginous than his overseers and the oil painting whose single point of view he now claimed to adopt. For there is no way to accept at face value the proposition that Taft was innately of papal or czarist stature. The idea that Paterno or anyone else genuinely believed that is outlandish. Despite his accomplished career, Taft never accrued the reputation of a man of exceptional charisma or talent or born leadership abilities. The hyperbole of Paterno is incredible once again. And yet the Americans in charge bought all the oil. They always do.

Return Engagement: *On the Arrival of Taft*

When Taft returned to the islands in 1905 as secretary of war in Theodore Roosevelt's cabinet, he was not making an international trip any more than when the secretary of defense visits Puerto Rico today. He was an American at home, not an American abroad, just as *Magdapio* is, among other things, an American opera written about American subjects, staged in America despite not being staged in St. Louis. The Philippines in 1905, like Hawaii and Alaska and other noncontiguous lands claimed by the United States, was part of America. And Paterno, who greeted the former colonial governor with a new musical play, was not a foreign subject but a domestic one. That play, entitled *Sa pagdating ni Taft* (*On the Arrival of Taft*), was presented, like *The Dreamed Alliance* and *Magdapio*, as reverence for a newly arrived power but in import was something quite different. The drama was yet another staging by Paterno in which he challenged colonialism face to face with the men bent on enforcing it. And like its predecessors, *On the Arrival of Taft* proved so polyfaceted that its multiple meanings were grasped distinctly, or not at all, by incommensurate audiences.

At this moment, there is no known extant copy of *On the Arrival of Taft*. It can be assumed that Paterno wrote and titled it originally in Spanish, the only language that he used to compose literary and historical texts. There may very well have been an English translation produced as well, as in the case of *The Dreamed Alliance* and *Magdapio*, to be vetted by American censors if for no other reason. But the only coeval text known to reference *On the Arrival of Taft* is a single, short article in the *Manila Cablenews* from August 6, 1905, entitled "Banqueros Are Heroes: New Musical Play by Sr. Pedro Paterno Honors the Arrival of Taft." The lead notes that the play is "a farcical comedy which is to be put on the boards in one of the local theaters in a day or two. The play is in Tagalog. . . . The musical accompaniment of the play is composed of purely Filipino airs" (12). The second and final paragraph explains that the protagonists of *On the Arrival of Taft* are struggling boatsmen (the "Banqueros") who "were at one time 'principales' of a provincial pueblo and are now compelled to perform the work they are doing on account of the poverty into which they have fallen as a result of the economic conditions of the country" (12).[24] The *banqueros* do not know how to resolve the problems that bedevil them and, by extension, the country at large, and so they turn for advice to an "old sorcerer" named . . . wait for it . . . Lapu (12). This sage "advises them to maintain the peace and to combine to make the reception of Mr. Taft a success. The banqueros then organize groups of persons prepared to make demonstrations; one of these groups asks for the independence of the Philippines, another for agricultural banks and a third for a school of the arts" (12).

This plot shimmers with subversion and sycophancy. As always, Paterno offers his guest of honor a bevy of sweet talk and bended knee. Surely Taft would favor such a play written and named in his honor, one in which, moreover, a wise elder encourages the protagonists to put on a great reception for the visiting dignitary. It is hard to kiss up that much in a single show, but Paterno did have decades of practice upon which to draw. And the visiting secretary of war would have been predisposed to enjoy the opera after a performance by Paterno that had taken place when the gargantuan federal delegation of seven American senators and two dozen congressmen landed in the Philippines (Cullinane 109). As the *Manila Cablenews* reported on August 3, the next day Taft would be received officially at the town hall of Manila, given a key to the city, and serenaded with the "singing of a song of welcome, composed by Sr. Paterno, by twenty school girls" ("Program" 3). Nobility in love with nubility, Paterno took great pleasure in waxing off about schoolgirls. He even dedicated his final ejaculations of fiction to them just before dying.[25] Taft too was probably quite pleased by the chorus put together for him. Front-page news in the *Manila Cablenews* on August 6, in fact, was not the announcement of *On the Arrival of Taft* (that preview was buried twelve pages in) but an account of the "delightful affair" that was the reception ceremony for the erstwhile head of the occupation ("Speeches" 1). Attending the event was not only the secretary of war but also the present colonial governor Luke E. Wright, his consort "Mrs. Luke E. Wright," and Alice Roosevelt, daughter of the 1898 war enthusiast President Theodore Roosevelt. During the festivities, according to the *Manila Cablenews*, "Don Pedro Paterno distributed copies of the vocal score of his hymn to Secretary Taft and Miss Roosevelt which was sung very charmingly by the choir" ("Speeches" 1).[26] One can only wonder if Mrs. Luke E. Wright was miffed at not getting a copy of the score herself. Taft, however, would have sat down to see *On the Arrival of Taft* with the "song of welcome" by Paterno and the schoolgirls still ringing "very charmingly" in his mind.

No known source actually confirms that *On the Arrival of Taft* was put on as scheduled or that Taft was in the audience. A program published on August 4 for his itinerary in Manila over the next week does not mention the play ("Program" 3). Yet this is hardly definitive. The slate of activities easily could have changed. Moreover, everything on it indicates endless opportunities for the kind of nattering among nabobs, both of the American and

Filipino variety, that Paterno spent his whole life enjoying immensely. If Taft were not intended to be in the box of honor, it is hard to imagine Paterno writing the play in the first place. And it seems unlikely that he would have gone ahead and staged the show without the secretary of war present. For Paterno, the whole point of fetishizing others was to fetishize himself in front of the high and mighty. But in any case, whether *On the Arrival for Taft* was performed or not, whether Taft saw it or not, the basics of the text remain rather more open to interpretation than first appears. The opera contains an array of elements that suggest something other than an unadulterated acceptance of American authority.

Readied for a performance almost three years to the day since Taft smiled weakly through *The Dreamed Alliance* and a year and a half since Wright grimaced through *Magdapio*, the latest Paterno opus rings with rebuttals to American rule. For starters, the macroeconomic conditions of the Philippines are awful, as former elites have sunk to the status of working stiffs. There is no hint that this took place under Spanish colonialism and so reads as a direct comment on the social and economic disorder wreaked amid the post-1898 governance of the archipelago by the United States. The self-congratulatory narrative of procolonial Americans such as Theodore Roosevelt and Taft routinely centered on the theme of uplifting the Philippines, so the downward spiral of the *banqueros* amounts to a sharp and bleak counternarrative.

More acutely still, the Filipino protagonists are stuck in their situation until they seek the counsel of Lapu, who encourages them to strive together. This is the same motif that drove the production of *The Dreamed Alliance* in August 1902. There too appeared a seer named Lapu, evocative of the indigenous king Lapu Lapu whose military had defeated the first Western imperialists on Filipino shores, those of Magellan. In *The Dreamed Alliance*, as Taft sat in the box of honor, Lapu advised Filipinos to unite in order to drive out an occupying force. The force in that case was an army of 16th-century Moors that allegorized to 20th-century Americans. In *On the Arrival of Taft*, Paterno retains the symbolism, the call for Filipino union, even the Tagalog translator, but dispenses with a degree of subterfuge. The *banqueros* are figures from 1905, not from the 16th century, and they plead directly for independence. Such audacity before the secretary of war is remarkable, given that Taft had headed the commission that in November 1901 had legislated that any Filipino who promoted independence would be subject to the death penalty or jail and heavy fines. Taft himself, in his principal speech to Filipino politicos during his 1905 return visit, underlined that he "favored retention of the Philippines. . . . He advised the Filipino leaders to set aside their quest for independence for the time being and join with the American government to make the Philippines a more prosperous land. Negotiations and plans for independence could come later" (Cullinane 109).

Paterno was taking a hell of a risk, and yet, given his familiarity with Taft and perhaps presumption of friendship, he may have thought himself to be taking no risk at all. Elites often have a way of thinking that they are on the same page. In the case of *On the Arrival of Taft*, however, that page was rather illegible to both parties in the first place. Paterno did not command Tagalog well enough to translate his own work for the performance, and Taft certainly could not comprehend a drama in that language put on in his honor. Playwright and theatergoer both would have been stumped by the true scope of the narrative before them. Perhaps certain echoes of the gala performance of *The Dreamed Alliance* would have been heard, such as the call for "a school for the arts" that sounds like the moment three years earlier when Paterno gave Taft the gate receipts for the night and the colonial governor urged him to use the proceeds to found "a conservatory of music for the benefit of Filipinos" ("Governor" 1). But other elements of *On the Arrival of Taft* would have remained perceptible only to those in the theater, whether backstage or onstage or in the crowd, who were in a position to grasp them. The call for the creation of "agricultural banks," for example, could be interpreted as a pun on *banqueros*, a hispanized locution that is evidently derived from the Tagalog *bangkâ*, or small Filipino boat or canoe. The *banqueros* read thus not only as "boatsmen" but also as "bankers," which is the standard meaning of *banqueros* in Spanish. Possibly there is a cry here for economic independence to match the political independence that is requested first for the archipelago and the cultural independence implied by the plea for a school for the arts. Or, more narrowly, all these requests could be interpreted as a petition against the policies of Wright, a man disliked and distrusted even by the collaborationist Filipino elites who had cozied up to Taft. They had lost ground under Wright and now saw in the return of his predecessor a chance to regain their standing (Cullinane 105–11). Paterno himself surely believed that elites deserved to remain elite. But regardless of the purpose of his play, if *On the Arrival of Taft* were indeed performed, there was enough flattery and servility in it to keep its author in the limelight and out of jail. And this was the case too with *The Dreamed Alliance* and *Magdapio*.

The inherent risks of parsing a single secondary account of a lost text are obvious. This is particularly so given the penchant of the *Manila Cablenews*, the source of that account, for sardonically depicting the nature of operas by Paterno. For instance, its characterization of *On the Arrival of Taft* as "a farcical comedy" is entirely inaccurate if the plot summary in the article is to be believed ("Banqueros" 12). The phrase seems to be written in the spirit of ridicule that marked the reviews of *Magdapio* in the same newspaper. Amelia Lapeña-Bonifacio implicitly discounts that derision, however, by reading the narrative of the *banqueros* as quite serious: "Of the [seditious] playwrights, Pedro Paterno was able to circumvent the strict laws against nationalistic plays by a drama which he entitled *Pagdating ni Taft* (On the Arrival of Taft) as a tribute to Taft. . . . Actually, the play was a grim statement of the dire state the Filipinos were finding themselves in after the Philippine-American war and an open advocacy for independence" (50). This interpretation could go further with consideration of the resonances of "Lapu" that strengthen greatly the call for archipelagic autonomy by the characters. The historical Lapu Lapu is the foundational freedom fighter of four centuries of Filipino anticolonialism. The Lapu of *The Dreamed Alliance* urges the creation of an alliance of Filipinos to fight for freedom. The Lapu of "The Honorable Taft and His Successor Governor Wright" recommends the opposite of freedom, but that advice is ironic. The Lapu of *On the Arrival of Taft* inspires Filipinos to unite for independence before foreign power. Such inspiration is not the stuff of "a farcical comedy."

Apparently, Lapu does counsel the *banqueros* "to maintain the peace" (12). This guidance is not commensurate with the explicit request for national independence but is consistent with the Paterno pattern of plausible defense. Should Taft react aggressively to the independence request, at least Paterno could claim that he supports peace above all. The advice, in essence, opens up a space of self-preservation for the playwright. And a similar space is created by the choice of language. After all, why not perform the play in English if the point is to appeal to Taft? Perhaps the appeal itself is too dangerous to be voiced so directly. A call for independence would sound a lot sharper to Taft in English than in Tagalog, which he would not comprehend. The play was not written in either language in the first place, so the choice of Tagalog over English is deliberate. Perhaps the true intended audience was not the foreign guest of honor but the native staff who prepared the theater for him. What could be more Jacobin in a Thermidorean moment than a call for unity and independence to a secretary of war in the stands who could not understand it even as the food vendors and cleaning crew did? Paterno, inside his texts and outside them, performs over and over again a paradoxical anticolonial-ism against an increasingly militarized and suddenly global Pax Americana. And so laugh about the man as one will, grin at his vainglory as one must, Paterno proves critical to the century to come. The subversions of his operas anticipate those of playwrights and players elsewhere, in other theaters, in other acts, in other stagings. No one may have ever seen *On the Arrival of Taft*, but from Manila then to Kabul now, the show has gone on along lines that he imagined first.

Anticolonialism and subversion more broadly, including the anti-American variants that have marked the world over since 1898, are necessarily contradictory and subjective phenomena. Revolution to some eyes is collaboration to others, and the uneven line between opposition and assimilation is fractalized at best. Ultimately, it cannot be concluded that the dramatic oeuvre of Paterno, like the man himself, was clearly one thing or another. It is representative of his unresolved tensions that the actor who played the native patriarch Botokan in the performance of *Magdapio* for Wright also played the role of the foreign usurper, King Bay.[27] To some extent, Paterno evidently intended *Magdapio*, and to some extent *On the Arrival of Taft*, to exude independence ideals. To some extent, some in his audiences picked up on that. At the same time, Paterno was a sycophant for all seasons. This was a man who previously, as Mojares puts it, had "devoutly wished to be a Spaniard" but who now, with the Americans in charge, was eager to sing a new tune (*Brains* 210). This was no more manifest than on August 10, 1905, just a day and a half after Taft perhaps watched the *banqueros* ask for Filipino freedom, when the Liceo de Manila, a Filipino school, made the former colonial governor its honorary president. In the ceremony, as the *Manila Times* reported, after badges were pinned on Taft and Alice Roosevelt,

> The irrepressible Pedro A. Paterno who was seated in the body of the hall, rose to his feet, and called for vivas for the newly elected honorary president of the Liceo which were given with a will. Secretary Taft, then arose from his chair and said, "I am compelled to exercise the functions of my newly elected office and tell my very dear friend Sr. Pedro A. Paterno that he is out of order." This excited great laughter.
>
> Senor Paterno then called out "will I be in order if I call for vivas for Miss Roosevelt?" "Si, si," responded Secretary Taft, and the vivas that were given shook the foundations of the building.
>
> After the exercises a body of school children sang "Philippines, my Philippines" to the tune of "Maryland, my Maryland," at the termination of which all adjourned to the sala for light refreshments. ("Taft" 1)

As the munching and quaffing commenced, it seems likely that everyone who participated in the ceremony, though not necessarily those who labored to build its set or strike it, accepted at face value the vapid *vivas* of Paterno. The gathered elites probably all felt that substituting the Philippines for Maryland in a schoolchild song made sense too. At the very least, the Filipinos onstage were prepared to purport as much. And Paterno probably sang louder than anyone else.

Revolutionary Passions: Freedom and *Gayuma*

Nevertheless, the operatic oeuvre of Paterno, when approached allegorically, reads as rebellious. This holds true too in *Gayuma*, yet another of his over-the-top productions. Although a Tagalog libretto of *Gayuma* survives, this opera is even less commented by scholars than *On the Arrival of Taft*, whose only known record of existence is the report of a single newspaper article. *Gayuma* was rendered into Tagalog, as now customary, by Roman Reyes, and set to music by Gavino Carluen. The composer was the youngest sibling of Alejo Carluen, who had scored *Magdapio* ("Carluen" 106).[28] The Tagalog translation is datelined as "Manila—1905," thus likely placing the opera in the same year as *On the Arrival of Taft*.[29] As with *On the Arrival of Taft*, however, it cannot be verified as of this writing that *Gayuma* was actually performed at any point.[30]

The extant text of *Gayuma* echoes the concerns and tropes of other Paterno plays. The main exception is the absence in the plot of a newly arrived foreign power akin to the Moors in *The Dreamed Alliance*, the Malays in *Magdapio*, or the American delegation in *On the Arrival of Taft*. The dramatic conflict instead features two Filipino villages, Antipolo and Kainta, which, according to the libretto, have been enemies for generations and which therefore have prohibited interactions among their peoples. There is even a rule that a person from Kainta who falls in love with someone from Antipolo "agad agad hahatulan ng parusang camatayan" ["is immediately punished with the sentence of death"] (Reyes trans., 5; Dela Cruz trans. 4). The principal characters are a 10th-century guru named Pitho, the bachelor Tupas from Antipolo, the bachelor Sitan from Kainta, the maiden Sinagtala from Kainta, and her father Makandola. Various villagers, warriors, and deities round out the cast.

In the opening scene, Pitho and the two bachelors together invoke Bathala, a precolonial Filipino god who appears as a major figure throughout the writings of Paterno. Tupas confesses that he has fallen in love with Sinagtala, so Sitan reminds him of "ang cautusang dakila" ["the great rule"] that proscribes such relations between individuals from the rival villages (Reyes trans. 5; Dela Cruz trans. 4). Sitan then storms off; Tupas pleads with Pitho for something to make Sinagtala be attracted to him; and the guru leads him in a prayer: "Magcasundo naua't magcaisang dibdib ang dalauang bayang nangag cacagalit maguing daan nila sa pinto ng langit ang cay Sinagtala't Tupas na pagibig" ["Hopefully the two villages that are angry with each other will unify and the love between Sinagtala and Tupas will become their [i.e., the villages'] door to heaven"] (Reyes trans. 7; Dela Cruz trans. 6). Pitho then makes possible the *gayuma*, or love charm. This first seems to be a flower plucked from a pot of boiling water surrounded by ancient gods, but then seems to be a spell that Tupas writes as he has been taught.

The results are, in all senses, dramatic. Sinagtala feels powerfully drawn to Tupas by forces she cannot identify or control. She knows he is from Antipolo and that falling in love with him is a capital crime, but she is helpless to resist. Her father, Makandola, and other villagers are aghast at the turn of events and prepare to kill her, as the law dictates. Her female friends beg her to love a Kainta lad such as Sitan and thereby avoid execution. Resolute, however, Sinagtala accepts a poisoned drink and announces, "Aco'i papayapa—¡Oh Sinagtala! di ca nalupigan hindi't ang puso mo'i lalong nagtitibay" ["I will be at peace—Oh Sinagtala! You are not conquered, you are not, and your heart is further strengthened" (Reyes trans. 19; Dela Cruz trans. 23). Tupas and his fellow Antipolo villagers arrive intent on saving her but appear just a moment late. Sinagtala is dead. Tupas immediately dies of anguish beside her. Their souls ascend to heaven. In the nine-day period of bereavement that follows, the two coffins are placed side by side before people from both Antipolo and Kainta. The villagers are all now united in mourning. The souls of Sinagtala and Tupas descend from heaven and the opera ends with the entire cast chorusing, "Ang pag-iisa'y mabuhay mag-isa tayong calooban at ng tayo'y magtagumpay sa pithayang calayaan" ["Long live unity, let us unite our hearts so that we will succeed in acquiring our desired freedom"] (Reyes trans. 23; Dela Cruz trans. 28).

Outside the context of Paterno and his era, *Gayuma* hardly seems subversive. There is no explicit revolt against foreign presences. For that matter, there are no foreign presences visible at all. Within his body of work, however, and within the sociopolitics of the early American colonial period, the play is rather rebellious. The key here is the discontinuity that marks the final full-cast chorus that dreams of "calayaan" ["freedom"] through unity. This sentiment makes no sense in a literal reading of the play as yet another Romeo and Juliet knockoff, transported by Paterno this time to the 10th-century Philippines. Throughout the plot, after all, there is no mention of a desired freedom anywhere, either individual or social. To climax *Gayuma* with an unexpected, collective call for liberty by newly united Filipinos therefore compels a different interpretation of everything that came before it. Trite lines about love and Bathala suddenly sound like pleas for archipelagic alliances based on shared precolonial culture. The ascension to heaven of Tupas and Sinagtala now suggests a utopian vision of what a united Filipino polity could achieve. This is no mean statement in any theater under duress, be the theater of war or of thespians, of statecraft or of stagecraft. In a military environment in which the United States had killed an estimated quarter million Filipinos in the course of crushing an independence movement, in a theatrical environment in which the United States had threatened capital punishment, incarceration, and harsh financial penalty to dramatists who yearned openly for freedom, the final cry for *calayaan* in *Gayuma* is revolutionary. A foregrounded presence of American power or an allegorical stand-in for that foreign force is therefore unneeded. Here, ringing loudly, is an unmistakable proclamation for liberty throughout all the land unto all the inhabitants thereof.

The overall audience for the opuses of Paterno, particularly those anti-colonial Filipinos attuned to his tropological tendencies, would have recognized the ties of *Gayuma* to the rest of his writings. Those who had seen *The Dreamed Alliance* and understood as anti-American its call for Filipino unity and Filipino freedom would have sensed direct parallels in *Gayuma*. Here too a wise and ancient prophet, now Pitho in the role of Lapu, cues divided villages into coming together via invocations of traditional divinities and spirits. Here too, in fact, are two of the exact same villages in question, for Kainta and Antipolo along with Pasig make up the three Filipino towns that eventually ally in *The Dreamed Alliance*. And, once again, the blood sacrifice of a virgin and her beau is required for archipelagic unification and freedom to triumph. In *Gayuma*, Sinagtala drinks the poison and Tupas dies shortly thereafter, just before the other Filipino forces sing for unity and liberty; in *The Dreamed Alliance*, it is Tining who drains the toxin and Tarik who quickly expires, this time just before the surviving Filipinos sing together, "The union has triumphed! Long live our women! Long live our Liberty!" (26). This sentiment endows with obvious political charge, at least for those who would recognize the relationship between the two operas, the climactic line in *Gayuma*: "Long live unity, let us unite our hearts so that we will succeed in acquiring our desired freedom"] (Dela Cruz trans. 28).

Such parallels exist between *Gayuma* and other Paterno productions as well. *Magdapio* too features an homage to precolonial Filipino culture (that of the Aetas), a maiden who commits suicide in the name of enduring freedom, and a male protagonist who dies while in love with her. The role of father of the virgin is played by Botokan in *Magdapio* and Makandola in *Gayuma*. The order of deaths in *Magdapio* is opposite—Mapalad the hero perishes before Magdapio the heroine—but the rebellious resonances of the earlier play would have been apparent to any anticolonial audience member who subsequently attended a showing of *Gayuma*. It is not clear as of this writing whether *Gayuma* was written before or after *On the Arrival of Taft*, but the similarities here too are evident: another ancient seer, another call for unity among Filipinos, another desire for freedom.[31] Filipinos who had seen both plays would recognize their thrust as one.

Furthermore, those Filipinos in the audience for *Gayuma* who had seen the seditious dramas written by other authors would pick up on the comparable use by Paterno of characters with allusive names. For instance, "Tupas" is also the name of the last autonomous Filipino king of Cebu, the major island of the central Philippines, who fought against the Spanish conquistador Legazpi in 1565 until the superior military forces of the latter left him little choice but to sign a treaty of submission. "Sitan" refers to a Tagalog deity of the netherworld and "Sinagtala" means starlight. In *Gayuma*, therefore, the last indigenous ruler of the central Filipino island flips colonial history upside down, defeating a god of hell by merging with starlight. How this would be understood by anticolonial Filipinos under American occupation is transparent. Simultaneously, though, that interpretation would be entirely opaque to any Americans in the crowd. Those theatergoers would understand neither the Tagalog of the production nor the significance of the character names. And so amid all its implications and intertextualities, *Gayuma* is a rare kind of revolutionary achievement: a literary text that urges national independence without ever invoking the forces against which it stands.

The subversive subjects of all Paterno acts, the strategized and the improvised, on stages inside and outside, in theaters of various physical and metaphorical forms, develop in ways that repeatedly come undone. The seeming oddities of his performances, those of his librettos as well as those in his own life, work against the kind of strictly ordered world that American censors and colonists in the Philippines sought to enforce. Indeed, sedition laws in any age and place do not tolerate ambiguity well, for it is the very multiplicity of potential meaning that most unnerves those who seek to control and discipline. Throughout the 20th century, the grandees who waxed grandiloquent in the White House and their lackeys, whether American or not, whether in Manila or Hanoi or Baghdad, or for that matter in Guatemala City and Havana in the 1950s or Santo Domingo in the 1960s or Santiago de Chile in the 1970s or Managua in the 1980s, not to mention Kabul today, could not stand a performance that danced out of control before their very eyes. That is why Paterno is important, why the hoochee-hoochee matters as much as the Katipunan robe of Botokan. When generals appear in a box of honor, they expect genuflection. Paterno loved doing that. And so everyone took him for a fool. Which he was. But it is the fool, of course, who gets the last word.

Conquerors are rarely greeted as liberators. Believing otherwise, however, proved to be a postulate of American decisions to shed the blood of non-Americans throughout the 20th century. This still holds true. Those who find themselves in the pools of that blood often do not possess the literal firepower to turn history otherwise. They do retain, nonetheless, the figurative firepower of the pen, and so their response to American might can be looked for in theaters and stagings of their own design. And that response is as much a part of the story of the United States as anything else. So is the Philippines. The protagonists in the post-1898 archipelago are not minor figures with marginal trajectories. Taft would leapfrog from the islands to become secretary of war and then president and then chief justice of the United States. No other man has achieved that. Wright would next serve as the American ambassador to Japan, right after that archipelago became the first Asian nation to defeat a Western empire at war (Cullinane 111).[32] And Paterno would stand forever as the author of the first Asian opera in Spanish and as a pivotal fin de siècle politico amid global powers from western Europe and North America.

Yet the players at center stage, wherever that stage is located, are not necessarily the most germane to grasping any drama. An operatic critique of imperialism in Manila is as important to understanding the United States at the start of the 20th century as fictionalized critiques of the meatpacking industry in Chicago and of frontier violence in Alaska. For Paterno is one of the three most important authors of the first decade of the American century, alongside Upton Sinclair and Jack London. *The Jungle* and *The Call of the Wild* and *White Fang* are the immediate complements of all the Paterno performances of the early 1900s and should be read as such. His anonymity ought be aligned to their fame. For in the works of Paterno, American global power hung in the balance. And if the far side of the planet did not succumb to that power, then in truth perhaps it could not be said to be global at all.

three

Metamorphoses of Mid-America

The Fictions of Guillermo Gómez Windham
(1920–1924)

✵

The stories of Guillermo Gómez Windham are sanctified and subversive texts. As the inaugural recipient of what would come to be the most re-nowned literary award in the archipelago, the annual Zóbel Prize for the best Filipino writing in Spanish, Gómez Windham bears the imprimatur of national institutionalization.[1] And so marked, his short fictions and novel-las might seem to be of only insular interest. Yet despite being canonized in oblivion, despite being stuck in the mother of all corners, these same texts travel vigorously across the Pacific Ocean and challenge all normative borders of American literary studies. These unacknowledged, unwilling, and entirely legal textual migrations surge past the disciplinary regimes of academia and do work that is foundational to the United States as well as to the Philip-pines. Nevertheless, few people on either side of the Pacific know that the writings by Gómez Windham exist.

A number of underlying premises about territorial lines of all kinds might collapse if the case were contrary. That would be a very useful thing. Ameri-can studies, for all of its global colonizations, is without consideration of the Philippines a hopelessly parochial endeavor. And at the moment, there are few if any graduate students or professors who realize that they can justify studying Asian literature in Spanish in an American studies program. Yet the American century was forged with the narratives of Filipinos such as Gó-mez Windham. The global power of the United States that waxes in the late 19th century and wanes in the early 21st century is incomprehensible without consideration of writings such as his. Investigations into Filipino literature in Spanish may seem to be an exceptionally academic pursuit. Yet nothing that calls whole worlds into question is likely to be, put another way, academic.

The absence of Filipino literature in Spanish is the greatest gap in American literary studies today. Since the 1960s, many previously overlooked people have made their way into undergraduate syllabi, graduate student reading lists, academic conferences, tenure-track jobs, and conversations around the copy machine during the latest paper jam. The long arc of History, for the moment, has bent thus slightly toward justice. Filipino writers in Spanish should not be discussed, however, due to judgments emanant from domestic politics of who should no longer be marginalized or ignored altogether, such as individuals of a particular ethnicity, gender, or sexual orientation. Rather, the archipelagic authors should be studied because doing so necessarily generates new thinkings of the ways in which modern arts, however seemingly national, are in reality globalized phenomena. Twentieth-century Filipino writers in Spanish dealt with globalization long before doing so became fashionable elsewhere. Consequently, they center the American century. Recent waves of border-crossing scholarship are a boon, to be sure. But, to take one example, transatlantic theorizations require transpacific ones as well, if only to gain meaning by differentiation. Likewise, South-North interweavings and interpretations, such as "inter-American" studies, demand East-West correlates to make sense, if only to reveal reliefs by juxtaposition.

Off with the Bootstraps: Rising and Falling in *Cándida's Career*

The Zóbel Prize, an Asian competition created to honor works in a European language written amid a North American colonization, rings as both a reflection and bellwether of the globalized 20th century. The first of the awards given out was for *La carrera de Cándida* (*Cándida's Career*), a collection by Gómez Windham that includes two novellas, four short character studies of people who may or may not be fictional, a theatrical dialogue with stage directions, a second dialogue without theatrical accoutrements, a fairy tale, and two brief essays. The anthology, according to Andrea Gallo, was published in 1921, likely in Spain, with Gómez Windham finishing its second novella, "La odisea de Sing-A," in September 1920 ("La novelística" 140, 143). *Cándida's Career* was awarded the Zóbel in 1922, that is, at the center point of an American colonization of the Philippines that would run from 1898 to 1946; that colonial era was interrupted only by a Japanese invasion and occupation of the islands from late 1941 to 1945. The eponymous novella by Gómez

Windham, "Cándida's Career," is thus flush with the reality of the American presence in the Philippines. The story features Cándida, a young, provincial Filipina who is influenced by Miss Jones, her teacher from the United States, to read feminist and suffragette magazines in English.[2] Cándida is associated as well with European cultural projections. Her name evokes the famous novella *Candide, ou, l'Optimisme* (*Candide, or Optimism*) by Voltaire—"Cándida" in Spanish, like "Candide" in French, means "naive"—and her physical features are those of an "ensueño de un Rubens malayo" ["fantasy of a Malay Rubens"] (6). Yet all the while she stands too as a representative village girl from the central Philippine island of Iloilo. Her doomed affair with Bert, a rich Filipino city boy, therefore yields a parable of social and class relations that are simultaneously local and international.

Domestic tensions in the narrative are irreducible from their foreign contextualizations. Cándida meets Bert after she strikes out for San Pedro, the capital of Iloilo, "con el fin de matricularse en un 'business course' o curso mercantil en uno de los más afamados institutos de dicha capital" ["with the goal of matriculating into a 'business course' in one of the most famous institutes of said capital"] (3–4). Curiously, despite the quarter-century of American colonization that already has passed, Gómez Windham evidently expects the readership of his novella to be linguistically challenged by a simple phrase such as "business course," which he immediately translates into Spanish in the original passage as "curso mercantil." This implies an older and somewhat isolated readership who would have been past their school years by the time the imposed anglicization of the archipelago went into full effect. Neither the young Cándida nor her steady would have been stumped by similar phrases. Bert, a fellow student at the institute, falls for Cándida. She is wary, however, thinking he might only be interested in deflowering a poor girl (10). Furthermore, a relationship with Bert would interfere with her "lema o grito de guerra (*slogan*) que escribió en un cartón y fijó en un lugar visible de su cuartito, y que procuraba tener siempre presente en su memoria: 'MY CAREER ABOVE AL' [*sic*] (mi carrera sobre todo)" ["motto or war cry (*slogan*) that she wrote on a piece of cardboard and put up in a visible place in her little room and that she always tried to keep present in her memory: 'MY CAREER ABOVE AL' [*sic*]"] (10). Bert improves his chances, nonetheless, when he declaims in a school oratory contest about "el nuevo estado (*status*) de la mujer en la sociedad moderna, después de la guerra mundial" ["the new state (*status*) of women in modern society, after the world war"], that is, World War I (12). Eventually, Cándida does requite Bert's love, but when his family learns with horror that he has fallen for the worst type of woman, a poor and modern one, they ship him off to MIT (18).[3] The abandoned Cándida sinks into life as a cabaret dancer and prostitute (23). And there the story ends.

The plot of the novella speaks to the kaleidoscopic nature of Filipino social identities as unstable products of inextricable domestic and foreign forces. By extrapolation, it is indicative in general of 20th-century identities, upon which the torques of American soft and hard power applied around the world. The endless negotiations in "Cándida's Career" among languages and geographies point to two global empires in historical motion, the Spanish and the American, whirling through an archipelago antipodal and assimilating to them both. For example, the imperial tongues explicitly enlisted in the citations above maneuver atop one or more Filipino languages implicitly in use by the characters. The fact that "Bert" is short for "Alberto" is not a matter of a simple sobriquet, for immense movements in global history cause both names to exist and for one to turn into the other. The invocations of World War I and the American suffragette movement are not throwaway bits either. In a globalized world in which no island, however insular, is out of touch with continents everywhere else, the most distant of struggles can prove of intimate importance, the most faraway of fields but a backyard plot.

That being said, the rise and fall of Cándida does not appear at first to be particularly subversive of America or the American century. What is most striking about the textual environment of the tale is the opposite: the absence of overt resistance to American culture and power despite their obvious omnipresence. The tumultuous turn-of-the-century era of Pedro Paterno and William Taft is manifestly missing. No armed insurgents, whether historical or fictional, emerge in the near or deep background of "Cándida's Career." And no edict of execution like the Sedition Law of 1901 exists any longer to surveil and discipline revolutionary intent by the author. Cándida only seems to be seeking her way through a stable, Americanized archipelago. There is no call for Filipino unity or freedom, unlike in the operas of Paterno two decades earlier, and there is no transposition to some invented Filipino past to safeguard the author from accusations of antagonism to American rule in the present. There does seem to be some light satire of the attempts of Cándida to Americanize herself, but the rhetoric is hardly biting. The tone is closer to parody than polemics. Most significantly, the apparently straightforward moral of the story, that those same attempts are what leads to her downfall, belies the story itself.

Demonstrably, the reason why Cándida becomes a prostitute is not because she has prostituted herself to America but because Bert has prostituted himself to the Philippines. He is the one with the Filipino family who cannot accept her social mobility, so American an ideal. He is the one who ultimately cannot accept a modern, self-made Filipina he meets in business school and who styles herself after American suffragettes. Bert does have the opportunity to form, metaphorically, a unified Filipino people by marrying his status as an elite to that of Cándida, the daughter of an "aparcero" ["tenant farmer"] and an "ignorante campesina que había sido toda su vida una sumisa bestia de carga" ["ignorant peasant woman who had been all her life a submissive beast of burden"] (3). But instead, Bert abandons Cándida and, by extension, the lower rural classes of the Philippines to their customary fate as usable bodies. The most cutting criticism in "Cándida's Career" is not of the emptiness of the new American values of Cándida but of the traditional elite Filipino values of Bert. Had he accepted her as a modern American woman, the story would have ended in romance rather than revulsion, comedy rather than tragedy. This may not have been the moral that Gómez Windham intended, but it is certainly the one he wrote.

Given that moral, "Cándida's Career" seems to be, if anything, pro-American. There is no coded sedition here, unlike in the operas of Paterno. Instead, there is a text that appears to criticize the Americanization of the archipelago but in reality does not. There is certainly no suggestion, which would be counterfactual in any case, that the wealthy urban cad Bert and the poor provincial Cándida could have begun and sustained an equitable relationship as lovers or spouses at any moment prior to the American colonization. And there is no illusory nostalgia in the failure of their relationship for some prelapsarian pre-1898 Philippines run by either Spaniards or Filipinos. The modern education of Cándida is actually the only thing that makes her a potential partner for Bert in the first place, the only thing that places them together in the same space, and the only thing that possibly could have saved her from prostitution after his parents send him away. In short, "Cándida's Career" would appear to be a sub-version of the American century rather than a subversion: "sub" in the sense of overlooked, buried, or backgrounded. As a sub-version, it offers an unfamiliar viewpoint of 20th-century America, that of a village girl in the Philippines whose encounters with an English teacher and business school are part and parcel of American history just as much as if they had unfolded in the forty-eight states then in the Union.

This argument would seem instinctive today if Cándida had been instead an Inuit in Alaska or an original inhabitant of Hawaii. Those other noncontiguous American lands in the Pacific eventually became states themselves, so through retrospective teleologies they and their peoples have been subsumed into American literary history. That statehood did not come to pass for the Philippines, however, does not mean that characters such as Cándida, fictional or otherwise, were not fully part of the narrative of America at the time. To read her story as a sub-version of the American century, therefore, is to see the United States altogether differently, from the margins of the margins. Such a reading is inherently political, innately subversive. It overturns customary ways of looking at the world. And yet treating Cándida as a sub-versive may not do full justice to her story either. Her education in the Philippines is a specifically American phenomenon. As such, it fails. Surely this is subversive in some deep sense, not merely sub-versive. Education, after all, is politics by other means. And when it founders, the educators are oft held to account. This does not happen explicitly in Gómez Windham, but suggestions of an accounting are hard to dismiss altogether.

A second novella in his prizewinning anthology, "La odisea de Sing-A" ("The Odyssey of Sing-A"), foregrounds a Chinese youth who smuggles himself into the Philippines, marries a Filipina, and enters the black market opium trade via Muslim middlemen. Eventually, Sing-A is deported for this activity under the laws of the American colonial regime, whereupon he lives out his life teaching a Filipino language in China. This story therefore seems to reveal globalization more than Americanization. This time the protagonist is Chinese, the title evokes ancient Greece, the language of narration is Spanish, the plot involves Islamic traders, and the legal code is overseen by the United States. Yet all the while, Sing-A stands as a Filipino in the making. His movements, his memories, his use of an island language, his domestic and economic activities all constitute him as an exemplar of an archipelago that is uniquely itself and at the same time originates amid cultural flows from around the world.

The narrative of Sing-A, compared to that of Cándida, is less obviously indebted to the Americanized realities of the Philippines a generation after 1898. There is no significant character from the United States such as Miss Jones, no intent by Sing-A to learn English, no matriculation to a business school or MIT. Unlike Cándida, who is surrounded by American influences simply by being born and raised in the post-1898 archipelago, Sing-A appears to be foreign to the islands from birth to denouement. His story begins and ends in China. Sing-A moves into Philippine space and, ultimately, out of it. And if he is not Filipino, he certainly cannot be American. Throughout the story, his conscious identification with American power of any kind, cultural or political or military, is nonexistent. Literally or metaphorically, Sing-A has no claim to American identity.

This conclusion is wrong. The opacity of America in "The Odyssey of

Sing-A," seen otherwise, is quite clear. It is relatively easy to conceive of Cándida and her story as American because that reading results readily and frequently from the explicit content of the text that produces her. Yet in the story of Sing-A, America does emerge to cue three pivotal moments: his landing in the Philippines, the discovery of his drug trafficking by authorities, and his deportation. In other words, this individual who is seemingly so foreign to the Philippines is defined by American rule at the start, apex, and end of his Filipino arc. For example, the same paragraph that announces his arrival in the Philippines opens by noting, "Durante los primeros años de la ocupación americana de Filipinas, la administración de los asuntos civiles estaba en manos del departamento militar" ["During the first years of the American occupation of the Philippines, the administration of civil matters was in the hands of the military department"] (3). And many years later, at a moment when Sing-A is enjoying maximum success in the islands, his ruin begins when the customs officer Inspector Rojo receives an anonymous letter accusing the immigrant of drug trafficking. This is significant because just prior to this juncture, Rojo appears as an overt symbol of the Americanization of the Philippines.

That symbolism is rooted in the backstory that Gómez Windham assigns to Rojo. Twenty years earlier, a moment that coincides with the initial decade of the American colonial regime, Rojo had entered the customs office as a youth straight out of school "para perfeccionarse en el idioma inglés" ["to perfect himself in the English language"] (22). He then rose in the anglophone administration from assistant statistician to chief statistician to on-site inspector of suspicious boats, to chief of the anticontraband police, to interim customs chief of a small southern port, to, now, customs chief of the large port of San Pedro (22–23). This is a chronicle that resembles Gómez Windham's own vocational trajectory (Ben-Aben). Its vertical linearity, if not the Filipino details, seems lifted straight from stock American narratives of upward mobility. And Rojo, it turns out, achieved his latest, highest post due to "la 'Nueva Era' en la política de América en Filipinas, inaugurada bajo el gobierno de Harrison durante la primera administración Wilsoniana" ["the 'New Era' in the policy of America in the Philippines, inaugurated under the government of Harrison during the first Wilson administration"] (23). Francis Burton Harrison was the U.S. colonial governor of the Philippines from 1913 to 1921. He instituted the "Filipinization" of the islands, a broad attempt to put Filipinos in civil service positions in lieu of Americans. It is thus clear that Rojo, from his English studies at the start of his career to his leadership position at present, built his professional success by pegging himself to the parameters put in place by American forces of language, culture, and politics. And it is the entrance of this American understudy into the drama that marks the moment when the life of Sing-A in the islands begins to collapse.

That fall from success, however, is not preordained. Sing-A bribes his assistant Chun Li into taking the rap for the opium peddling, a maneuver that necessitates their telling the court that Chun Li is actually the entrepreneur and Sing-A a mere manual laborer. The strategy is set to spring Sing-A from all penalty until Inspector Rojo reminds the prosecutor about Law 702, "aprobada en 1902, mandando que todos los obreros chinos en Filipinas se proveyeran de Certificados de Residencia y castigando con la deportación su 'negligencia, falta o negativa'" ["approved in 1902, mandating that all the Chinese laborers in the Philippines obtain for themselves Certificates of Residence and punishing with deportation their 'negligence, error, or refusal'"] (28). Sing-A is caught, in other words, by his own defense, for while Chinese workmen were subject to Law 702, Chinese businessmen were not. His guise of being the employee of Chun Li makes him subject to legal legerdemain by Rojo, the American proxy who has assimilated attentively to the American administration. The dating of Law 702 to 1902 places it as a product of the Taft regime that established American legal frameworks in the Philippines. That was the same year in which Theodore Roosevelt declared American victory over Filipino revolutionaries and in which, shortly thereafter, Pedro Paterno offered his opera *The Dreamed Alliance* as a paradoxical rebuttal to the guest of honor, Taft himself. Although Sing-A is deported to China for his alleged foreignness to the Philippines, his expulsion is provoked by a law issued by American leadership and executed by American surrogates. This is a fundamentally Filipino narrative of the early 20th century, which is to say that it is a fundamentally American narrative as well.

American Genealogies

Such an interpretation of "The Odyssey of Sing-A" as an American story bypasses a separate and far larger logic: literature by an American national is, by definition, American literature. And Gómez Windham was certainly considered by the United States to be an American national. All Filipinos were at the time. Soon after the war of 1898 and the consequent rule by the United States over other islands such as Puerto Rico, individuals from those places began demanding a variety of rights from American courts in what became known as the Insular Cases. The U.S. Constitution did not provide ready answers for the questions that came up in these suits. The cases that were brought, and the verdicts returned, were often not parallel. Nonetheless, the upshot for Filipinos became fairly clear within the first few years of the 20th century: they were American nationals, that is, members of "a new class of Americans with an unusual civil status" that distinguished them from both citizens and aliens (Schlimgen 35). As early as 1901, in fact, the U.S. attorney general had been working under the assumption that Filipinos were American nationals (Schlimgen 35). The meaning of this status varied in practice during the forty-plus years that remained of the U.S. colonial period but not the status itself. Filipinos remained regarded not as aliens but as a kind of Americans. As Veta Schlimgen writes, "'American national' as a civil status would continue to override all other civil classifications that the U.S. extended to Filipinos during the decades of U.S. colonial governance. Both within and outside U.S. dominion Filipinos were American nationals first" (61). She concludes, "Filipinos lived under U.S. jurisdiction and were held to be a part of the United States" (73).

Just as literature by the famous American contemporaries of Gómez Windham is taught in American studies classrooms regardless of its foreign place of composition (say, Paris) or foreign setting (say, Spain) or, for that matter, foreign national affiliations (say, Great Britain), the Americanness of stories by Gómez Windham does not depend on the plots of their texts but on the person of their author. He could have written about anything at all—he could have mangled Chinese ideograms like Ezra Pound or mangled Spanish bulls like Ernest Hemingway—and it still would have been American literature. And this is the most liberating potential of "The Odyssey of Sing-A" for American students, who need to know that a short story by a Filipino in Spanish about a Chinese immigrant is just as constitutive of American literature of the 1920s as anything written by F. Scott Fitzgerald. This is not a matter of expanding existing grasps of the United States and U.S. literature but of unclenching that grasp—it is bare-knuckled and unconscious—altogether.

Of course, Gómez Windham was not only American. He was also Filipino, of course, and who knows what else he might claim, given that that his family background was also Spanish and Irish. Quite conceivably, he might not have wanted to be considered American. The idea might have repelled him. So too might have the idea of analyzing his writings as American literature. Perhaps he would have seen such an approach as the action of just one more American imperialist come to his islands to strip mine local resources and, insult to injury, strip them of themselves. There is an argument here, yes. But it is a weak one. It is entirely viable to study the fictions of Gómez Windham within as strictly regional or archipelagic traditions as possible, or within a genealogy that only includes authors commonly taken to be "Filipino." Yet the moment this strategy is enacted, the problems and limits of defining what is "Filipino" become self-evident. It is not as if Gómez Windham is a product of indigenous Filipino traditions. The alphabet he employs is from the West. The language he uses is from the West. The first Filipino fictions in Spanish, for that matter, date back just a few decades before his own. Moreover, those texts for the most part were written in Europe, published in Europe, circulated in Europe, and read mostly by Europeans. Gómez Windham, as a fictionalist who writes in Spanish from the Philippines and for Filipinos, is hardly participating in some kind of archipelagic heritage that stretches back into time immemorial. He is not a traditional Filipino writer so much as an inventor of Filipino written traditions. And his many francophile influences are the icing on the gâteau.

Regardless of personal preferences, the frames that authors can force around their own output are permeable at best. And Sing-A too was American whether he recognized it or not. His Americanness, like that of his creator, exists evidently despite not evidently existing. Put another way, his Americanness comes into being and never quite disappears. Being American is not a fixed ontological category but a provisional state that one can move into and out of through any number of legal and metaphoric means: immigration, exile, naturalization, renunciation of citizenship, and so forth. Cándida, like Gómez Windham, was an American national because America had come to include the Philippines. And the actuality of the American nationality of Filipinos was recognized by American courts for nearly half a century. As Allan Punzalan Isaac states, "Filipinos were, in fact, part of the U.S. domestic sphere" (16). And so Sing-A becomes American when he enters the American space that was the Philippines. His life in the Philippines is his life in America. His home in the middle of the archipelago is his home in the middle of America. And since he never ceases being Filipino in his mind—long after his involuntary return to China, Sing-A continues to dream of the Philippines and his Filipino self—he never ceases being American in his mind either.

The Chinese background of Sing-A does not make him less Filipino or less American. At stake here are multiple and overlapping identities, not exclusive racializations or nationalizations. For the last five centuries at least, Chinese immigrants and their legacies have been just as constitutive of Filipino culture as anything else. The Spanish colonial period was marked by successive waves of Chinese labor that was, just as successively, bloodily repressed and then admitted to the islands once again. The Filipino national hero José Rizal was of Chinese ancestry, as was Paterno, as is a large swath of the Philippine political and cultural elite still today. And Sing-A, upon coming to the archipelago, becomes Filipino, that is, American, like other immigrants to the United States, however they assimilate, whatever identities they travel with or without, regardless of whether they ultimately return to the place their younger selves left. The symbolic proof of the enduring Filipinization of Sing-A, which is to say, his enduring Americanization, is that once he is deported to China, he becomes a Filipino language teacher to others intent on striking out for the Philippines—that is, for America—in order to initiate their own attempt there at going from rags to riches (33–34). They too are Filipinos in the making. They too are about to become Americans. Horatio Alger, meet your doubles. The comeuppance of nouveau riche social climbers that Gómez Windham metes out to Cándida and Sing-A is of a kind with that which condemns their contemporary Jay Gatsby. There are other long islands in America in the 1920s beyond that in New York. There are other meretrices who start out as monogamists. And the most American egg of the East is balut.

All national identities have porous borders and none more so than those of the Philippines. The shorter texts in Gómez Windham's prizewinning collection correspondingly reveal an unsettled admixture of Western and Asian elements beyond those mentioned above.[4] For instance, there are constant evocations of canonical European authors and literary tendencies, to the point where the short essay "Un día en Manila" ("A Day in Manila") relays the musings of a flâneur. France in particular seems to stand out as lending meaning to Filipino space and time more often than even Spain and the United States, the historical foreign powers in the archipelago. Yet of course, francophile predilections do not make Gómez Windham any less American than the anglophile or hispanophile leanings of his contemporaries such as T. S. Eliot and Hemingway. Another piece in the *Cándida's Career* anthology, "La infinita estulticia" ("The Infinite Foolishness") is subtitled by Gómez Windham as a "Dialogo socratico" ["Socratic Dialogue"], and its topic is the new entertainment technology that is the silent movie. The cultural line from Socrates to the Philippines is hardly straight. The nascent film industry is imported from a Western elsewhere as well. Yet such components do not make Gómez Windham any less Filipino than his writing in Spanish and using a Western alphabet in doing so. These too are technologies from an abroad that has become domestic. This is all to say that the Western world is refracted here through an antipodal author. For that is what Gómez Windham is:

antipodal and American at once. He is also, simultaneously, francophile and Filipino. His is a quintessentially 20th-century subject position.

Given the fictions of Gómez Windham, the putative purviews of American studies stand out as parochial. Who teaches the moveable feasts of American literature in the 1920s—the buffet of Eliot, Pound, Gertrude Stein, Hemingway, Fitzgerald, and so on—by moving Paris to a province in the Philippines? Which teachers realize that they can broaden dramatically the American world of their students by assigning Asian literature from that decade instead, and in Spanish at that? The issue is not informed diversity and not ivory tower charity. Rather, the narratives of Gómez Windham should be read out of a need for acute inquiry where it rarely if ever has been suggested, much less developed. His inclusion generates new questions, not old answers. His work puts under suspicion, instantly, conventional historical and literary narratives of Spain, France, the United States, China, and other geopolitical entities that do have dedicated wings in the academic infrastructure of the West. Gómez Windham is a writer of cosmopolitan import who, like Filipino authors in Spanish in general, transforms most landscapes ever sketched of the Spanish-speaking world. And he does all this not only as an American subject but as an American national as well.

The significance of Gómez Windham extends, in sum, far beyond the Philippines to other sides of the world. But certainly, this is not how he has been envisioned within the archipelago either, where he is remembered (and barely at that) only as a signpost of a mostly vanished national tradition in Spanish. A revisionist consideration of Zóbel winners such as Gómez Windham would therefore invigorate some senescent suppositions among literary scholars everywhere. The public letter by the Zóbel patriarch announcing the establishment of the prize reads in part, "Así queremos nosotros que se haga Patria" ["Thus we want Fatherland to be made"] (Brillantes, *81 Years* 37). This notion of making a nation and national identity by building it a literature has a long history among intellectuals in the Americas, but few if any researchers who have delved into such questions have offered transpacific analyses. Such juxtapositions, though, would provide vibrant new frameworks for approaching the many Latin Americanist novelists of the 1920s, all of them direct contemporaries of Gómez Windham, who likewise sought to create fictions that were uniquely Colombian or Argentine or Venezuelan. Why not contrast a Filipino attempt in Spanish to make "Patria" via fiction with those of peer efforts across the Atlantic such as José Eustasio Rivera in *La vorágine* (*The Maelstrom*) from 1924, Ricardo Güiraldes in *Don Segundo Sombra* from 1926, and Rómulo Gallegos in *Doña Bárbara* from 1929? The worst that would happen is that somebody would learn something. The best would be exciting and creative considerations of dusty debates that in turn would inspire new thinkings about the myriad relationships of nations and national literary traditions.

The authors in a position to compete for the Zóbel award were in a fluid and complex historical position. They were part of the only relatively broad generation of Filipinos to have learned Spanish even though Iberian claims to the archipelago dated back to Magellan in 1521.[5] And when these authors reached adulthood, a different Western language, English, was compelling the attention of all subsequent generations. How this compares to what Puerto Rican writers have faced since its own colonization by the United States in 1898 remains an open question. More widely still, investigations are needed to argue how the simultaneously postcolonial and colonial situation of 20th-century Filipino writers in Spanish can be related to all Latin Americans who have written in Spanish since the early 19th century amid the pervasive, and often expansive, hemispheric influence of the United States. Yet the fictions of Gómez Windham are never considered in their transatlantic and global import. Perhaps this is because they usually seem so focused on characters in the Philippines. Most of the narratives of Gómez Windham are set neither in Manila, the national metropolis, nor in Cebu, the geographically central island of major historical and cultural importance, but in Iloilo, a province northwest of Cebu. His characters probably speak Filipino vernacular languages among themselves more often than not, perhaps exclusively in the case of those from lower socioeconomic classes. Any conversations in those tongues, though, are only alluded to in his texts beneath the omnipresent Spanish and occasional English. In other words, Gómez Windham is a provincial writer who is not provincial at all. He recasts the world. His narratives, as a result, might illuminate the work of various Latin American authors of his era and earlier, not to mention writers from other marginalized regions of the planet, who likewise sought to navigate in their letters far beyond the apparent periphery that seemingly confined them.

In his person, Gómez Windham presented a globalized Filipino subjectivity. According to Andrea Gallo, his father was a descendant of Spaniards as well as Tagalogs, and his maternal grandfather was a native of Ireland who reportedly worked as a British consul in the Philippines ("Guillermo" 3). Born in 1880 and thus entering adulthood amid the 1898 conflagrations, Gómez Windham responded nimbly to the protean realities of the archipelago (Gallo, "Guillermo" 4). He must have spoken Hiligaynon (also known as Ilonggo), which is the vernacular of Iloilo, surely Cebuano, and likely Tagalog as well, plus apparently a certain amount of French (Gallo, "Guillermo" 4).[6] His English seems to have been unusually good, given that "al llegar los americanos a Iloílo, eran ellos, los hermanos Gómez Windham, los únicos que podían hablar inglés, a excepción del cónsul británico" ["When the Americans arrived in Iloilo, it was they, the Gómez Windham brothers, who were the only ones who could speak English, with the exception of the British consul"] (Gallo, "Guillermo" 4).[7] The early travels of Gómez Windham were worldly too, possibly including visits, according to Gallo, to Hong Kong and Spain ("Guillermo" 4). Manuel García Castellón affirms that Gómez Windham actually pursued advanced studies in commerce in Hong Kong in 1899 or thereafter (225). In 1904, furthermore, "tuvo un relevante papel en la representación filipina de la Exposición Internacional celebrada en San Luis de Missouri, Estados Unidos" ["he had a relevant role in the Filipino delegation at the International Exposition celebrated in St. Louis, Missouri, United States"] (García Castellón, 225). This is the same world's fair for which Pedro Paterno was the only Filipino on the organizing board and at which his opera *Magdapio* was supposed to be staged. Had that happened, Gomez Windham probably would have seen it performed on the Philippine Reservation there.

In the Philippines, Gómez Windham crafted a long career as a customs officer. This profession made him acutely aware of the foreign inputs and outputs that affected daily archipelagic life, from the wares that smugglers tried to sneak past his oversight to the fluctuations in the world sugar market that directly impacted the economics of the islands. Iloilo, though not the political or historical center of the Philippines, was still an important nexus of commerce and so could function as an open window from which Gómez Windham could evaluate the world. For instance, in a 1925 opinion piece published in the Manila newspaper *El debate*, Gómez Windham spoke of "las tres principales capitales, Manila, Cebu Iloilo" ["the three principal capitals, Manila, Cebu, Iloilo"] and argued, with reference to owners and laborers in the Philippine maritime industry, that "capitalistas y obreros no son ni pueden ser enemigos, como se creia durante el siglo XIX, sino asociados, tan necesarios los unos a los otros como son el fuego y el agua para producir el vapor que da fuerza, movimiento y progreso . . . podran realizar su noble funcion de estrechar y apretar cada dia mas los lazos que unen a las diversas regiones de la patria" ["capitalists and workers are not and cannot be enemies, as was believed during the 19th century, but associates, the one as necessary to the other as are fire and water to produce the steam that creates force, movement, and progress . . . they will be able to fulfill their noble function of strengthening and tightening each day more the ties that unite the diverse regions of the fatherland"] (8). Though residing in a province, in other words, Gómez Windham apparently felt well positioned to assess the macro and micro interrelations of economic and cultural forces within the Philippines and beyond.

It is tempting to read the biography of Gómez Windham into his fictions and see their worldliness as a relative outlier. The English and business school education of Cándida, the transnational movements of Sing-A, the career in customs of his character Inspector Rojo, the detailed attention to financial accountings and legal and political maneuvers, all suggest roots in the experiences of an unusually cosmopolitan man whose writings are therefore, arguably, unrepresentative of a larger literary tradition. Yet this conclusion is questionable, and not only because relying on the biography of any author for the interpretation of his texts is a fallacy long established. Gómez Windham may have been particularly suited to gauge a world in flux from the docks of Iloilo, but the international currents that washed up and over his home port are proper not to him alone but to the archipelago as a whole. Owing to the pedagogic juggernaut of the occupiers, mixing vernaculars and English was common among many Filipinos by the time *Cándida's Career* appeared. Further fluctuations in Spanish were surely prevalent among those who spoke that tongue as well. Most Filipinos, not just Gómez Windham, moved among multiple languages then and still do today. The development of an archipelagic class with the professional skills needed to work with the American colonizers and their economic interests extended far beyond customs officials such as Gómez Windham, to wit the formation of business school student populations in "Cándida's Career." It is true that Gómez Windham traveled all the way to St. Louis, but that was for a sojourn. Thousands of other Filipinos subsequently would cross the Pacific to spend many years as laborers in the western United States. In short, Gómez Windham was in no way unique as a Filipino who negotiated the globe from his island vantage. Given standard imperial relationships involving the extraction of natural resources on one hand and the creation of colonial markets for value-added products on the other, the whole of the Philippines, not just customs officers, was attuned to import/export dynamics. Gómez Windham may have channeled his particular brand of worldliness into fiction, but the local communities he wrote about were worldly already without him.

That worldliness had developed along American lines in the Philippines since 1898. By the time of the Zóbel Prize awarded to Gómez Windham, the United States was well into its third decade of occupying the archipelago. In the 1920s, in fact, America was cementing its hold on the islands. Back in

Washington, the sequence of three Republican presidents after the elections of 1921 resulted in policies that pushed against moves by preceding Democratic administrations to cede more power in the Philippines to Filipinos, such as the Filipinization efforts of Harrison. Shortly before leaving office, the Democratic president Woodrow Wilson had gone on record as favoring Philippine independence, but his Republican successors Warren Harding and Calvin Coolidge made significant efforts in the opposite direction (Kramer 387–88). And as degrees of political autonomy receded for Filipinos, so did measures of cultural autonomy as the work of two decades of English teachers and American mass media wedged ever more deeply into archipelagic society. The creation of the Zóbel contest was a conscious attempt at countering the compounding Americanization of the Philippines by promoting a hispanized island culture that was increasingly distanced from its historical origins.[8] The fictions of Gómez Windham, by virtue of being in Spanish, stand today as a reminder that the United States took the colony in an intraimperial struggle. To audiences at the time, however, his texts appeared as an innate argument against all the assimilations that the United States had sought to impose in the archipelago since 1898.

Earlier Filipino writers working in Spanish had grappled aggressively with the deployment of American authority in the islands. It is not a coincidence that the operas by Paterno offer plots whose starting point is usually the arrival of foreign powers in the Philippines: the Moors in *The Dreamed Alliance*, the Malays in *Magdapio*, the U.S. secretary of war in *On the Arrival of Taft*. By the time Gómez Windham wrote *Cándida's Career*, however, the American occupation was a fact of life, a background context that was neither newly erected nor visibly coming to an end. His protagonists, as a result, face their challenges within social, economic, and political systems that already operate in established networks and matrices. The familiarity of those systems is why the characters try to navigate through their worlds rather than overturn or substantively modify them. The operas by Paterno, in contrast, all begin with sudden upheaval in social order that needs to be put right. They therefore are comedies in the sense of ending in resolution and optimism. The good guys do tend to win one way or another, despite the setbacks they suffer, with even Magdapio, notwithstanding her suicide, remaining morally and bodily pure and committed to her beloved. Communal bonds are forged in Paterno. Filipino fraternity triumphs. In Gómez Windham, existing social orders are relatively stable in the first place, and the struggles of his protagonists are as individuals to succeed within them. When they do not, they tend, unlike the players in Paterno, to become antisocial antiheroes, losers in a social Darwinian world for not having figured out how to conform to the rules effected by force majeure. Cándida and Sing-A are characters whose lives end in alienation rather than communion. Indeed, perhaps their rise and fall as primarily individual rather than social subjects is the most markedly American thing about them. And perhaps Gómez Windham is at his most American as an author for structuring their stories as bildungsromans in the first place.

Unresolved Narratives: "Aunt Pasia" and Beyond

Although Gómez Windham is often cited in the Philippines as the inaugural winner of the Zóbel Prize and thus of historical importance, substantive criticism of his texts is almost nil. Searches for scholarship on 20th-century Filipino literature in Spanish usually need to begin with the three books that offer the most comprehensive surveys of the tradition: *Historia analítica de la literatura filipinohispana (desde 1566 hasta mediados de 1964)* (*Analytical History of Filipino-Hispanic Literature (from 1566 to the middle of 1964)*) by Estanislao Alinea from 1964, *La literatura filipina en castellano* (*Filipino Literature in Castilian*) by Luis Mariñas from 1974, and *81 Years of Premio Zóbel: A Legacy of Philippine Literature in Spanish* by Lourdes Castrillo Brillantes from 2006. Yet Alinea barely mentions Gómez Windham in passing and only as an essayist at that (105). Mariñas places Gómez Windham as one of the top three Filipino novelists in Spanish during the American colonial period but limits his half-page commentary to biographical details, quick descriptions, and a twice-repeated observation that the texts are "de carácter sentimental y moralista" ["of a sentimental and moralistic character"] (57). The overview by Brillantes is a self-translation of her *80 años del Premio Zóbel* (*80 Years of the Zóbel Prize*) from 2000, but the two texts differ in their section dedicated to Gómez Windham and the earliest years of the award.[9] The closest either offers to analysis is a short paragraph that describes "Cándida's Career." And Florentino Hornedo does not interrogate Gómez Windham at all in his important essay, "Notes on the Filipino Novel in Spanish."[10]

As of this writing, the only studies that focus on Gómez Windham appear to be the essay by Gallo that is entitled "Guillermo Gómez Windham: Líneas bio-bibliográficas y unos poemas" ("Guillermo Gómez Windham: Bio-bibliographic Lines and Some Poems") and its follow-up on Gómez Windham's five novellas. The "bio-bibliography" is the favored genre of scholarship on 20th-century Filipino literature in Spanish. It chiefly entails three elements: a heavy investment in the details of the lives of the author and his family, a list of titles, and a presentation of some poems and/or prose excerpts. Criticism that goes beyond this usually only does so in order to provide a few phrases that summarize themes or aesthetic inclinations. Sometimes a scholar also will decide to contextualize the author within a larger literary taxonomy. In such veins, Gallo delineates in his "bio-bibliography" the life trajectory of Gómez Windham and those of his relatives. He then reproduces all the poems he was able to locate by the Zóbel winner and his brother Felipe. He concludes, "El intento de este ensayo ha sido, ofreciendo datos desconocidos, sacar de nuevo a la luz a un autor y unos textos que en su día construyeron el gusto de aquella época" ["The intent of this essay has been, by offering unfamiliar data, to bring to light anew an author and some texts that in their day built the taste of that distant epoch"] ("Guillermo" 22).[11] The subsequent article by Gallo on the novellas implicitly follows a similar rationale. After deciding to treat the five fictions as "una unidad textual" ["a textual unity"], Gallo describes all of them and then ends by saying, "En conclusión, Gómez Windham demuestra no sólo no ser un autor menor de la literatura filipina, sino que prueba cómo la creación literaria en este país alcanzó una autonomía estética y una madurez de autorreflexión ya en tiempos lejanos" ["In conclusion, Gómez Windham demonstrates not only that he is not a minor author of Filipino literature but also proves how literary creation in this country already reached an aesthetic autonomy and a maturity of self-reflection in distant times"] ("La novelística" 140, 149).

In his bio-bibliography, along with recovering lost verse, Gallo chronicles the literary production of Gómez Windham. The body of work splits into a burst of prose (mostly fiction) in the first half of the 1920s and then a dozen poems and a few articles that appeared in print in a single periodical from May 1949 to May 1950 ("Guillermo" 29–31). The prose includes the twelve texts that constitute *Cándida's Career* and a second anthology, *La aventura de Cayo Malínao: (Novelas filipinas contemporáneas)* (*The Adventure of Cayo Malínao: (Contemporary Filipino Novels)*). This latter collection comprises an eponymous bildungsroman that at some seventy pages is Gómez Windham's longest known text; a shorter bildungsroman entitled "Los ascensos del Inspector Rojo" ("The Ascents of Inspector Rojo") about the rise of the customs officer who appears in "The Odyssey of Sing-A"; and a complicated story of nightmares and vengeance entitled "Tia Pasia" ("Aunt Pasia"). Notwithstanding the 1924 publication date of the anthology, most or perhaps all of this material was written closer in time to *Cándida's Career*.[12] The last page of "The Adventure of Cayo Malínao" is dated August 1922, and the last page of "The Ascents of Inspector Rojo" is dated September 1922; "Tia Pasia" is undated

(77, 128). Along with the smattering of poems and articles that were published in the twelve-month stretch a quarter-century later, this is pretty much all the literature currently known by Gómez Windham.

Surely, however, he wrote much more than that. The structural complexities of his novellas and his confident narratorial voice in them suggest an author working with a substantial amount of literary experience. In 1916, half a decade before penning the first of his longer fictions, Gómez Windham characterized himself as "Periodista antiguo" ["a former journalist"] and recalled, as if it were distant, the "comienzo de mi vida literaria" ["start of my literary life"] (Gómez Windham, "Sr. Gregorio" 67). A journalist who interviewed him in 1931 referred to "sus varias novelas, sus ensayos de drama, sus discursos y el sinnúmero de artículos que con su firma han cotizado muy alto los valores en nuestro mercado literario" ["his various novels, his essays about drama (or, possibly, "his dramatic works"), his speeches and his innumerable articles that with his signature have been reckoned as of very high value in our literary market"] (Ben-Aben). An article by Tony Fernández from 1966 therefore seems likely to be accurate in its retrospective on Gómez Windham, who by that point had been dead for nearly a decade: "Durante sus ratos libres, no dejaba de escribir novelitas, cuentos cortos, artículos y otras obras literarias, mucho de las cuales se publicaban en revistas y periódicos de Iloilo y Manila" ["During his free time, he never stopped writing novellas, short stories, articles, and other literary works, many of which were published in magazines and newspapers in Iloilo and Manila"].

There are hints of a continuing involvement by Gómez Windham in literary circles during those long periods when, given the bibliography by Gallo, no creative writings of his seem to be known. In 1940, for example, Gómez Windham participated in a conference held on the first anniversary of the Philippine Writers' League as a member of an aging generation of writers, or as Federico Mangahas put it at the time, "representing the veterans' point of view" (100). Gómez Windham spoke to the attendees about "the probable effects of the Tagalog translation of Cervantes' 'Don Quijote' on Filipino life and thought" (Mangahas 100).[13] That year, he published an article on the same subject.[14] And in 1953, he served as one of the judges of the Zóbel competition (Brillantes, *81 Years* 189). Dedicated sifting through various periodicals seems likely to reveal more aspects of his literary life and environment. A hitherto unknown book review by him from 1923, for example, reveals his lament for an archipelagic cultural scene in which even a published book of high literary value "pasa desapercibido casi siempre, sin revisteros que lo describen, sin críticos que lo analizen [*sic*] y casi sin lectores que lo cometen [*sic*] y lo saboreen" ["passes almost always unperceived, without magazine writers who describe it, without critics who analyze it and almost without readers who comment it and savor it"] ("Siembra" 2).[15] The quest for such lost publications by Gómez Windham is a worthwhile endeavor but should serve as a prelude to analysis, not an end unto itself. As things stand, though, this is rarely the case.[16]

Of the three novellas that Gómez Windham published in 1924, "Aunt Pasia" is the most complex and open ended. "The Adventure of Cayo Malínao," despite its length, offers the most simple of all of Gómez Windham's plots in its depiction of a humdrum man of average talent who leads a routinized life at work and home until one day he is happened upon by Vicentito Martínez, a bullying childhood schoolmate now become a dashing politician dedicated to amassing "episodios pintorescos en todos los cuales intervenían como factores importantísimos el vino, el juego o las mujeres" ["picturesque episodes in all of which wine, gambling, or women intervened as very important factors"] (34–35). Encouraged by Vicentito, Cayo suddenly becomes obsessed with gambling and, as a result, ruins his family, his career, and his life. A noteworthy early episode in this sequence is when he commits adultery with Cándida, still a cabaret dancer and prostitute, whom Vicentito describes as "¡muy dispuesta! ¡muy dispuesta a divertirse!" ["very ready! very ready to enjoy herself!"] (35).[17] "The Ascents of Inspector Rojo" also resurrects a character from *Cándida's Career*, the titular customs officer, who in "The Odyssey of Sing-A" figures out how to legally ensnare the protagonist for his opium smuggling and have him deported to China. As in "The Adventure of Cayo Malínao," a relatively linear tale propels "The Ascents of Inspector Rojo." The plot in this case follows Inspector Rojo as he does everything by the book until one day he allows his sympathies for a Spanish woman who wants to immigrate to get the better of him: he lets her land on Filipino soil when technically he should not. This bending of the rules torments him, but all is eventually resolved in his favor.

In short, "The Adventure of Cayo Malínao" narrates the fall of a hard-working but, from Gómez Windham's perspective, mediocre man who fails to improve his station both by licit and illicit means. "The Ascents of Inspector Rojo" recounts the opposite, with the final promotion of Inspector Rojo to the highest rank in the local customs office in sharp contrast to the culminating incarceration of Cayo in a Manila penitentiary described as "un buitre hambriento con la boca siempre dispuesta a engullir su ración de carne corrompida" ["a hungry vulture with a mouth always ready to gulp down its ration of corrupt flesh"] (77). Though some commentators identify the moralizing tendencies in Gómez Windham as particularly characteristic of his prose, the principles apparently at stake often seem to dissolve. This is most noticeable in that those characters who upgrade their station are applauded, whatever the means they use to rise. The ethics behind such success are irrelevant. Vicentito is surely more corrupt, for instance, than Cayo, but he never receives even a hint of comeuppance. Similarly, the other drug traffickers who are ancillary characters in "The Odyssey of Sing-A" prosper freely despite being far more invested in the illegal trade than the protagonist. Agile socioeconomic maneuvering is rewarded in the oeuvre of Gómez Windham far more than adherence to a strict system of values or morals. All the main figures in the novellas, even those who begin wealthy, work energetically to adapt their original class positions to the changing Filipino and global realities under American hegemony. This is to say that the Iloilo of Gómez Windham offers a stratified but not ossified class structure. Cándida, Bert, Sing-A, Cayo, Vicentito, Inspector Rojo, and many minor characters all strive to obtain or maintain elite status in a rapidly altering world. It is the failure of consolidating upward mobility that is condemned and, correspondingly, the inability to be versatile enough before the demands of a globalized colony. Scorned is not, as the stories superficially seem to propose, the intent per se of non-elites to rise above their station. Rigidity to any code, be it moral or linguistic or otherwise, would be a poor fit for a protean planet and the polities it produces.

Perhaps the most remarkable narrative by Gómez Windham, "Aunt Pasia," does center around an inflexible individual. She is pursued by nightmares in consequence. This novella is the only one that does not follow the life story of a character from birth to dramatic climax. It is also the one most deeply rooted in imperial historicity. With its literal hauntings, rich and ambiguous symbolism, and peripatetic narratorial eye, it departs more sharply from the conventions of realism than the other novellas. Moreover, its Gothic ambience and themes of sadism and vengeance rely on affect as a dominant mode. The tone contrasts sharply with the intellectualized, somewhat wry depictions of Cándida, Sing-A, Cayo, and Inspector Rojo. The result is a text of particular literary depth, compelling in its strangenesses and the perplexing catharsis with which it ends. The starting point is the formal but incomplete triumph of American troops over Filipino rebels who sought independence for the archipelago in the early 20th century. The first paragraph thus reads, "El día que se rindieron, con mucha ceremonia, las fuerzas regulares revolucionarias de San Pedro, que comandaba el General Plaza, ante las fuerzas superiores del ejército norteamericano de ocupación, allá por el año 1902, la provincia de X . . . quedó 'pacificada' oficialmente, pero no del todo en realidad" ["The day in which, with much ceremony, the regular revolutionary forces of San Pedro, commanded by General Plaza, surrendered before the superior forces of the North American army of occupation, around the year 1902, the province of X . . . became officially 'pacified' but was not entirely so in reality"] (131).

San Pedro is the capital of Iloilo and the central space in the overall narrative world of Gómez Windham, but "Aunt Pasia" is evidently not just a local story. Instead, the opening lines put forth a trilateral macrohistorical moment in which the transition from the old Spanish empire (implied by the language of the text itself) to the new American empire is concluded with the surrender of island patriots. The supposed pacification is not comprehensive, though, because some Filipino irregulars refuse to concede, particularly one band led by Captain Palás, "que fué medio cuatrero, medio bandido, en tiempo del gobierno español, y a quien los jefes revolucionarios habían tolerado en sus filas" ["who was half rustler, half bandit in the time of the Spanish government and whom the revolutionary chiefs had tolerated in their ranks"] (132).[18] Palás, struggling to survive in the countryside, demands protection money from locals, who comply at first but then ignore him as they start falling in line with the American regime. To counter this trend, Palás kidnaps and executes Ramón Pañoso, whom "las nuevas autoridades acababan de nombrar vice-presiente [*sic*] municipal" ["the new authorities had just named municipal vice-president"] (134). The grief of Ramón's widow, Pasia (short for Bonifacia), then causes General Talberg, the American military commander in the area, to pursue Palás obsessively. Palás is caught and condemned, but as he walks toward the hangman he catches sight of Pasia in her window. They gaze at each other, and then Palás "con paso firme y actitud altanera" ["with a firm step and haughty attitude"] heads to the noose (136). Afterward, Pasia feels cheated out of her rightful vengeance:

> Hubiera querido que los del consejo de guerra la hubiesen entregado a Palás y la hubiesen dado el arma misma con que mató a su marido para castigarle ella por su mano; para herirle donde hirió, para causarle los dolores que causó; para recrearse en el espectáculo de la sangre del asesino fluyendo lentamente con su vida miserable . . . (137; ellipsis in the original)

> [She would have wanted those in the war council to turn Palás in to her and give her the same arm with which he killed her husband,

so she could punish him by her own hand; to wound him where he wounded, to cause him the pains that he caused; to enjoy the spectacle of the blood of the assassin flowing slowly with his miserable life . . .]

A month later, Pasia sells the property left her by Ramón and moves to San Pedro for good. She is thirty years old, a childless widow, and an orphan as well, and the look from Palás as he strode to his death will haunt her for decades to come.

This chapter, the first of four, frames the story in metaphorically suggestive ways. What the structures and figures symbolize, however, and what the ideological impetus of the author is, seems deliberately blurry. Authors of war fiction tend to take one side of the conflict at hand or another, particularly if national independence is on the table, yet the initial paragraph of "Aunt Pasia" seems to honor not only the Filipino revolutionaries but also their surrender. Moreover, foreign armies of "ocupación" ["occupation"] are rarely portrayed positively, but here their regional commander is the man who captures Palás, a scourge of average Filipinos. Yet at the same time, it is a Filipina who really wields power by impelling the American general into action. This implies a subtly subversive triumph in which a colonial subject, seemingly in a position of weakness, gets the colonizing power to exert force on her behalf. This gesture, however, is upturned by the fact that Ramón, in whose name Pasia cues the foreign police power to act, is a collaborator with the occupying regime in that he accepted a political post under their aegis. Complicating matters further, the choice of Spanish as a medium for the narrative, given that Gómez Windham surely could have written it in Hiligaynon and perhaps English, implicitly may carry with it a nostalgia for pre-1898 ways of writing the Philippines. None of this appears to hold together organically.

As for Aunt Pasia, though the eponymous character and therefore presumptive protagonist, she enters the story only belatedly and not as an aunt in any biological sense.[19] Her persona, nevertheless, seems to signify vast issues in tension. Is her retrospective desire for a personalized and bloody vengeance a sublimation onto Palás of an allegorical rage at being orphaned not so much by her parents as by Spain, the dead and gone *patria*? Or is her fury really at being widowed not so much by Ramón as by the United States, the present power that has rubbed out the revolution? "Pasia" seems to directly evoke "Pasiam," the nine-day period of bereavement that was customary in the Philippines and which does take place for Ramón (134).[20] The macrohistoricity of the opening transfer of power in the story implies that "Aunt Pasia" is not a story just about Aunt Pasia, focused only on the lamentings of one young wife for her husband. The concern rather seems to be with mourning work of a complex symbolic nature and large-scale import.

This supposition is reinforced by her given name, which echoes with revolutionary fervor cut short. "Bonifacia" sounds like a female version of Bonifacio, that is, Andrés Bonifacio, the original leader of the Filipino insurgency against Spain who was summarily tried and executed by a rival faction. Allegorical movement for independence seems to be hinted at here. Judgments seem to be implied. There are in this opening chapter no fewer than three courts, all of them kangaroo to greater or lesser degrees. Palás tries and convicts and executes Ramón; the foreign general does the same to Palás; and a native force of some kind does the same to "Bonifacio/a." The move of Pasia(m) to the provincial capital, San Pedro, marks a centralization of mourning. In truth, the whole story seems to be an extended interplay of afterlives of one sort or another. Yet how to read the interactions of the posthumous, be they the ghost of Palás (for he keeps returning) or, say, of the Spanish empire or the Filipino revolution, is never clearly resolved even though the narrative ends in what appears to be a definitive catharsis.

The second chapter of "Aunt Pasia" depicts the city life of the title character as she throws herself into Catholicism and church goings-on. Her bitterness at the dead Palás deepens. She prays nightly before an altar in her room that features a "calvario fantástico" ["fantastic calvary"] that includes the dagger that killed her husband, his portrait, and an image of Saint Michael the Archangel stepping on the devil (141). Her sadistic thoughts surge as

> dedicóse con más ahinco que de costumbre a fantasear sobre su tema favorito : el de que no se había vengado lo suficiente del malvado que la redujo al estado de viudez y soledad. Complacíase en imaginarse que se lo habían entregado, bien atado de pies y manos, y que ella, con la misma arma asesina, le hería donde él hirió, contemplando gozosa sus dolores y su lenta agonía . . . (141–42; ellipsis in the original)

> [she dedicated herself with more effort than customary to fantasize about her favorite theme: that she had not taken sufficient revenge on the villain who reduced her to the state of widowhood and solitude. She pleased herself by imagining that they had turned him in to her, his feet and hands well tied, and that she, with the same assassinating arm, wounded him where he wounded, contemplating happily his pains and his slow agony . . .]

Amid these fantasies, the ghost of Palás begins to make appearances before her, corporealizing more and more as the weeks go by. By 1920, many years after the events that launched the story, "aquello había llegado a constituir una pesadilla, una obsesión constante para tía Pasia" ["that [Palás's ghost] had turned out to constitute a nightmare, a constant obsession for Aunt Pasia"] (143). This is no encounter with the uncanny by a lone widow but rather the repeating emergence of the specters of 1898. These revenants are multiple and of expansive sociopolitical and macrohistorical dimensions. Palás was a figure of disorder to three distinct armed forces in conflict at the turn of the century, and he haunts their respective projects as much as Pasia's nights. His posthumous recurrences decades after the dust supposedly had settled on the fin de siècle wars threaten far more than an individual, Pasia, upon whom he looked only once. The American colonial order was inextricable from the Philippines by the 1920s, as stable as such occupations get. And yet a specter hovers at night.

When the third chapter commences by veering into the story of a shoe-shine boy who plies his trade before the National Bank, "Aunt Pasia" cross-hatches the transoceanic war grid of Spain and the Philippines and the United States with the economic globalizations of the first quarter of the century. The urchin, though named Pablito, is referred to as "Amboy" for no given reason. The nickname seems to mesh syllables of "America" and "boy," but the symbolic import of that is difficult to decipher. He is described as orphaned because his father dies when he is eight years old and his mother moves in with a man who repeatedly hits him on the neck, causing Amboy to run away when he is ten (146). Amboy, like Cándida, heads to San Pedro and tries to pull himself up by his bootstraps. He works first on the docks as an informal porter for travelers and then converts his earnings into the equipment necessary to become a shoeshine boy. As he is "relativamente fuerte y de natural levantisco" ["relatively strong and naturally rebellious"], he outhustles his ragamuffin peers and succeeds outside the National Bank while shouting in Spanish and English, "¡Limpia, señor! *¡Shine, sir!*" (146–47). The local businessmen and nearby landowners who leave the bank with "sus créditos aprobados y sus préstamos concedidos" ["their credit approved and their loans granted"] are happy to take Amboy up on his bilingual cry, and "llovían las propinas" ["the tips rained down"] (147).

In this sudden introduction to the life story of an unexpected character, Amboy proves truly an American boy. He leaves behind his wretched situation in life and makes his way to a bustling city, where he takes the lowest job available in order to make ends meet. By working hard, he is able to save up enough money to buy himself a little capital and advance up a notch to shoeshine boy. He seeks out a wealthy customer base and lifts himself up still higher, learning enough English to improve his chances of landing any particular shoeshine job. This is a fictional story of Horatio Alger, of Cándida, of America. After all, a tale of upward mobility by a poor but independent subject is hardly a narrative of the pre-1898 Philippines as run by Spain. The use of English alone in his cry of "*¡Shine, sir!*" is a telling marker of the Americanization of his clientele, for there is no suggestion that the businessmen and landowners who enter and exit the Philippine National Bank (PNB) are investors from the United States. The bank, in fact, was a relatively new institution designed to capitalize local initiatives at a time when, as Frank Hindman Golay writes, "For the most part, foreign-owned commercial banks operating in the Philippines concentrated their loans on financing foreign trade . . . The PNB rapidly expanded its network of branches and agencies until it became the dominant commercial bank in the Philippines and the principal source of funds for Filipinos and their enterprises" (190). The patrons of the bank to whom Amboy pitches his services in English are Filipinos who, now two decades after the start of the American occupation, are anglicized enough to heed a call in that language. Amboy surely does not know any more English than that and probably no more Spanish either, for the priests who had dominated the archipelago before 1898 had striven to keep the language outside the skill set of islanders. What stands out here, therefore, is that a Filipino boy who surely speaks only an indigenous Filipino language attempts to author his own Horatio Alger story by communicating with other Filipinos only in languages thrust upon them by empire.

As for the Philippine National Bank, though intended for Filipinos, it was not created by them. It too is inescapably American. The idea for the bank came from the American colonial governor of the time, and its first president was an economics professor from Columbia University (Golay 190, 212). It was a "national" bank, yes, but not of the nation it presumed to represent, which did not exist. The bank opened in May 1916 and expanded exponentially during a boom in the Philippine economy that resulted primarily from demand by the Western powers fighting World War I on the other side of the planet (Golay 213). Easy credit flowed to the Filipino elite, and perhaps as a result so did their willingness to rain tips on shoeshine boys such as Amboy. The end of demand stemming from the war, however, and a consequent global crash in commodity prices, plunged the Philippines and the bank in particular—which was poorly run to begin with—into a full-blown crisis in 1920–21 (Golay 219–20). This collapse, driven by transoceanic macroeconomics, directly affects Amboy, for it causes the suits leaving the bank to forgo shoeshines. As Gómez Windham puts it, "Vino la crisis, la fatal crisis de mediados del veinte, y las cosas cambiaron radical y rápidamente. Los que salían del Banco llevaban los ceños fruncidos, la mirada hosca, el paso inseguro de quienes van sumidos en amargas preocupaciones, y pasaban de largo sin escuchar el canto de las sirenas del betún, o contestando, si lo oían, con un seco y malhumorado 'déjame en paz!'" ["The crisis came, the fatal crisis of mid-1920, and things changed radically and rapidly. Those who exited the Bank had furrowed brows, a gloomy look, the unsteady step of those who are sunk in bitter preoccupations, and walked on by without listening to the song of the sirens of shoe polish, or answering, if they heard it, with a dry and ill-humored 'Leave me in peace!'"] (147). Hungry and impoverished, Amboy tries to rob some hats but has to flee from a watchdog. In the process, he loses his shoeshine equipment, that is, his only capital (148). Early the next morning, en route to church for mass, Pasia passes by the crying boy and decides to take him in as a servant and religious pupil. Amboy, who is barely literate in his native language, struggles mightily to learn prayers in Spanish and Latin as she commands. One day, frustrated by his mistakes, Pasia hits him, the second pseudoparental figure to do so. Again Amboy runs away, this time to join other former shoeshine boys who now survive by petty thievery (151).

This entire sequence, read allegorically, raises new and important questions. Why does a lumpen figure abruptly enter and dominate the novella? What are the class implications that follow? Why are the events of lost capital at the macro and micro levels, that is, the national bank and the shoeshine equipment, so tightly paralleled? It is the latest crisis in international capitalism that causes Amboy to lose a most local of markets for his trade. Why does Pasia, who appears unexpectedly late in the narrative that bears her name, now disappear suddenly before the protagonism of yet another "orphan" whom she nonetheless victimizes? If the Catholic stringencies of Pasia are a manifest legacy of the Spanish friars who prevailed in the archipelago before 1898, are they rejected here in favor of the most seemingly isolated Filipino in Gómez Windham's oeuvre, a monolingual waif with no access to Cándida's anglophone educations or Sing-A's transnational opportunities or Cayo's white-collar diurnalities? And what does the revenant of Palás have to do with any of this?

The answers emerge obliquely, though hardly definitively, when the fourth and final chapter of "Aunt Pasia" opens with a decision by a new character, Copio, the leader of a Dickensian band of street children, to write with Amboy an anonymous letter to Pasia threatening to kill her for her evil ways. For a surface on which to construct this note, they choose "un espacio relativa-mente plano en la base de cemento de la estátua de Rizal" ["a relatively flat surface on the cement base of the statue of Rizal"] (152).[21] The significance of this scene is manifest and murky at once. Rizal represents nationalism and martyrdom incarnate in the Philippines. In 1920, Gómez Windham himself had mentioned Rizal in the same breath as Saint Paul, Mohammed, Zara-thustra, and Abraham Lincoln, and concluded that "the spiritual wealth of our own country would certainly be considerably poorer had our great Rizal not been gifted with the ability of clearly expressing his ideas in writing" (Gómez Windham, "An Open" 11). In general in the archipelago, Rizal is singularly identified with national freedom and unity, regardless of the many conflicts with that image that are evident in his paper trail. The ghost of Rizal hovers everywhere in the Philippines. As a result, ectoplasm of immensity and instability is created when dispossessed (in all senses) children conspire atop a literal foundation of Rizal against an individual possessed by a persis-tent ghost that unnerves her after unsettling the Spanish empire, the Ameri-can empire, and the Filipino revolution. Pasia herself guesses that either the dead Palás or the vanished Amboy composed the letter. This juxtaposition of the two figures symbolically conflates them as her conjoined antagonist, as that which haunts her as someone linked to both imperial regimes via her theocratic comportment and her collaborationist husband.

It turns out, therefore, that it is not necessary to be on one imperial side or the other in an 1898 narrative. At stake are interwoven inheritances of the broadest social, political, and economic kinds. These inheritances, not Iloilo, are the true province of all powerful specters. Palás and Amboy, though radi-cally different characters who never meet and who play distinct roles in the story, both personify the threat of power coming from outside all constituted social orders. Such orders include those of Spain and locals and the church and the United States. The horror they represent to Pasia is that of anarchy and entropy. By extension, this is the national nightmare of a Philippines never able to cohere into an organically constituted self, whether forged from within or imposed from without. Since the unending shifts of forces in the archipelago are of global range and often antipodal sources, the phantasma-goria that pursues Pasia is modernity itself. And that modernity is marked more than anything else, and in the Philippines more than anywhere else, by the round-the-world reach and repercussions of American empire.

The night that Pasia receives the death threat, "medio paralizada de horror y a la luz vacilante de la lamparilla de aceite de coco que ardía ante el crucifijo, vió al espectro avanzar decididamente hacia ella, siempre con los dedos abiertos y como preparándose a buscar su cuello" ["half paralyzed with horror and by the flickering light of the little coconut oil lamp that burned before the crucifix, she saw the specter advance decidedly toward her, always with his fingers open and as if preparing to search for her neck"] (157). Yet with a sudden determination reminiscent of "sus primeros años de matrimonio, cuando se imponía a los obreros de su hacienda" ["her first years of matrimony, when she imposed her will upon the workers on her ranch"], she grabs from her altar the dagger that Palás had used to kill her husband and she thrusts it into the chest of the ghost (158). Gómez Windham then inserts a line of periods to indicate a section break, after which Pasia awakens to see "su mano derecha, la que empuñaba el puñal, llena de rasguños que manaban sangre" ["her right hand, the one that gripped the dagger, full of scratches that streamed blood"] (158). She realizes that the image of Saint Michael the Archangel is in pieces and that the head of the devil he had been stepping on is now rolling on the floor. The struggle between good and evil has ended in defeat for both, but what good and evil might allude to in the narrative remains an open question. Only Pasia has won, for the last line of the novella proclaims, "Ni aquella noche ni ninguna otra desde entonces volvió a aparecérsele a tía Pasia el espectro de Palás" ["neither that distant night nor any other since then did the specter of Palás return to appear to Aunt Pasia"] (159).

This scarcely amounts to victory or redemption. Pasia, with her Gothic obsessions and imperiousness toward a street child and her former "workers on her ranch," is never represented in positive terms in the story. A possible reading in which she stands as a local figure who emerges triumphant as the macro forces of Spain (represented by the saint) and the United States (as the devil) mutually self-destruct just does not seem to hold up. After all, the lumpen characters who literally base themselves on Rizal, the national hero, are her antagonists. It would take an aggressive psychoanalytical conjecture to argue that since the letter of Amboy and Copio, written upon the statue of Rizal, leads to the fright out of which Pasia destroys both Saint Michael and the devil, the real agent of the symbolic destruction of both Spain and the United States here is the revenant not of Palás but of Rizal.

The climactic catharsis may satisfy Pasia but not the reader, for whom nothing is resolved. A conclusion that the fears and fantasies of Pasia represent nothing more than the manias of a single individual with a traumatic past, that the visitations of the revenant are but projections of the material figure of the devil on her altar, that this story is nothing more than a Filipino ghost story in the age of Freud, is suspiciously superficial. The opening frame of the story is too political and involves too many vast forces for such an isolating interpretation. The personas of Palás and Amboy are too estranging for a microscopic, literal explanation to tie up loose ends so cleanly. Pasia may no longer be haunted after the last page of her story, but the Philippines certainly is. And if the Philippines is haunted, then so too is the United States. For those entities cannot escape from each other any more than from the specters of Palás and Amboy and 1898 in general. It does not matter how wide the Pacific. Ghosts do, of course, walk on water.

The openness of "Aunt Pasia" remains for the reckoning. And the oblivion of Filipino literature in Spanish is at such odds with the scales on which it operates. The point of reading Gómez Windham should not be to insist on his past importance but to propose his future impact. His fictions render inadequate the continental narcissism of conventional notions of American literature. Dissolving in his wake as well are the transatlantic currents that cause many investigators of America to perch eastward in a crow's nest scanning the horizon for another, wrong continent, the wrong islands off the wrong coast. American literature may begin as an offshoot of English literature, but it becomes a product of Filipino literature. In Spanish. Go West, old men with doctorates. And these days, some aging women. And then board a boat and go further West, until you hit the East. Because that is where the West is. The Philippines launched the American century, transformed the United States from across the Pacific. Though of course, the Philippines was no longer across the ocean at all. The archipelago arose in the aorta of America. In the heartland itself.

The output of Filipino authors who wrote in Spanish under American colonization is often difficult to obtain. Archival investigations even in the Philippines can meet resistances of many sorts. Simply trying to get a photocopy of a Gómez Windham story in a Manila library in order to read it elsewhere tends to present challenges of mock epic proportions. Among the results of such access issues is the persisting problem of how to write creatively and yet responsibly about texts that most other readers cannot consult and cross-check. Nevertheless, much 20th-century Filipino literature in Spanish still can be sleuthed out via a combination of determined detective work and chance. And contacts still can be made that could allow rare, noncirculating texts such as those by Gómez Windham to rematerialize one way or another. These efforts should be undertaken by American studies scholars, among others. Those who cannot read Spanish need to learn. The story of America makes no sense without it. More particularly, the story of America in the 1920s, so often told, so well known, is actually not quite told, not quite known at all. Not until you read Gómez Windham and read America from him.

To be sure, it is an uphill struggle for most Americans to attempt gleaning sense from the tales of Gómez Windham, their settings so unfamiliar, their cultural contexts so seemingly alien. And the initial efforts to make way through that world may fail like those of Cándida and Sing-A and Cayo. Still, better to fail than to achieve a myopic self-satisfaction like Pasia, thinking that all pertinent issues have been resolved. There is nothing to lose but the boundaries that confine us all.

four

Assimilating the Antipodes
in Peace and War

Mariano de la Rosa's *Fíame*
(Filipinas-América) ([1936?]–1946)

꙰

The National World War II Memorial on the Washington Mall features fifty-six granite pillars of equal size and shape, each dedicated to a geopolitical entity that fought under the American flag. Naming the states and territories and the District of Columbia, the pillars testify to the wartime contributions of all those places that mark July 4 as a date of national independence. One of them, however, is now another country. The Philippines stands thereby as the only foreign nation honored between the Capitol and the Lincoln Memorial. And yet in 1945, the year in which the Pacific ground campaign culminated with the annihilation of Intramuros, the old Spanish walled city of Manila, the Philippines was not sovereign. All Filipinos were Americans at that point as much as were all Alaskans and Hawaiians and Puerto Ricans in that none of those people lived in states of the United States either and yet were also formally subject to laws and policy coming out of the federal government in Washington. A memorial pillar erected by a colonizing power does not amount to justice, but it does at least grant recognition in the metropolitan center to the dead and destroyed of the colonized land.

Such recognition is virtually absent in cultural histories of both the imperial and national kind when the subject is Filipino literature written during World War II in Spanish, the language spoken by much of the Intramuros population that was obliterated amid the bombing of Japanese forces by the

United States. This small but important body of literature remains nearly unknown on all sides of the Pacific despite its unique involvement in the joint story of the United States and the Philippines and its refractions, via unfamiliar vantages, of larger dynamics of colonizing and colonized peoples. Wartime Filipino writings in Spanish linger in oblivion in large part due to their chronological context. By the 1940s, formal Iberian power in the Philippines had been extinct for nearly half a century. Consequently, when war arrived, the last of the Filipinos born before 1898 who were native Spanish speakers were already middle-aged or older. After the war, not many survivors remained who could read or create literature in the tongue of the erstwhile empire. And since the audience and media to keep texts in Spanish in public circulation had for the most part vanished, recent or new literature in that language tended to disappear into the void. This in turn led to gaps in the occasional overviews of 20th-century Filipino literature in Spanish that subsequently appeared. For instance, the few scholars who paid attention to the tradition supposed unanimously that *Los pájaros de fuego* (*The Birds of Fire*) by Jesús Balmori was the lone archipelagic novel in Spanish to be written during and about World War II. But Mariano L. de la Rosa, a Filipino judge, began composing *Fíame (Filipinas-América)* (*Trust in Me (Philippines-America)*) before the cataclysm commenced, kept working on it during the war, and completed it a year after the atrocities ended.

Both novels complicate considerably any familiar definitions of the modern contours of literature from the United States and the Philippines. They are therefore of exceptional significance despite their dearths of readership. The texts merit serious and sustained analysis, especially *Trust in Me*, for up until recently it had not been known to exist. The typescripts of *The Birds of Fire* remained buried in archives for over half a century but nonetheless garnered scattered commentary over time. In 2010, moreover, the novel saw light at last in an annotated, published edition. *Trust in Me*, however, insofar as presently known, is the only World War II Filipino novel in Spanish to be published in or close to its era of composition. This more or less makes it the single most marginalized major American novel of the war.

As for de la Rosa, he was evidently an amateur creative writer who began his foray into fiction only in his later years. If he contributed short stories or poetry or drama to any of the many prewar Filipino newspapers and magazines, they remain to be discovered. Yet ultimately, de la Rosa may be deemed to have produced in *Trust in Me* a novel of more lasting interest than *The Birds of Fire*. This is despite the fact that Balmori, by contrast, had been a well-known poet and fictionalist for four decades. Much of the attention to his novel stems from issues of biography and reception: the reputation and prolificacy of the author, the manuscript unpublished and often unfound. But de la Rosa, though practically invisible to literary historians, deals with World War II in *Trust in Me* in a way far more closely connected to the present and future of an interwoven world than Balmori in *The Birds of Fire*. This is to say that the internationalized text of the novel, not the fame of the author or the seductions of a long-lost manuscript, would be the primary impetus for any decision to read and study it.

Despite the horrors of World War II in the Philippines, in which death figures are regularly assumed to exceed one million Filipinos, the plot of *Trust in Me* is rather chipper.[1] The novel opens in November 1935 with the inauguration of the Commonwealth, a political entity designed by power brokers in Washington and Manila to transition the Philippines gradually from colonial rule by the United States to independence a decade later. The heroes of the novel are four well-connected young people, the strapping lads Harry and Max and the coquettish virgins Rosy and Nena. Harry and Rosy are Americans passing through Manila, he as a "guapo oficial del ejército de los Estados Unidos" ["handsome official of the army of the United States"] and she, "del vergel americano, la nítida flor" ["of the American orchard, the clear flower"], as an assistant to the congressional delegation that has arrived to celebrate the birth of the Commonwealth (11, 5). Max, "un apuesto joven filipino" ["a good-looking Filipino youth"], is a member of the reception committee for the visiting officials, while Nena is his childhood friend (5). Like Rosy, she is an undeflowered flower: "Orquídea oculta . . . ignorante de su belleza y fascinación, su virginal modestia es su mejor encanto" ["A hidden orchid . . . ignorant of her beauty and fascination to others, her virginal modesty is her greatest enchantment"] (11). Max and Rosy meet each other at the welcoming ceremonies and flirt at the inaugural ball of Manuel Quezon, the incoming president of the Commonwealth, "ella con su blonda femenidad, y él, con su continente varonil, moreno" ["she with her blonde femininity and he with his dark, manly build"] (6). Harry, who is also blond, falls for Nena, the Filipina orchid, at the same inaugural ball.

The clichéd descriptions of these protagonists may seem laughable to readers today, but de la Rosa is quite serious about the symbolic extrapolations at hand. The development of the twin interracial romances, which provides the fictional infrastructure of the novel, represents the unity of the Philippines and the United States throughout the Commonwealth period and World War II. The thesis of *Trust in Me*, as stated repeatedly by de la Rosa, is that era natural que en los primeros días de la ocupación existiese desconfianza entre unos y otros [i.e., filipinos y estadounidenses]. Además, las diferencias en usos, costumbres y, sobre todo, la cuestión de raza, que siempre ha dado lugar a lamentables disensiones, se han interpuesto para impedir un contacto más íntimo. Pero, la mutua comprensión acabará con tal estado de cosas, que no tiene razón de ser en una sociedad civilizada. (32)

[it was natural that in the first days of the occupation there was distrust between some and others [i.e., Filipinos and Americans]. Besides, the differences in manners, customs, and, above all, the racial question, which always has created space for lamentable disagreements, have come between to impede a more intimate contact. But mutual comprehension will end that state of things, which has no reason for being in a civilized society.]

This desired surmounting of the "distrust" produced by cultural and racial differences yields the anagrammatic title of the novel in Spanish. The word *Fíame* translates in English as the heartfelt imperative "Trust in me" while combining eurythmically the first syllables of "Filipinas" ["Philippines"] and "América" ["America"]. The romances of Max and Rosy, Harry and Nena, function as allegories of Filipinos and Americans as unified. This synthesis in turn represents a particular realization of the universal harmony among all people(s) that is the ultimate ideal championed by de la Rosa.

For that utopian aspiration to be consummated, the dystopia of World War II will need to be overcome first. The novel begins in peacetime, though, and the relations among the four youths initially play out at the level of a romantic comedy. Their quick and easy friendship is foregrounded while the gigantic forces leading up to war swell in the background. As *Trust in Me* proceeds, however, the relative prominences of the two plots interchange. The standout historical figures and episodes of the war become covered in a fashion that is nearly journalistic. But the small- and large-scale stories are complementary and intertwined from the very beginning, starting with the meeting of the four youths at the prewar political arrangement that is the Commonwealth. De la Rosa thereby keeps his fictional characters and events implanted within the specific news frames of the era.

Such inextricability of plot and geopolitical context is fundamental to Filipino fiction in Spanish. This is true regardless of whether the plot and the context appear to be directly related to the American presence in the archipelago or not. The moment America extended its authority to the Philippines, Filipino writers automatically became writers of America, in all senses. Their texts, regardless of their content, irrespective of their explicit engagements with anything, immediately redefined American identity and power; this is to say, redefined America. The most ancient of settings in the operas by Pedro Paterno are simultaneously the most contemporary. The Spanish and Chinese and French forces in the fictions of Gómez Windham, not to mention the native Filipino characters, are all equally American. In the case of de la Rosa and *Trust in Me*, however, no such extrapolation needs to be argued because the American and Filipino characters are embedded so obviously with each other in the first place. Their unity, moreover, appears organic and pure.

Class Acts

The presence of such unity corresponds to the nonorganic and unpure 20th-century history of Filipino elites, who remained elite precisely because they were so content to be in bed with their American counterparts. The favor was returned by such men as Douglas MacArthur, who as an aging military leader bedded a teenage Filipina starlet named Isabel Rosario "Dimples" Cooper, carried her across the Pacific to Washington, and stored her secretly in a room because he was afraid his mother would find out. Eventually, he abandoned her; years later, though still at an age younger than that of MacArthur when he cached her, she committed suicide. The story of Dimples Cooper remains a roughly apt metaphor of the macrohistory of the United States in the Philippines in between the two mass blood-sheddings of Filipinos by the American military that frame the U.S. colonial period: the war against Filipino freedom fighters at the turn of the century and the war against entrenched Japanese at midcentury. Sexual relationships between Filipinas and American soldiers have a brutal and hyperbolic history that includes entire towns next to U.S. military bases in the Philippines that were dedicated to servicing servicemen. De la Rosa, nevertheless, found none of this problematic when imagining Filipino/American romances in the form of his four chirpy heroes or elite bilateral political and military alliances. He exalts the American presence in the Philippines at just about every turn.

Perhaps this is because de la Rosa did so well professionally during the American occupation, carving out a prestigious career within one of its governmental branches at that. As an individual from the provinces who rose through the ranks of the judiciary between 1924 and 1953, he seems to have moved with great success within the systems of the regime. But this is just a guess, for little is currently known about him. According to the dust jacket of his novel *La creación* (*The Creation*) of 1959, "Only the constitutional age limit of 70 years prevented his further promotion to the Supreme Court, the highest tribunal of the land." His birthdate in 1883 means that he was already a young adult by the time the United States began sending shiploads of English teachers in the early 20th century to the islands it had just grabbed. The native languages of de la Rosa would have been Spanish and, presumably, a dialect of Bikol, the main language of the Camarines Sur province where he was born. To succeed in such a sphere as the judiciary, he surely also would have had to have spoken, or learned to speak, Tagalog, the vernacular of the Manila region, even though it was not until 1937 that that language was declared a national idiom in a slightly adjusted form called Filipino. Meanwhile, since the American colonial regime emphasized the use of English throughout public sectors, de la Rosa would have faced limited professional prospects had he not adapted to that reality too. The dust jacket of *The Creation* duly notes that after passing the bar in 1906, "Without the assistance of a tutor, he learned to speak English." Given his long and fairly prominent career, archival investigations in the Philippines might turn up additional biographical information on de la Rosa that could situate him more specifically within the sundry Americanizations of his social and professional contexts.

While de la Rosa was rising as a jurist under the American occupation, thousands of Filipinos in a rather distant stretch of the socioeconomic spectrum were making their way to the contiguous forty-eight states and becoming migrant laborers. The most famous of them is Carlos Bulosan, for he wrote a novelized autobiography in English entitled *America Is in the Heart* that since has achieved canonization among Asian American studies and U.S. ethnic studies in general. The account by Bulosan of his travails during the Depression, published in 1943 and therefore composed while de la Rosa was working on *Trust in Me* in the Philippines, is most remarkable in the eponymous passage:

> We are all Americans that have toiled and suffered and known oppression and defeat, from the first Indian that offered peace in Manhattan to the last Filipino pea pickers. America is not bound by geographical latitudes. America is not merely a land or an institution. America is in the hearts of men that died for freedom. . . . America is also the nameless foreigner, the homeless refugee, the hungry boy begging for a job and the black body dangling on a tree. America is the illiterate

immigrant who is ashamed that the world of books and intellectual opportunities is closed to him. We are all that nameless foreigner, that homeless refugee, that hungry boy, that illiterate immigrant and that lynched black body. All of us, from the first Adams to the last Filipino, native born or alien, educated or illiterate—*We are America!* (189)

This America, as depicted by Bulosan, is transhistorical and unbordered and marked by interrelated stories of struggle. It is not so much a nation or a place as an idea that links diverse oppressed peoples across time and space. The original inhabitants of Manhattan and lynched African Americans and Filipino agricultural workers all participate in the common narrative of a concept that outstrips its own boundaries, for "America" is not really in America but wherever the story of America, of its conquered but not defeated, is told.

The metaphoric flexibility needed for acceptance of that definition of "America," however, is merely an expansion of the particular case of the colonization of the Philippines by the United States. Neither Bulosan nor the "last Filipino" to which he refers had to emigrate across the Pacific to join in the story of that America. For that matter, Bulosan did not emigrate at all. No Filipino did who arrived in the United States between 1898 and 1946. Like everyone born in the Philippines in the early 20th century, Bulosan was *already* in America. The United States included the archipelago because it claimed both the land and its people. As Oscar Campomanes observes, Filipinos in the Philippines "moved to the continental states not as nationals of a sovereign nation but as *U.S. nationals* of a territory 'appurtenant to' but considered as 'belonging to' the United States. It is kind of like the movements Puerto Ricans make now from the island to New York" (Tiongson 41). The status of Filipinos in the Philippines as American nationals existed from 1900 to 1946, that is, from the early consolidation of the American victory in 1898 right up until the formal independence of the islands (Schlimgen 2).

Campomanes points out that "the term 'Filipino American' is a redundancy" that "can be a signifier just as descriptive of the modern and U.S. colonial period formation of Filipinos as it is of an emergent and self-empowering political subject in U.S. multiculturalism" (Tiongson 42). The implications of this idea extend to all Filipinos who never left the colonized Philippines for the continental United States, including those who wrote in Spanish such as de la Rosa. Yet while the story of Bulosan has been swallowed into the service of existing American and Filipino genres of immigrant literature and the sociopolitical structures they perpetuate, the texts in Spanish of his contemporaries in Manila, and of de la Rosa in particular, are left out of the narratives of both nations. Many bookstores in the two countries keep *America Is in the Heart* ready for purchase on their shelves. In Manila, the text is often available in both a Tagalog translation and in the original English. This stands in sharp contrast to the absence on retail shelves everywhere of any Filipino literature in Spanish, notwithstanding the length of the tradition (seven decades into existence by the time de la Rosa published *Trust in Me*) and its contemporaneity with the life of a figure such as Bulosan. The lone Filipino author who worked in Spanish whose texts are accessible by the general public is José Rizal, the 19th-century national martyr and foundational writer. Yet his novels precede the imperial shift of 1898 and, in any case, appear in archipelagic bookstores only in translations into English and vernaculars. In short, Filipino literature in Spanish of the American colonial era has no place in the imaginary of either country as separate entities or as the single one they formally were for nearly fifty years. Most scholars in the United States would be astonished to learn that Filipino literature in Spanish exists at all, much more so to find out that it gives a singular take on the World War II history of America from *inside* America.

This is why *Trust in Me* deserves a readership and analysis: it redefines imperial and national narratives of literary history. And its rewritings happen even as de la Rosa tries to align the text within existing American order. This paradoxically assimilationist effort is representative of the larger history of Philippine elites who adapted to the post-1898 balance of power in the islands. Once the United States had defeated Spain and then Filipino revolutionaries, the archipelagic upper classes quickly moved to strengthen ties with the new imperial rulers rather than entrench in antagonistic positions. They were motivated primarily by opportunism but also by a sense of realpolitik. After all, Theodore Roosevelt had proposed as early as 1899, then as governor of New York, that Filipinos who desired independence from Washington be crushed. As he pithily put it, "The first and all-important work to be done is to establish the supremacy of our flag. We must put down armed resistance before we can accomplish anything else, and there should be no parleying, no faltering, in dealing with our foe" (188–89). Roosevelt spared no tolerance either for Americans who opposed U.S. colonialism, asserting,

> I have scant patience with those who fear to undertake the task of governing the Philippines, and who openly avow that they do fear to undertake it, or that they shrink from it because of the expense and trouble; but I have even scanter patience with those who make a pretense of humanitarianism to hide and cover their timidity, and

who cant about "liberty" and the "consent of the governed," in order to excuse themselves for their unwillingness to play the part of men. (188)

Roosevelt, who assumed ultimate responsibility for the Philippines in September 1901 when he rose from vice president to president of the United States after the assassination of William McKinley, made it quite clear to the Filipino elite where their alliances should lie. His point man in the islands, William Taft, the future president and chief justice of the Supreme Court, reinforced the message with such edicts as the Sedition Law. This decree, which entered into effect less than two months after Roosevelt became president, provided for the death penalty, incarceration, or significant fines for any playwright convicted of pleading for Filipino independence. The American presence in the islands that would come to be regarded as salvational by the end of World War II began half a century earlier under the threat of a very big stick.

Under the American regime, anglicization of the Filipino population was rapid and widespread, to wit the education of Cándida by Miss Jones in the story by Guillermo Gómez Windham. Although archipelagic elites continued for some time to produce their major governmental documents in Spanish, English increasingly became the dominant lingua franca among all Filipino classes. And as the decades passed, the United States developed a corps of civil partners with Filipino oligarchs, among whom the final sovereignty of the islands was always a pending question. Gómez Windham, writing in the early 1920s, was distant enough from both 1898 and the prospect of an officially autonomous Philippine state to take colonization as a status quo backdrop for his fictions. A decade and a half later, however, it would have been illusionary to do so. The advent of formal geopolitical change at the macro level was clearly around the corner. This is because power jockeying among various parties in Manila and Washington led to the creation of the Commonwealth in 1935, presided over by Quezon and charged with a slow, stable transition to independence. That gradualism exploded when World War II came to the Philippines a matter of hours after it came to Hawaii, the other significant American island holding in the Pacific.

Today, Hawaii and the Philippines seem to be unrelated geopolitical entities. At the time of Pearl Harbor, though, as imperial territories there was little substantive difference between them. Both were Pacific archipelagos that the United States had seized in the late 19th century for economic exploitation and military utility. Japan acknowledged as much by bombing them in quick succession; the builders of the National World War II Memorial in

Washington likewise were justified in recognizing each equally. *The Onion*, a satirical newspaper of the 21st century, merrily launched their retrospective fake coverage of Pearl Harbor with a most incisive headline—"Dastardly Japs Attack Colonially Occupied U.S. Non-State"—and proceeded to explain that "Japanese planes also attacked the U.S. territories of Guam, Wake Island, and Clark Field in the Philippines, all areas rightfully considered U.S. brown-people holdings . . . [Franklin D.] Roosevelt cautioned that, after this attack, 'All oppressed peoples in lands under U.S. territorial and military rule may be in danger of foreign territorial and military rule'" (60). *The Onion*, which makes everything up, thereby rendered accurately the common situation of the Philippines and Hawaii.

Yet there was nothing to laugh about, however darkly, in the aftermath of the twin bombings of the colonies. Horrors followed in the Philippines when the Japanese occupation of the archipelago from 1942 to 1945 turned out to be one of the more atrocious chapters in human history. Douglas MacArthur, leader of American forces in the Philippines, ended up retreating to Australia, where he pledged that he would return someday and drive Japan out. It was in fulfillment of this famous personal promise, not military advisability, that he decided to stage climactic land battles with Japan in the Philippines. The result was that hundreds of thousands of Filipinos died unnecessarily, many in the most brutal ways imaginable. In the course of these human events, Manila and its environs were destroyed. This, nevertheless, scarcely dents the MacArthur legend in the United States, where the main blotch on his record, his conflict with President Harry Truman during the Korean War, still seems considered by many to be not a blotch at all. In Filipino popular culture as well, MacArthur tends to come off as immaculate or nearly so. Despite his grisly legacy, two sweeping conclusions about the American wartime involvement in the islands remain commonplace in the archipelago: (1) In 1945, MacArthur saved the Philippines, and (2) in 1946, the United States proved its fundamental benevolence by granting independence to the Philippines through a peaceful legislative process rather than, say, by being forced into doing so after a bloody revolution. *Trust in Me* by de la Rosa is a text that operates on both premises.

Once World War II ended and Philippine independence was recognized, social order in the archipelago came under new pressures. The Hukbalahap rebels, better known as the Huks, who had formed as a guerrilla army against the Japanese, now strove to change the national balance of forces in which a clique of Filipinos arrogated nearly all wealth and power while the rural masses remained impoverished. Manuel Roxas, handpicked by MacArthur to become the first president of the independent Philippines and, like most of the oligarchs, a collaborator with the Japanese—he was even a cabinet member of the puppet Philippine Republic, set up in midwar by Japan—trounced the Huks with the consent and assistance of the United States. Although official colonial rule ended in 1946, the United States had no intention of allowing a broad democratization that might jeopardize its economic, political, and military interests in the Philippines, nor those of the domestic elites with whom it ran the archipelago.

That American position emboldened the Filipino oligarchs as the Cold War surged and Red Scare zealotry followed. Barely a year after Senator Joseph McCarthy in early 1950 had begun accusing the U.S. State Department of harboring communist infiltrators, a now extremely crotchety and hyperbolically racist Arthur Stanley Riggs—the same gentleman who had lambasted the opera *Magdapio* by Pedro Paterno in 1904—published an article in which he accused the Huks (or, rather, the alleged communist conspirators behind them) of resorting to subversive plays just like their evil peers of half a century earlier: "That the sinister power behind the Hukbalahap forces ranging the provinces should in some instances use seditious plays as a means of furthering disorder reveals a definite knowledge of native history and a shrewd analysis of the native temperament and reactions" ("Seditious" 202).[2] A resurrection of the prewar status quo in the archipelago was far more desirable to the United States than a postwar change in sociopolitical order. Thus Frank Hindman Golay notes that "MacArthur had used his power and prestige while in the Philippines in 1945 to restore the collaboration-tainted Quezonista faction to power and promote Roxas as Quezon's successor" (480). He adds that at the independence ceremonies on July 4, 1946, "There was MacArthur, who had used his brief reign in the Philippines to ensure that the Quezonistas and the economic elite behind them would continue to monopolize power in the Republic" (483). Similarly, Stanley Karnow writes that MacArthur "aborted change in the Philippines by reinstalling the traditional dynasties, whose primary aim was to protect their vested interests" (324).

The actions nearly half a century earlier of Arthur MacArthur, military governor of the Philippines and father of Douglas, provide continuity here. In 1900, he helped squash a speech by Pedro Paterno that favored independence for the archipelago. He also issued a policy manifesto that led to the programmatic obliteration of rural Filipinos in regions thought to harbor anti-American guerrillas (Kramer 136–37, 152–53). By contrast, de la Rosa glorifies the work of irregulars. Yet of course, given the context of World War II, those particular guerrillas were working with the United States, not against it. Chronologically, *Trust in Me* stops shy of the postwar reconsolidation of the traditional Filipino elite and their American backers. The last page of *Trust in Me* refers to the end of World War II in August 1945 and concludes its time frame with the independence of the Philippines the following July.[3]

Fore!

In the opening part of *Trust in Me*, the four young protagonists play golf together while exchanging repartee by the walls of Intramuros, the old Spanish colonial center of Manila. They tee off on a modern course that was once a fetid swamp (21). The symbolism here is that amid the Spanish legacy (the Intramuros walls) in the islands, Americans and Filipinos now forge together socioeconomic progress (the swamp turned golf course) and an egalitarian future. With the Commonwealth celebrations over, meaning that Rosy must now return home with the congressional committee while Harry ships off to China, the foursome found a friendship club intended to double as a movement dedicated to eliminating worldwide "de las sociedades prejuicios de raza y clase" ["prejudices of race and class from societies"] (43). The utopian goals of this movement, the novel suggests, have already been realized in certain places in the Philippines such as Baguio. This locale is the first and framing stop of a looping tour around lands north of Manila that Max, Nena, and Rosy undertake after Harry has departed. Baguio is a setting associated closely with the American presence in the archipelago because the first U.S. colonial governments built it up as a mountain retreat. Correspondingly, Baguio features prominently in artistic re-creations of American power such as the opera *Magdapio* by Paterno and the late science fiction novel *The Creation* by de la Rosa himself. Since de la Rosa thinks highly of the American presence in the Philippines, Baguio resonates as a positive place of transpacific union in his texts rather than as a colonial imposition. He thus describes it in *Trust in Me* as "la Ciudad-jardín . . . una conjunción filipino-americana" ["the City-garden . . . a Filipino-American conjunction"] (52–63).

This space of common bond, it turns out, united America and the Philippines even in prehistory, for Max says, with apparent sincerity, that the indigenous Filipinos of the area were blood relatives of Native Americans. The two populations used to be connected geographically, he hypothesizes, by the ancient continent of Lemuria that existed in the Pacific Ocean before sinking in a cataclysm (64). It is not a coincidence, therefore, that on a stop on the northern tour that begins in Baguio, Max receives a charm from an old indigenous Filipina who is later referred to as a priestess and whom he has saved from an accidental fall (74–75, 127).[4] He saves here, by his own logic, both a metaphorical Native American and a figure who represents Filipino traditions. In so doing, he seamlessly melds prehistoric indigenous cultures on both sides of the Pacific with the modern Philippines, as incarnated by himself, and modern America, as represented by Baguio. Amid this fusion, he also achieves the transcendent goal to which the new friendship club is dedicated, namely the overcoming of differences of ethnicity, class, status, and so on. And this happy project soon takes on a new form in the way Max proves his affections for Rosy after she leaves the Philippines with the congressional delegation: he beats her to San Francisco and waves at her from the dock when she arrives (84). Such harmonious scenes are rudely interrupted at the start of the second part of the novel by the Japanese bombardments of Hawaii and the Philippines.

As de la Rosa, who wrote this part during World War II itself, chronicles the military campaigns of the Pacific, his reportage of macrohistory tends to background the previously dominant flirtatious banter and the idyllic evocations of a racially harmonious world.[5] The adventures of the protagonists do not disappear altogether, though. Max is wounded in an early battle but is saved because shrapnel that would have pierced his heart is blocked by the amulet given to him by the aged indigenous priestess (126–27). He is transported to Australia to recuperate (126). There he is found by Rosy, who is now a Red Cross nurse. When Max regains his health, he is hired onto MacArthur's staff. Since MacArthur proclaimed, "I shall return" in Australia, Max is now foreshadowed by association as likewise eventually arriving anew and in triumph in the Philippines. Meanwhile, Harry ends up leading Filipino irregulars back in the archipelago. He is helped at times by Nena, who provides key information leading to the successful assassination of a Japanese commander (137). At the end of the novel, allied American and Filipino troops defeat the Japanese, and the foursome, together again, marry soon after the atom bombs fall. They, presumably, live happily ever after. So do, by extension, the United States and the Philippines.

This triple wedding of characters and countries is one and the same. The novel thereby puts forth a symbolic family for the Philippine future. Strikingly, Filipinos such as de la Rosa who were born before 1898 and therefore under Spanish rule do not seem to be relevant in *Trust in Me*. No characters of parental age or older play a substantive role in *Trust in Me*, excluding historical figures such as Quezon and MacArthur. The Philippines projected by the novel is to be constructed by the young and hopeful with nary a look back at even the pre-Commonwealth decades of American colonial rule. De la Rosa offers fresh-faced protagonists to show that equality, particularly the version ostensibly evinced by Filipino-American union, is a bright and surging wave. The common military struggle against Japanese aggression is waged ultimately as a moral cause in favor of egalitarianism among all. The four youths are elites, of course, but of a relatively democratic bent. They do not possess the inherited wealth of, say, robber baron progeny or archipelagic oligarchs, and they do not ally and wed because of preexisting ties of blood or power. On the contrary, they are close to political figures but of the elected sort, and they are not politicians or power brokers themselves. Yet they are urban and hip and charged with more or less creating a binational and planetary zeitgeist while personally and relationally embodying it. They are the most modern of global citizens who intend to spread their version of modernity across all borders. This surely will include passing their egalitarian values on to their own children, though the consummation of the double marriage is safely relegated to the unwritten space after the wedding ceremony on the last page. Everything about these kids bespeaks a fruitful future.

In the principles of fraternity that inspire all the pairings in *Trust in Me* may be undertones of Masonic ideals of international brotherhood. Like many members of the Filipino elite, de la Rosa was a Mason. In fact, according to Teodoro Kalaw, he was one of the three founders of a Masonic lodge in his home province (241).[6] In 1917, the Filipino and U.S. lodges in the Philippines combined in what Kalaw terms "the fusion." The first deputy grand master of the joined lodges was none other than Manuel Quezon, the future president of the Commonwealth (T. Kalaw 250). He became the grand master of the postfusion lodges in 1918; it seems that Filipinos and Americans alternated the top position in that era (T. Kalaw 250). In 1920, Kalaw described the merger in terms that would echo strongly in *Trust in Me* a generation later: "The fusion of Filipino and American lodges, under the jurisdiction of the Grand Lodge of the Philippine Islands, was an event joyfully celebrated by everybody. . . . It established union and harmony, not only between Americans and Filipinos, but also between Americans, Filipinos and foreigners" (204). Notably, Americans are so immixed with Filipinos here that they are excluded from the concept of "foreigners" in the first place.

The embraced fusion of Americans and Filipinos both in the Masonic fraternity and in the plot of *Trust in Me* is striking alongside the de facto dismissal by de la Rosa of the much older and longer presence of Spain in the Philippines. This tacit exclusion seems unexpected, given the language in which he chose to write the novel despite the several more publicly active ones that he had at his disposal. For a polyglot, it takes a certain act of will to compose in an imperial tongue nearly half a century after the empire in question collapsed. Guillermo Gómez Windham too had a variety of languages in which he could fictionalize and also decided upon Spanish, but this seemed to reflect a certain affinity with, or perhaps nostalgia for, pre-1898 sociocultural patterns. On the contrary, de la Rosa treats the first Western power to colonize the archipelago as a dusty historical marker amid all his fraternal and romantic embraces of the second. America is everywhere explicit in *Trust in Me*, from Harry and Rosy as main characters to the pivotal military battles now also memorialized in stone on the Washington Mall. Linguistically, the United States is ubiquitous too, for example via the commingling of languages on the golf course as follows:

> En el segundo *tee*, Nena, ya tranquila *draiveó* tan perfectamente que su pelota voló ondeando, como una golondrina.
> —Excelente!—exclamó Rosy.
> —*Perfect!*—dijo Harry.
> Lo hiciste admirablemente, Nena—agregó Max. (22)

> [On the second *tee*, Nena, now tranquil, *drove* her ball so perfectly that it flew undulating like a swallow.
> "Excellent!" exclaimed Rosy.
> "*Perfect!*" said Harry.
> "You did admirably well, Nena," added Max.]

In this exchange, everybody understands everybody, whether Max is praising in Spanish or Harry ejaculating in English. The same holds true of a reader attentive to Spanglish: "draiveó" is a hispanized spelling of an English word, a linguistic unison and union that complements a round of golf played on a modern Americanized course by ancient Spanish walls in the heart of the Philippines. The history of Spain in the archipelago provides the novel with a backgrounded landscape and a foregrounded language, but both are manifestly static. All the movement and energy of culture and politics, at the micro as well as macro level, is tied to the United States.

Meanwhile, the very name "Rosy" suggests that of Rosie the Riveter, the archetypal embodiment of the contribution of American women to the war effort. And most importantly, de la Rosa makes a pivotal geographic move when he transports the plot to California. He achieves this by having Max travel to San Francisco aboard the *China Clipper*, a hydroplane, on the first commercial transpacific flight in history. There is a *Spirit of St. Louis* feel to this jaw-dropping sequence, with de la Rosa extolling the "exitoso vuelo inaugural de un servicio de aviones, que establecía la vecindad, anulando la distancia entre América y Filipinas" ["successful inaugural flight of an airplane service that established a common neighborhood, annulling the distance between America and the Philippines"] (83). In reality, that distance had long since been annulled by William Taft, Arthur MacArthur, Pedro Paterno, Cándida and her teacher Miss Jones, and many others.

The evaporation of distance and difference, however, does not blind de la Rosa to particularly American racial dynamics. He is quite aware that all Americans are not as open minded as Harry and Rosy. In San Francisco, Max encounters various Americans who doubt he is equal to them due to his skin tone. Through a combination of handsomeness, charm, and the occasional feat of strength, he convinces all the racists otherwise. It is easy to smile grimly at the naïveté of such solutions for bigotry. The fact that de la Rosa tackles the subject, though, suggests that a lot more is going on in *Trust in Me* than an unthinking embrace of a romanticized colonial power. Swimming pools may not strike 21st-century readers as political spaces, but when Max leaps into one in San Francisco and saves the pretty white daughter of a powerful national politician, the scene is potent (92). The interracial taboos of the era are being roundly denounced at a symbolic level whatever the superficial silliness of the scene. De la Rosa does not hold up the United States as a colorblind ally in order to create a contrast with the racism of imperial Japan. When Max, flying to San Francisco, "creía ver la estatua de la Libertad, con su antorcha en alto" ["believed he saw the Statue of Liberty with her torch held high"], he was heading to a place that, though "un eden" ["an Eden"] also would present him with "días de prueba" ["days of testing"] (101). An image of the Statue of Liberty suspended midair over the Pacific and signaling a garden ahead is rather less utopian before the simultaneous recognition that the gates of Eden do not automatically open in America for dark people.

Another maneuver by de la Rosa that destabilizes his apparent enthusiasm for the United States and its presumptive egalitarian partnership with the Philippines is his repeated inversions of symbolic relations of power between the two lands. Notwithstanding his appreciation for the ongoing American influence in the archipelago, his characters neither accept American supremacy as natural nor ignore an asymmetrical geopolitical reality under the guise of equality. For example, Max, the Filipino, is accepted as the natural head of the four youths, not Harry, the American: "Ninguno propuso la nominacion de un *leader*, porque Harry, Rosy y Nena, virtualmente reconocían y se sometían al liderato de Max" ["No one proposed the nomination of a *leader*, because Harry, Rosy and Nena virtually recognized and submitted themselves to the leadership of Max"] (44). Later, Rosy even tells Max, "Eres genuino leader, porque todos te seguimos, espontaneamente" ["You are a genuine leader because we all follow you spontaneously"] (53).[7] That a Filipina such as Nena might be deemed the natural leader may be too much to hope. Still, there is a consensus verdict here that a Filipino civilian and not a GI is the most innately qualified person to assume leadership of the foursome and their campaign for global harmony. This amounts to a counterproposal to the actual distribution of power during the American colonization of the Philippines.

In another notable moment of role inversion, Nena jumps into a river to rescue a fat U.S. senator who has fallen overboard. He, energized by "su buena voluntad" ["her goodwill"], musters the forces to get up from the riverbed (56). Nena then congratulates him: "Vd. se levantó por sí mismo" ["You stood up by yourself"] (56). Everyone chuckles during this episode, but, allegorically, this scene is not light at all. First, it foreshadows the later incident in the California swimming pool when Max saves from drowning the white girl with the powerful father. Second, it flips the Commonwealth relationship that the senator had come to the Philippines to recognize. Here, a personified America figures out how to stand on its own, inspired by the gracious spirit of the Philippines. Procolonial propagandists from the White House on down had long cast the occupation in exactly opposite terms. Now all that bunk about benevolence belly flops into Filipino waters like the corpulent senator.

On a correlate track, Harry and Rosy are Filipinized more than Max and Nena are Americanized. Although Harry does end up leading Filipino guerrillas during the war, he often goes native when doing so by operating according to long-standing military techniques of the rural Igorot people who instruct him. Rosy, for her part, is routinely depicted as becoming as Filipina as Nena, if not more so. At a shrine to Andrés Bonifacio, the radical and martyred early leader of the Filipino revolution against Spain, "Rosy y Nena depositaron, piadosamente al pié del monumento sus collares de sampaguita, blanca y fragante, flor nacional" ["Rosy and Nena piously deposited at the foot of the monument their rings of sampaguitas, white and fragrant, the national flower"] (53). It is safe to say that when Rosy first arrived in the Philippines, she had no idea who Bonifacio was. Now she pays him reverence. The sampaguita stands in Filipino literature for national identity, its whiteness for innocence and purity; Pedro Paterno was particularly fond of such associations. Who has metamorphosed into what in *Trust in Me* therefore gets an unexpected twist when later "Max y Nena mismos pusieron en el cuello de

Rosy los collares de sampaguita que traían para ella" ["Max and Nena themselves put around Rosy's neck the rings of sampaguitas that they brought for her"] (80). With these white flowers synonymous with both Filipinas and with the Philippines as a collective ideation, the frequent associations of Rosy with sampaguitas throughout *Trust in Me* betoken a Filipinization of her that upends any facile notion of a novel in which Filipinos unhesitatingly pattern themselves after American cultural norms. Referring to Rosy, Max even goes so far as to say to Nena, "Es más filipina que tú" ["She is more Filipina than you"] (79).

At the macrohistorical level, de la Rosa dismisses as "propaganda" the Greater East Asia Co-Prosperity Sphere, the shell created by Japan to portray its imperial expansion as a continental and racial alliance (110). And he refers sarcastically to the Philippine Republic, the purportedly independent state set up by Japan, as "una panacea, la píldora dorada" ["a panacea, the golden pill"] (132). Furthermore, when a Japanese ruler announces the creation of the Philippine Republic in Luneta (now Rizal) Park, the symbolic center of the archipelago, de la Rosa switches momentarily into Tagalog, followed by a parenthetical translation into Spanish, to show how Filipinos in attendance used their own language among themselves to jeer at the Japanese pronouncement. All these gestures against Japanese policy are rooted in a Filipino nationalism that is not mediated by America. In other words, the United States, which had been the primary political referent in the archipelago since 1898, is not relevant to these anti-Japanese asides. Filipino polemics emerge here with tenets that are obliged to neither the latest empire to seize the islands nor the previous one.

The long view of history in *Trust in Me* also can be mustered to marginalize America. For instance, de la Rosa invokes the legendary battle offshore Mactan Island in which Magellan, the first European to reach the archipelago, fell in 1521 to the forces of a local king named Lapu Lapu. When Max is wounded by the Japanese, although he is saved fortuitously by the amulet of the indigenous priestess, he is saved logistically by a hospital ship dubbed the *Mactan* (126). And when MacArthur returns to the islands in realization of his monomaniacal pledge, he does so in the wake of 1521, "entrando por la misma ruta que el hado llevara al gran navegante Magallanes a los mares interiores de Filipinas" ["entering via the same route that fate had carried the great navigator Magellan to the interior seas of the Philippines"] (152). This embrace by a Filipino writer of both the inaugural Iberian invader and the indigenous resistance to him, that is, of Magellan and Lapu Lapu as jointly heroic, appears in another barely known Filipino text in Spanish of the late 1930s and early 1940s, Félix Gerardo's unpublished collection of short fiction entitled *Justicia social y otros cuentos* (*Social Justice and Other Stories*).[8] In *Trust in Me*, the swerve to 1521 places the American era of the Philippines within a much older archipelagic history, decentering the U.S. period by revealing it to be merely the latest chapter in a rather long saga. In short, whether by Filipinizing his American characters or dislodging the United States from its self-awarded imperial role as the indispensable nation, *Trust in Me* is a text whose whetted words pare all its superficial sympathies for the American century.

Circulations

Despite the complexities of the novel, de la Rosa scarcely appears in the main catalogings of Filipino literature in Spanish.[9] Luis Mariñas, in his important overview of the tradition, mentions *Trust in Me* in passing (77). And Lourdes Castrillo Brillantes notes that *The Creation*, his science fiction novel, was one of nine entries for the 1961 Zóbel award for the best Filipino literature in Spanish (*81 Years* 218). De la Rosa might have submitted *Trust in Me* too for a Zóbel Prize had the contest not been suspended from 1942 to 1952 due to World War II and its consequences. Archival sleuthing may yet turn up mentions of *Trust in Me* in high-society periodicals right after its completion in 1946. At that juncture, however, Manila lay in ruins and its surviving elites were busy positioning themselves to profit in an era of formal independence. Reading novels, or at least acknowledging them, may not have had a high profile amid the grasping for spoils left by the dead.

As of this writing, it is unclear whether *Trust in Me* was published right after the war or half a decade later. At issue here is that the novel carries a copyright date of 1946 but no actual publication year. Ramon M. Velayo writes in a biographical note that accompanies *The Creation* that *Trust in Me* was published in 1946. Velayo, however, may have been misled by the copyright date, for the only known edition of the novel includes a prologue by Manuel C. Briones that is dated December 1950. It therefore seems probable that the manuscript did not appear as a bound book until 1951 at the earliest. But even at that point, *Trust in Me* may not have been commercially distributed or much remarked. The book appears to have been self-published. The print run must have been rather limited. Copies may have circulated only hand to hand.

Yet even if just a few people obtained *Trust in Me* and commented on it in private, the connections of de la Rosa with other elites imply that the readership was a powerful one. The prologuist Briones, for instance, began his career as an editor of Spanish-language newspapers in the central Philippine island of Cebu, then became a lawyer who rose to serve many years in the House of Representatives. According to the website of the Senate of the Philippines, "Briones was also member of the Philippine Independence mission to the United States in 1930. From 1931 to 1935, he served as senator. He was a delegate to the Constitutional Convention in 1934, and he was one of the seven that composed the Committee of Wise Men, which drafted the Philippine Constitution. The Nacionalista party mad [*sic*] him vice-presidential standard-bearer in 1949, but he lost. In 1951, he was again elected to the Senate and he was subsequently chosen Senate President Pro Tempore up to 1957" ("Manuel"). With a figure such as Briones lending his prestige to the novel as its prologuist, de la Rosa was pitching his product by proxy to peer elites. Anyone interested in the worldview of the governing class of Filipino society throughout the critical 1930s and 1940s—a period that includes the Commonwealth, the Japanese occupation, and formal national independence—should read *Trust in Me* for its assimilations to and of American power. Subtly in this novel, antagonism to two colonialisms, not just the Japanese, does assert. The United States had come to produce Americanized subjects such as de la Rosa, yes. But the Philippines had come to produce Filipinized subjects such as Harry and Rosy and, for that matter, MacArthur too.

The elites among whom *Trust in Me* circulated also could live in yet another country with an imperial legacy in the Philippines. Inked onto the title page of one of the extant copies of the novel is a handwritten dedication.[10] The signatory remains to be deciphered but the dedication itself is clear: "A Doña Adelina Gurrea, filipina pulcra e intelectual, que honra a su país, dedico este regalo, con la autorización del autor. Madrid, a 12 de Junio de 1952" ["To the esteemed Adelina Gurrea, beautiful and intellectual Filipina who honors her country, I dedicate this gift with the authorization of the author. Madrid, June 12, 1952"]. Gurrea is probably the most famous Filipina writer in Spanish, but she spent almost the entirety of her adult life in Spain and wrote from there. Her *Cuentos de Juana* (*Short Stories of Juana*) appeared in Madrid in 1943, that is, at the same time that de la Rosa and Balmori were writing their Spanish-language novels in Manila. The dedication therefore suggests the social tightness of prestigious Filipinos despite transoceanic distances. The gift-giving signatory was surely also a member of that class who personally carried a copy of *Trust in Me* with him to Spain at the behest of de la Rosa. If the novel had been sent by mail, de la Rosa would have had no need of an intermediary. Moreover, in accord with the prologue by Briones datelined

December 1950, the handwritten dedication implies that *Trust in Me* was probably published in 1951 or, at the latest, early 1952.[11] Either way, the date of the dedication reveals that one of the first things that de la Rosa did was ensure that a copy was hand-delivered to a fellow writer from the Philippines who lived on the other side of the world.

Yet it would be a misstep to conceive of *Trust in Me* narrowly in national terms, or in the national terms of one class. After all, the novel itself takes an internationalized approach to the conflict that was the most globalized in all of human history. And Briones was not merely a Philippine politician but an American politician too: he was an American national who achieved lofty ranks in governments established and legitimized by the United States. And de la Rosa was likewise anything but a solely national writer. His positionalities were far more fluid and complicated than that. He was an individual who spent his youth as a subject of one empire and much of his adulthood as a subject of another. He was an American judge as much as a Filipino one. In fact, during the first half dozen years of his career, he served on a judicial hierarchy whose highest figure was none other than William Taft, the former colonial governor of the Philippines and now chief justice of the U.S. Supreme Court. Under the Commonwealth, the political status of de la Rosa altered somewhat but he remained an American national, as was the case of all Filipinos. And with the Japanese occupation in World War II, he became a subject of a third empire. With the formal independence of the Philippines in 1946, he became a postcolonial author of a new nation, but *Trust in Me* was all but wrapped up by that point. And that independence took place on the Fourth of July. Not all independences are created equal.

Whenever a reader turns to modern Filipino literature, the reader turns to modern American literature. *Trust in Me* was finished after the war during the last stretch of when America held ultimate power over the archipelago in legal as well as realpolitik senses. The consideration of Carlos Bulosan within Asian American studies, and American studies more broadly, is incomplete without the apposition of de la Rosa, his contemporary and fellow American national. De la Rosa too offers a transgeographic concept of America that, in its own way, considers the fraternity of culturally different people as the fundamental definitive at stake. Viewing both *Trust in Me* and *America Is in the Heart* as American literature does not mean that they are not Filipino texts but that the meaning of "Filipino" can encompass that of "American," not only the other way around. Such a vantage allows for necessary inversions of understanding, if not hard power. American culture is deepened and complicated when recognized as including the arts produced in its colonies by the people—by its own *nationals*, for that matter—who live there. This is important. The British, for the most part, are well aware by now that Indian history and British history cannot be extricated from each other, regardless of where particular Britons stand ideologically on that reality. The Indian mark on British life is not only permanent, it is long since innate. The French, for the most part, know instinctively by now, with loathing or without, that Algerian history is not only inseparable from French history but from its future as well. The land to the north is forevermore defined by the land to the south at least as much as vice versa. The consequences of these facts are everywhere visible. But the United States and the Philippines? Who reading these words accepts intuitively that the America of the 20th century, the America of today, the America of tomorrow, is what it is *because* of the Philippines? Yet that is the case.

World War II is still fought every day, the battles having shifted to classrooms and to myriad continental calculations and concentrations of power. De la Rosa speaks to all the ongoing operations. The United States continues to dominate in the Philippines. Its military continues to run missions in the archipelago, with or without the consent of Filipinos, and its mass culture continues to penetrate deeply every level of Filipino society. Meanwhile, the descendants of the old elite continue to rule, with the president of the Philippines as of this writing the grandson (on the paternal side) of a Cabinet member of the puppet Philippine Republic of 1943 and (on the maternal side) of one of the richest sugar barons in the archipelago, not to mention son of another president.[12] America may or may not be in the heart, depending on how one reads that phrase, but America is definitely in the archipelago and *América* certainly was. Studying unread Filipino (American) novels in Spanish may seem like a dusty academic exercise, but there is rarely anything more relevant than the workings of writers who have witnessed the wrack of the world.

five

The Radical Reactionary

Jesús Balmori's *Los pájaros de fuego* ([1942?]–1945)

The trajectory of modernity is incomprehensible without studying the Philippines. It was in the Philippines that at the end of the 19th century, the empire of Spain, once the largest in the world, was forced to withdraw from the most distant of its colonies. It was the imperial adversary of Spain, the United States, that in seizing the Philippines established its global reach that was to mark the entirety of the 20th century. It is from the Philippines that, at the end of that century and the start of the next, emerged a labor force of staggering size that scattered around the world as the human infrastructure of the latest phase of international capitalism. And it is the Philippines where the most globalized conflict of them all, World War II, was drenched in blood by the last major land battle between American and Japanese forces. The carnage climaxed in Intramuros, the old walled town of Manila built by Spanish colonialists and, until the moment of its obliteration, the home of the largest Spanish-speaking community in Asia. Yet grasping the planetary dimensions of all these phenomena is impossible without attempting to understand the art produced by locals who witnessed them. Modernity is written not only by those who wrest power on foreign shores but also, and more importantly, by people from those shores who respond with narratives of their own. A Filipino novel written in Spanish during World War II, such as *Los pájaros de fuego* (*The Birds of Fire*) by Jesús Balmori, is therefore critical to any reckoning with the world in welter that is ours. Composed in the tongue of a European empire while under the duress of an East Asian empire and amid the colonization of a North American empire, this novel is inherently a landmark of world literature. It is also inherently a landmark of America, written by an American national in an American property about the conflict most central to the American century. And the unsuspected subversions of Balmori and his novel reside most radically in their reactionary refusal to accept American impact in the antipodes in the first place.

The significance of *The Birds of Fire* correlates inversely to its lack of an audience. Balmori finished the novel in 1945 but did not publish it. The text was purchased by the Filipino government of the time and effectively disappeared. Over the decades, most of the few scholars who knew of it assumed it had been lost forever. There is proof, however, that one individual, Florentino Hornedo, did read it in that timespan, and likelihood that another, Estanislao Alinea, did as well.[1] That is it. Lourdes Castrillo Brillantes, writing in 2006, observed that "according to Pilar Mariño, former professor of the University of the Philippines and translator of Balmori's short stories, his last novel is in the possession of the Philippine Government and, until 1987, was known to be still unpublished" (*81 Years* 69). In other words, all Brillantes could do as late as 2006 was point to a reference some two decades earlier to the unpublished status of *The Birds of Fire*.

A measure of the current state of scholarship on Filipino literature in Spanish is that a number of the texts whose titles but not contents are known are not lost at all but available in the most likely places to anyone who might look for them. A microfilm of the typescript of *The Birds of Fire* survived for years, perhaps decades, in the library of the Ateneo de Manila University, yet not until recently did researchers independently find it.[2] It is prefaced by an unpaginated note apparently from Hornedo (it is initialized by "F.H.H.") dated 1979 that indicates that the typescript is "a copy of the original" text bought by the Philippine government and held at the National Library of the Philippines ("To The Reader").[3] One of the rediscoveries of the novel led to the publication of a critical edition in 2010 by the Cervantes Institute, a cultural organization of the government of Spain. The edition is a traditional philological effort in that it offers introductory prose on the author, a large bibliography of his writings, elucidations of various historical and cultural references by Balmori, and a discussion of all extant versions of the novel. It does not, of course, situate Balmori and his text as American literature by an American author.

The edition also does not, counterintuitively, make the novel much more accessible to Filipinos than it was during the more than half-century of its disappearance. For starters, the publication was meant primarily for archival existence, not retail. Major bookstores in Manila did not stock it and, as of this writing, it still remains unavailable, even on the used book market, via mammoth Internet sites such as Amazon. The continuing invisibility of *The Birds of Fire* is related directly to the fact that the published edition is monolingual in Spanish, a language now far more distant from a potential Filipino audience than even when Balmori was typing in it. Had the intention been to make the novel available to be read by Filipinos, the edition would have been published in a translated version or in a bilingual format inclusive of either of the two national languages, English and Filipino (which is the official version of Tagalog), or Cebuano (the next most widely spoken archipelagic language), or for that matter any of the dozens of Filipino languages that are more widely understood today in the islands than Spanish. The disconnect of a purely Spanish edition with a Filipino audience is furthered by the oddities of the novel appearing as one of two texts to launch a collection dubbed *Clásicos hispanofilipinos* (Hispanofilipino Classics) by the Cervantes Institute.[4] It is the rare classic that has a total transhistoric readership next to zero.

Due to the disappearance of *The Birds of Fire* after World War II and the prominence of its author, scholars in the interim had to describe a text of which they had only heard. Balmori had been a leading literary figure for four decades, and the novel was his last major work. Until the discovery of *Trust in Me* by Mariano de la Rosa, it was also believed to be the only Filipino novel in Spanish written during and about World War II.[5] For such reasons, simply ignoring the text was an unappealing option. But without a manuscript in hand, the critical attempts could not help but be lean. Brillantes writes that "his third and last novel, *Pájaros de Fuego*, shows its principal character accepting the existence of God, society and its limitations, and displays fervent patriotism" (*81 Years* 69). This single-sentence summary is so vague that it does not mention World War II, the context of the plot.[6] Alinea, writing in 1964, provides a more detailed description of the novel, which he terms "esta obra que es la más lograda en prosa de Jesús Balmori" ["this work that is the most accomplished in prose of Jesús Balmori"] (97). Hornedo is rather less sanguine, saying that *The Birds of Fire* "promises by its title more than it delivers" ("Notes" 412). Isaac Donoso Jiménez, editor of the published version of the novel, states in contrast that *The Birds of Fire* is "una obra cardinal" ["a cardinal work"] (l). These sources offer just about the only commentary in existence on the text.

Scholars of American literature have not written about *The Birds of Fire*. And yet Balmori was an American national and, as such, probably the most accomplished American author to both witness and fictionalize the epicenter of the American war in the Pacific. He wrote, quite despite himself and his own inclinations, not to mention those of the few academics to regard him, in the long line of American artists who experienced the horrors of war firsthand and turned them into fiction. Read him against war stories from Ambrose Bierce through Joseph Heller and beyond: how does American war literature look now? For that matter, read him against Norman Mailer, his young archipelagic neighbor who was serving in the American military in a less turbulent region of the Philippines at the exact same time that Balmori was writing *The Birds of Fire* in Manila and burying the pages in crystal jars in his garden so that violent Japanese searches of his home would not find them (Balmori 5; all page references to *The Birds of Fire* correspond to the published edition of the novel).

Balmori was born in 1886 and became one of the most renowned of the Filipino literati to come of age under American rule. Owing to his early stardom, much is known about his biography and many of his texts survive. In 1904, when still a teenager, he published *Rimas malayas* (*Malay Rhymes*), his first book of poems. In 1908, barely into his twenties, he won a high-profile poetic competition and, according to Donoso Jiménez, "A partir de este momento Jesús Balmori pasará a ser figura principal de la creación poética filipina" ["Beginning at this moment Jesús Balmori would become a principal figure of Filipino poetic creation"] (xvii). Also in 1908, he finished writing the novel *Bancarrota de almas* (*Bankruptcy of Souls*), publishing it in 1910.[7] This text is generally if mistakenly accepted to be the first Filipino novel in Spanish since José Rizal's *El filibusterismo* (*Subversion*) of nearly two decades earlier.[8] In 1924, Balmori engaged in a series of public verse competitions with Manuel Bernabé, another esteemed Filipino poet who penned in Spanish. These contests were denominated as jousts and are considered a high point of a phenomenon referred to by various scholars as the Golden Age of Filipino literature in Spanish. In 1926, Balmori received the annual Zóbel Prize for the best Filipino literature in Spanish. And in 1940, he won a national award for what is often considered his greatest work, *Mi casa de nipa* (*My House of Nipa*]) a thick volume of poetry.[9] He died in 1948, just two years after the Philippines gained independence from the United States and three years after finishing *The Birds of Fire*, his early promise having been borne out at least in terms of prolific output and widespread recognition.

Put another way, the work of Balmori in a range of genres matches chronologically the entire span of the American regime. And as a subject of the United States who worked in the tongue of a preceding worldwide empire, he is a writerly incarnation of global American colonization. At the same time, within the strictly archipelagic context (actually, there is no such thing) of Filipino literature in Spanish, he was a contemporary of virtually everyone who ever wrote. Born a year after Pedro Paterno published *Nínay* (the first Filipino novel in any language) and a year before Rizal published *Noli me tangere* (the foundational novel of the nation), Balmori would have been old enough to witness the execution of the latter and attend the operas of the former. His chapbook *Malay Rhymes* came out the same year, in fact, as Paterno staged *Magdapio*. The two men both joined the leadership of the new Nationalist Union Party a short time thereafter, with the inaugural issue of the party newspaper in December 1906 listing Paterno as the treasurer and Balmori as a member of the Press Committee ("Partido" 8).[10] As older men such as Paterno eventually left the scene and younger authors emerged, Balmori remained prominent. In the mid-1920s, his public poetic jousts with Bernabé took place just two years after Guillermo Gómez Windham won the inaugural Zóbel for *Cándida's Career* and the same year that Gómez Windham released the short story "Tia Pasia" ("Aunt Pasia"). And by the time Balmori was finishing *The Birds of Fire* some twenty years after that, his career had spanned the same period as many illustrious, fellow American writers who also redefined America through their work in the 1930s and 1940s: William Faulkner, John Dos Passos, John Steinbeck, Richard Wright, Henry Miller, and so on.

Characters of War

Aesthetically, *The Birds of Fire* is a melodrama whose Romantic pretensions struggle to keep pace with a reality more savage than anything a belletristic poet like Balmori was likely to imagine on his own. The plot revolves around the Robles, a wealthy Filipino extended family headed by Don Lino, who reveres Japanese culture, and his pragmatic brother Don Ramón, who discerns presciently the threat to the Philippines of the expanding Japanese empire. Don Lino has two young adult children who are also central to the goings-on. His daughter, Natalia, plays the role of innocent Filipina virgin that is apparently obligatory in every Filipino narrative written in Spanish by a male author; his son, Fernando, is an astute and patriotic lad who commits himself early to the national defense. Natalia has an Italian suitor, the irascible and pretentious music teacher Bruno Anselmi, who claims that Mussolini is his relative in order to impress the Robles. Natalia has paired up instead, however, with Sandoval, a cosmopolitan yet worthless doctor. He has degrees from universities in Tokyo, Berlin, and Vienna but no patients. Sandoval is a gold digger who represents a nonhereditary and rising professional class that is styled in the novel as so much nouveau riche rubbish.

Balmori was very much an elitist but, judging from *The Birds of Fire*, he much preferred the traditional aristocracy of Spanish-era descent rather than the various parvenus who ascended during the U.S. occupation. Such anachronistic inclinations amount to antipathy to modernity. They are but one component of his insular insurrection against everything that accompanied the American military into the archipelago. Notwithstanding the rise of an elite Filipino class in the last half-century of Spanish rule that could send its Spanish-speaking sons to Europe, the pre-1898 colonial period was not marked broadly by social mobility. American rule, for all its sponsorships of certain individuals and institutions over others, allowed much wider spaces for nonaristocrats to advance than had its imperial predecessor. Mariano de la Rosa, a man who taught himself English and succeeded as a judge in the American colonial system before becoming the other known Filipino World War II novelist in Spanish, was just the sort of individual who would be dismissed in the pages of *The Birds of Fire*.

Balmori favors instead characters such as Marta, the fiancée of Fernando who is as pure as Natalia but stands for the eternal goodness of Filipinas of indigenous and rural stock. She represents the peasantry phenotypically and therefore metaphorically even though her family is wealthy. The challenge of treating peasants as national symbols, from a reactionary standpoint, is that they are poor; this was certainly the issue with Cándida, the Gómez Windham character of two decades earlier who was rejected by the rich family of her boyfriend Bert. Balmori neatly solves this problem by making Marta the best kind of allegorical peasant, a prosperous one. Her family has land and means, but the symbolic role she plays for Balmori remains evident: "Belleza dulcemente indígena, de expresión soñadora y ojos lánguidos de mirar de esclava . . . se educó en su casa, en su pueblo, en el santo amor a Dios y en la sencillez y la virtud de las costumbres campesinas" ["Sweetly indigenous beauty of a dreaming countenance and the languid watching eyes of a slave . . . she was educated at home, in her village, in the saintly love of God and in the simplicity and virtue of peasant customs"] (25). Marta, supine and supple and sumptuous, is the erotic and eternal body of the indigenous Philippines and of Filipino peasant culture. As such, her loveliness rebuts the value of change of any kind to existing class hierarchies and their presumptively timeless archipelagic customs.

In earlier texts by Paterno and Gómez Windham, as well as in the contemporary *Trust in Me* by de la Rosa, the Philippines and Filipino culture are deeply affected by American power of diverse kinds. Not so in the novel by Balmori. Those who wreak change in *The Birds of Fire* are not Americans but instead the symbolic representatives of the Axis powers. These include a couple of Japanese gardeners who actually are secret agents with semiotic bents. They plant chrysanthemums, the emblematic flower of imperial Japan, over the lands of Don Lino in the opening scene. The Italian rogue Anselmi, meanwhile, is friends with the German physician Fritz Von Kauffman. Both of them personify the shifting wartime balances of power in the world and, by extension, in the Philippines. Alterations to existing sociopolitical order in the archipelago, however, also can be threatened by the masses of Filipinos who do not enjoy the hereditary wealth of the Robles family. To ward off such rebellion from below, Balmori inserts a priest among his protagonists who counsels lower-class Filipinos to abandon their armed uprising against the Japanese occupation.

The relative absence in the novel of American impact on the archipelago dovetails with the absence of the 20th-century history of the Philippines in general. The cast of *The Birds of Fire* is affected by post-1898, pre–World War II phenomena only in the most glancing of ways. The overarching reality of the Philippines after the turn of the century is that the United States imposed various cultural and political regimes while running the colony both directly and via a proxy alliance with an array of local elites. Factions within the elites increasingly competed to bring home an independence deal from Washington, and the winning cohort was led by Manuel Quezon, who claimed victory after the passage in the U.S. Congress of the Tydings-McDuffie Act of 1934. This legislation established a transitional entity known as the Commonwealth of the Philippines that would come into existence in 1935 and terminate with the formal independence of the archipelago in 1946. Quezon duly won the Commonwealth presidential elections of 1935. It was in honor of the fifth anniversary of the Commonwealth, still run by Quezon in 1940, that a national literary competition was held and won by Balmori with his capstone book of verse, *My House of Nipa* (Alinea 87).

The gradualism of the Commonwealth transitional period evaporated in early December 1941 when, hours after bombing Pearl Harbor, Japanese pilots attacked the United States' "biggest air armada anywhere overseas," the fleet commanded in the Philippines by Douglas MacArthur (Karnow 288). His father, Arthur MacArthur, had been the American military governor of the archipelago who, four decades earlier, had helped squash a proindependence speech by Pedro Paterno meant for William Taft, the civil governor of the colony and future U.S. president. The Japanese assault on the Philippines that deepened with the land invasion of Manila in January 1942 proved to be a particularly brutal episode in the history of humanity. Lowlights included the Bataan Death March that April. Amid the devastations, Japan pushed the concept of the Greater East Asia Co-Prosperity Sphere, which was a euphemism for its imperial holdings that included Taiwan, Korea, and Manchuria. And in 1943, co-opting the always pliable Filipino elite and trying to hoodwink the general population, Japan established the allegedly independent Philippine Republic, a puppet government.

In 1944, Douglas MacArthur unnecessarily committed his troops to fighting the Japanese in the Philippines. He did this only in order to fulfill his famous pledge, "I shall return," made after retreating from the Philippines to Australia in March 1942. His counselors warned against the massive strategic error, but military advice was one thing and the murderous megalomania of a MacArthur was another. Narcissism was ever the handmaiden of empire. The decision to wage full battle again in the Philippines led to the deaths of perhaps one million Filipinos or more, the obliteration of Intramuros, and, in a brutal climax, an apocalypse described by Stanley Karnow as follows: "Trapped in the chaos, the Japanese embarked on an orgy of atrocities matched only by the pillage of Nanking in 1937. They impaled babies on bayonets, raped women, beheaded men and mutilated the corpses. Setting houses ablaze, they shot the fleeing inhabitants, and started fires in hospitals after strapping patients to their beds" (321).[11] All these historical phenomena—Quezon and the Commonwealth, the Bataan Death March, the Japanese occupation of Manila, the Greater East Asia Co-Prosperity Sphere, the Philippine Republic, the horrific finale—necessarily must charge any analysis of *The Birds of Fire* even though Balmori highlights instead the saga of the Robles. The tensions between the macroscopic history in the background and the melodramatic family in the foreground are what produces the ideological resolutions and irresolutions of the text.

Early in *The Birds of Fire*, Fernando is driving to visit his beloved Marta but is held up by "una gran parada militar en honor al Aniversario del Commonwealth . . . Marchaban nuestros soldados confundidos con los de América" ["a great military parade in honor of the Anniversary of the Commonwealth . . . Our soldiers marched mixed together with those of America"] (25–26). This scene establishes the fact of American military presence in the Philippines in entirely positive terms but without any specific reference to the four-plus decades of American culture or history in the archipelago. Fernando follows the military parade to Luneta Park, the symbolic center of the nation as the site of the execution of Rizal, where "estaba hablando el Presidente. . . . decía que en cualquier instante, Filipinas estaría dispuesta a luchar junto a América en defensa de las Democracias y a morir junto a América, si hacía falta dar la vida, por la libertad del mundo. Fernando pensó entonces que el tío Ramón no había hablado por hablar" ["the President was speaking. . . . he said that in any moment, the Philippines would be ready to fight together with America in defense of the Democracies and to die together with America, if it were necessary to give lives, for the liberty of the world. Fernando realized then that Uncle Ramón had not been talking just to talk"] (26). The unnamed president is Quezon, and the allied Filipino and American troops indeed will die together when World War II arrives.

Those casualties, however, do not negate the misrepresentation by the fictionalized Quezon that the Philippines was one of the "Democracies" to be defended. The archipelago was, after all, a colony of a great power and had been so for nearly four centuries. The historical Quezon was acutely aware of that when, decades earlier, he had fought with Filipino revolutionary forces against the United States. Subsequently, Quezon had worked as a defense lawyer for Aurelio Tolentino, one of the most important writers of anti-American "seditious" plays, when he was arrested for treason against the United States after staging his drama *Kahapon, Ngayon at Bukas* (*Yesterday, Today, and Tomorrow*) in May 1903 ("Tolentino" 376–77). The peers of Tolentino included Pedro Paterno, whose own anticolonial operas appeared in the same era. The acquiescence of Filipino politicians to American authority, however, would come to mark Quezon and just about every other member of the ruling archipelagic class throughout the 20th century. As a result, the juggernaut of Japan jeopardized his power far more than the continuation of American colonization.

Balmori does not consider any of this when assessing archipelagic history. Instead, he suggests after the Quezon speech, via an internal monologue by Fernando, that "España puso los cimientos formidables de nuestra estructura nacional y América coronó más tarde el edificio con sus modernas galas y sus adornos prácticos. A las dos les debía Filipinas su orgulloso pasado y su triunfal presente" ["Spain lay the formidable foundation of our national structure and America crowned the building later with its modern trappings and practical adornments. To both of them the Philippines owed its proud past and its triumphal present"] (27). He then repeats the canard that with the United States "aún nos unían lazos de Gobierno y la gratitud eterna y enorme de una libertad que sólo nos costó pedir y sólo nos costó querer, a diferencia de otros pueblos, de todos los pueblos, de los propios americanos, que tuvieron que conquistar su libertad a tiros" ["ties still united us of Government and of eternal and enormous gratitude for a liberty that cost us only the asking and that cost us only the wanting, in contrast to other peoples, to all peoples, to the Americans themselves, who had to conquer their liberty with bullets"] (27). All of this is not a cover-up of 20th-century historical reality so much as its erasure altogether. The whitewashing takes place via two techniques: (1) overlooking all actual details of the decades of American colonization; Balmori sweeps up all those years as simply the prologue to a "triumphal present," and (2) ignoring that the relatively peaceful decolonization path offered via the Commonwealth papered over the immense amount of Filipino blood spilled by American soldiers during the young adulthood of Balmori himself. After 1898, Filipinos tried very hard, and with many bullets, to gain their liberty from the United States. An estimated quarter million of them died as a result (Kramer 157; Campomanes 138). But Balmori is not interested in recalling any of this or, for that matter, anything particular at all about the American occupation. The topic that truly seizes his attention is not even the devastation of the Philippines during World War II. Most significant to him is instead the destruction of a certain group of elites whose way of life the war alters irrevocably.

That archipelagic aristocracy is nearly helpless when Japan invades the Philippines as a gleeful sadist: "La deseaba con el furor sensual del sátiro a la ninfa hermosa. . . . Soñaba en devorarla, en embriagarse y festejarse con su sangre rica y generosa, como el lobo a la gacela" ["He desired her with the sensual fury of the satyr falling upon the beautiful nymph. . . . He dreamed of devouring her, getting drunk and partying with her rich and generous blood, like the wolf falling upon the gazelle"] (144). The stark aesthetic politics of this description—the sexualized brutalization of Japan as an insatiable rapist, the feminization of the Philippines as a defenseless, sublime creature—obscures a deeper historical reality. After all, the same general conclusion, minus the orientalizing stereotypes, could be reached regarding the American arrival in the archipelago in 1898 and extending through today. The United States, of course, always pontificated that its policies toward the Philippines were profoundly benevolent. The poor and peasant Filipinos it assaulted and annihilated, whether via main arm or proxy, from the Katipunan rebels at the turn of the century to the Huk rebels at midcentury, rose and fell in counterpoint. So too did the hundreds of thousands of Filipinas whose most viable economic option for decades after formal national independence was to enter the sex labor market for American military men. A case can be made, therefore, that the Japanese violation of the islands from 1941 to 1945 is not quite the outlier it seems. After all, an observer with a broader view than

Balmori might argue that the United States penetrated the Philippines in 1898 and has stayed inside ever since, a predation as lupine over the long haul as anything Japan attempted in the short term. The sadism of conquest is not unique to any nation. And the courtesans of conquest, the true ones, are not the camp followers but the classes who kowtow in congresses high above.

In *The Birds of Fire*, amid the ravages and ruinations that follow the Japanese invasion, one by one the cast of the novel is demolished. Fernando, the most active participant in the resistance effort, is wounded while fighting in Bataan.[12] He then survives a "campo de concentración" ["concentration camp"] qua passion play by remembering the angelic Marta, ends up leading irregulars in the countryside, recants that campaign at the advice of a priest, and ultimately dies by a relatively random Japanese bullet (164). At the family mansion, his sister Natalia is gang-raped by Japanese soldiers as her horrified father, the nipponophile Don Lino, listens (174–75). He dies afterward out of grief and shock, a sympathetic figure for Balmori to the end despite never having understood anything at all about the giant contending forces of World War II or the class and social tensions of Filipino society. Sandoval, the boyfriend and then husband of Natalia, is taken prisoner and later perishes when the hospital where he works is bombed by the Japanese (153, 189).[13] Anselmi the Italian and Von Kauffman the German are slain by their allegorical allies in the vicious retreat of the Japanese from Manila.

What stands out amid all these gruesome episodes is the narrow lens that Balmori focuses on them. Unlike de la Rosa in *Trust in Me*, Balmori never steps backward for a macroscopic view of the context of the war in the Philippines, such as the movements of American forces in the Pacific. In following closely the Filipino characters and their enemies, Balmori keeps his gaze shuttered. The war is reduced to a plot whose dramatic tension rides on whether a particular family of extremely elite Filipinos will be able to maintain their class position against all comers. Their nemeses include not only the Japanese invaders but also the upstart peasants, who are now free to organize by virtue of the sudden weakness of their traditional overseers. The implicit antagonists of the Robles are also the backgrounded Americans of the preceding half-century who had loosened up enough the sclerotic Spanish social order to make men like Sandoval viable contenders for the hands of the daughters of the landed plutocracy.

As the novel weaves through purple prose about virgins, flowers, and butterflies, there are fleeting allusions to wartime entities such as the Greater East Asia Co-Prosperity Sphere and the puppet Philippine Republic. Yet these are usually not named directly, much as Quezon is not when the president of the Commonwealth speaks. The effect is to underline the allegorical rather than realist aesthetics and logics of the novel. *The Birds of Fire*, whose title alludes to Japanese bombers, thus ends with the appearance in Filipino skies of other symbolic birds:

> Un día, después de muchos tristes días, las águilas de América velaron con sus alas el resplandor del sol . . . ¡Salve, América, buena, grande y poderosa . . . ¿En dónde estaban, en tanto, los pájaros de fuego? ¿En qué entraña de qué abismos se habían refugiado despavoridos el cinismo, la osadía y la mentira enormes del Japón? Pasó la noche, pasaron la traición y el crimen. Esta era América, señores japoneses. Las águilas volvían a su nido. (203)

> [One day, after many sad days, the eagles of America veiled the brightness of the sun with their wings . . . Salutations, America, good, great, and powerful! . . . Where were, meanwhile, the birds of fire? In which hiding place of which abysses had the cynicism, impudence, and enormous lies of Japan taken terrified refuge? The night was over, treason and crime were over. This was America, Japanese misters. The eagles were returning to their nest.]

The novel, which begins with a Commonwealth anniversary parade in which American and Filipino troops march as one, so finishes with a reassertion of American power. The United States indeed had nested in the Philippines for a long time by that point, nearly half a century, and for that matter had left many a fertilized egg in the process. Yet none of the massive transformations wrought by the United States on the archipelago in all arenas of life beyond the military obtain more than a passing reference in *The Birds of Fire*. And even the military exists in the novel in some kind of fantasy world in which its only purpose in the Philippines is to preserve freedom. This is counterfactual. Freedom cannot be preserved in a colony, particularly not one whose brutal subjugation was the condition of its colonization in the first place. Freedom can only be gained.

Ejecting Modernity

The pervasive exclusion of the United States by Balmori from nearly all aspects of Filipino life is tantamount to a full rejection of the same. In diametric contrast to *Trust in Me*, only one character with lines in *The Birds of*

Fire is American, an unnamed lieutenant who appears fleetingly to arrest Kauffman and who is given twelve words to speak and is never mentioned again. And of all the protagonists, only Natalia is associated with American soft power in the archipelago. Early in the novel, she is depicted as "una muchacha moderna, práctica, muy a la americana, devota de los deportes y de las cosas útiles. Nada de sueños ni romanticismos. ¿Poesía? ¡La del cine! ¿Música? ¡La del baile!" ["a modern girl, practical, very à la American, devotee of sports and useful things. Nothing of dreams or romantic things. Poetry? That of the movie theater! Music? That of dance!"] (17). Yet Balmori goes no deeper or more specific than this. In one throwaway sentence, he has her accompany Sandoval to a dance "en honor de la oficialidad americana" ["in honor of the American officers"]; in another, she compares Fernando in his military uniform to "un general de Hollywood" ["a Hollywood general"]; in another, she rides in a Lincoln car; in another, her wedding dress is revealed to be ordered from Hollywood (39, 80, 91, 110). None of this is substantive or sustained. Natalia goes on her honeymoon to Baguio, a mountain resort town closely associated with the American occupation, but Balmori never sets any scene there (116). She is said to be a devotee of sports, but she is never shown playing any. She allegedly likes the movie theater but she is never seen by the reader in one. She seems to knows no English despite her purported fondness for colonial culture and forty years of the anglicization of the archipelago. She is a Filipina virgin with an American veneer; that is it. The scene with her that most rings true is when Fernando comes upon her in the family garden gathering sampaguitas, the white flowers symbolic of an innocent Filipino national identity and of innocent Filipinas (80). Natalia represents a kind of modernity without, well, modernity, just as her counterpart Marta symbolizes the peasantry without being a peasant herself.

The novel gives off the impression that Balmori, though writing in the middle of an all too real 20th century, felt more comfortable with the middle of an imaginary 19th century. And this is despite his adulthood coinciding with the entirety of the American colonial period. *The Birds of Fire* is nostalgic for a nonexistent, static time when landed Filipinos succeeded outside of any colonial order, when mute peasants accepted their lot, when all sexpots were virgins, when priestly power was pure, and when no evil empire prowled. That evil empire for Balmori is primarily the Japanese, against whom the "good, great, and powerful" American eagles make an appearance at the end to banish back to Mordor. But notwithstanding the historical fact that the American military in 1945 did chase its Japanese counterpart from Manila, these aquiline pilots do not equate so much to the actual American air force as to a deus ex machina that is brought forth to resolve the plot of the novel and the war. All the praise by Balmori of this potent but hollow god machine exists only to counter the darkness that he attributes to its more or less satanic opposite. There is no embrace of anything else America did during its own and much longer invasion and occupation of the Philippines. It is as if the first half of the 20th century had not quite happened.

In sharp contrast to the spotlight in *Trust in Me* on youthful protagonists, *The Birds of Fire* foregrounds the older generation of Robles as much as their would-be heirs. The elderly Robles represent a caste who speaks Spanish among themselves and adheres to pre-1898 codes of conduct, even to the point of maintaining the honorific title "Don" ["Sir"] inherited from Spain. They lead a romanticized and somewhat medieval life on an immense estate with hundreds of workers. They provide a touch of noblesse oblige for the local priest and his chapel. On the eve of World War II, therefore, the Robles family borders on the anachronistic. Their wealth is based on old agricultural holdings rather than any industrial, technological or otherwise modern sector of the economy introduced by the United States. Most of the clan are oblivious to domestic and international realities and live in a cocooned high-society world. In historical truth, midcentury Filipino elites such as the Robles were embedded within the American colonial order and turned all the tricks thus required of them. The Robles, nevertheless, somehow still prevail amid a hispanized, quasi-feudal landscape in which American culture has scarcely changed anything.

Although Balmori does seem to criticize the Robles, and Don Lino in particular, as a relatively effete and clueless lot compared to preceding aristocratic generations, they emerge as clearly preferable to the professional class that is evidently taking their place in Manila. Every individual in the novel who professes formal training or an actual skill set is dismissed by Balmori with a sneer, from Sandoval the doctor to Anselmi the music teacher to Von Kauffman the physician to Andrade, a journalist who collaborates with the Japanese. All are depicted as quacks of one kind or another. At one point Fernando, who takes turns with Don Lino and Don Ramón at voicing sociopolitical positions, even says of a group of minor characters who represent "la flor y nata profesional del país, todos doctores" ["the professional crème de la crème of society, all doctors"] that "aquella sociedad le resultaba grosera, indeseable" ["that society struck him as vulgar, undesirable"] (85, 86).[14] Fernando himself "odiaba los estudios" ["hated studying"] (24). That was just fine by his father Don Lino, who felt that "el país estaba lleno de profesionales que no servían más que de estorbo. Robles con sus vastas propiedades y sus millones en los Bancos, tenía por demás asegurado el porvenir de sus hijos" ["the country was full of professionals who were good for nothing except being a nuisance. Robles [i.e., Don Lino] with his vast properties and his millions in the Banks had the future of his children assured anyway"] (24). The professionals are no match for Balmori's romanticized peasantry: "¡Cuánto más dignos aquellas rústicas campesinas y aquellos ignorantes gañanes de la hacienda!" ["How much more honorable are those rustic peasant women and those ignorant peasant men from the estate!"] (86). Throughout the novel, Balmori does not qualify much or at all such class prejudices as these. The "ignorant peasant men" cease being "honorable" the moment they grasp the war situation better than Don Lino and the instant they reject the archconservative advice of the paternalistic priest.

The ultimate eradication of the Robles bloodline implies grimly that the hereditary landowning classes have been annihilated by the war. Don Ramón, the lone but childless survivor, effectively voices this conclusion after the deaths of most of his family by implying to Andrade, the turncoat reporter, that he should no longer be referred to with the honorific "Don" but just as "Ramón Robles" (187). The "Robles" patronym translates from Spanish to English as "Oaks." These trees, symbols of strength, have burned to the ground beneath the birds of fire. The destruction has been aided by Filipinos like Andrade, who became editor of a pro-Japanese newspaper. Yet his real sin is not betrayal of the nation so much as of the aristocracy. Andrade is pegged by Balmori as a malcontent even before the war when, on class grounds, he resents having to cover the high-society wedding of Natalia and Sandoval (112–13). The American colonization of the archipelago, relative to Spanish rule, allowed for democratizations of assorted cultural and political kinds. Balmori in *The Birds of Fire* rejects all of that. This is why his novel is a work of mourning for an oligarchy now apparently as powerless as the empire that had produced it.

Given the disinterest of Balmori in reformulating sociopolitical orders, it remains unclear in the novel who might take the place in the postwar Philippines of the Robles and the rural aristocracy for which they stood. In historical reality, no one did. The surviving members of the class scooped up the land and capital of the dead and maintain their position today. But Balmori was not invested in the future in any case. The novel ends with a coda that looks backward to Columbus, not forward to a Philippines that would become independent just a year later. *The Birds of Fire* is essentially an eschatological text, a processing through fiction of the wrenching social end of a useless Spanish-speaking elite nearly half a century after Spain itself had been ejected from the islands.

In this deeply reactionary text is subversion of the most anti-American kind. Ignoring almost entirely the U.S. presence in the Philippines after forty years of its penetrating every major aspect of Filipino culture amounts to a defiant stance against the status quo. In *The Birds of Fire*, there is barely any indication of the mixing of English and Spanish words that had started appearing decades earlier in archipelagic literature and among the flesh-and-blood Filipino elite. The Robles live in a Spanish colonial world long after its collapse, and the Japanese destroy them before they comprehend clearly what is going on. The markers of their class would seem recognizable to readers of 19th-century Latin American literature: rich landowners in whose service toil nameless peasants; vigorous young men who come and go in the family mansions bearing news of the outside world; and the chaste daughters of the gilded class who spend their time playing European classical music on the piano or enjoying Edenic gardens or bathetically longing for their sweethearts. The virgins can be counted on to plead frequently for intercessions from Mary on behalf of their beloveds and to otherwise exude piety. There is virtually no assimilation of anything here that could pass as modernity, much less acceptance of it. America appears as a military force for the Japanese to reckon with but not as a force of any other kind for Balmori himself to reckon with. He ignores the soft power of the American century altogether and a great deal of its hard power as well.

The contrasts with de la Rosa and his war novel are sharp, save for the mutual malarkey about maidens. Writing in the same place, at the same time and about the same subject as Balmori, de la Rosa goes out of his way to acknowledge the long American presence in the Philippines and all its effects on archipelagic society, from its linguistic and wider cultural impacts to its literal and figurative geopolitics, economics, and underpinning logics. The turning toward American power by de la Rosa counters the turning away of Balmori and yet undermines it none the less. This is because de la Rosa, who pairs his Filipino protagonists with Americans as deliberately as Balmori does not, upends the assumed hierarchy of colonizer and colonized by construing the latter as equally potent and often more so. If Balmori subverts the American century by portraying it as irrelevant, military power aside, to the insular lives of his characters, de la Rosa inverts the American century by representing the Philippines as indispensable to American senses of self.

Neither author is particularly moved by historical reality despite writing about current events they knew to be destined for History, though de la Rosa pays a lot closer attention to the documentable events of the war. Both men, really, are fantasists at heart. Balmori is wishful that the present and recent past be replaced by an idealized deeper past. De la Rosa, instead, imagines that the present and recent past be substituted for an idealized deep future. This latter optimism, however groundless, at least retains the allure of possibility, for the future cannot be disproven until it actually plays out. Balmori, in contrast, knew full well that the autarkic elites and accommodating peasants that he adored were counterhistorical chimeras. By the time he was writing *The Birds of Fire*, those landowners had long since secured their class position by servicing the American export market and navigating adeptly through American economic and political policies in the archipelago. And those upstart peasants did not rise for the first time amid the social chaos caused by the Japanese occupation. Their traditions of revolt were steeped in decades of anti-American efforts, the most powerful of which surged around the turn of the century when Balmori was initiating his literary career. And those anti-American endeavors were rooted directly in the preceding periods of anti-Spanish agitation.

One way to counter the blinkered focus of *The Birds of Fire* would be to read the novel not from the stock aristocratic characters at its center but from the figures on the margins, such as Sandoval and Marta. These supporting actors imply integration into the Robles clan and therefore class. Their respective unions with Natalia and Fernando suggest how the old hispanized elite of the islands might endure by fusing either with the new professional class (Sandoval) or the ancient peasant class (Marta). In the novel, Marta comes off better than Sandoval, but neither one ultimately represents a way toward survival of the aristocracy via class cross-fertilization. Sandoval claims to have impregnated Natalia on their honeymoon, but Don Lino can see no sign of it. And, anyway, both newlyweds die in the war. So much for the future of the hereditary elite with the new petit bourgeoisie. As for a potential merger with the peasants, Fernando and Marta never do marry because he joins the army out of patriotism before any ceremony is held (55). Later, after recovering from battle wounds, Fernando has an opportunity to be with Marta again. He gazes upon her through a window as she prays to an image of Mary. Rather than join her, however, he chooses to reenter the war out of his duty to his *patria* and to his dead father and sister (190). Subsequently, Fernando leads guerrilla forces, "más de mil hombres decididos y bravos" ["more than a thousand determined and brave men"] against the Japanese and becomes something of a folk hero (192). Balmori, nonetheless, judges that his decision to leave Marta again was a grave error. Faced with dedication to the survival of his country versus dedication to the survival of his class, Fernando should have opted for the latter. He did not, however, and so even though the priest finally convinces him to abandon the anticolonial fight, Fernando dies at the end of the novel without having wed Marta (197–99, 209). In consequence, he, like Natalia, will not produce a real or symbolic heir. The elites will not be saved by (pseudo) peasants either.

Balmori also considers the possible reproduction of the Robles family and their class by offering an option external to the archipelago. Strikingly, this allegorical alternative is not with the United States, as in the case of de la Rosa, but with Japan. Don Lino is a widower who longs for Haruko, a woman in Kyoto whom he had courted there five years earlier. With unadulterated orientalism, Don Lino describes Haruko to his brother as "bella como un templo de oro, suave como la seda y los pétalos de las flores del cerezo. Me hizo feliz con su amor tímido y reverente. Esas mujeres saben amar. Si alguna vez necesitas a tu lado una mujer amante, ¡búscate una japonesa!" ["beautiful as a golden temple, soft as silk and the petals of the flowers of the cherry tree. She made me happy with her timid and reverent love. Those women know how to love. If at some point you need at your side a loving woman, look for a Japanese woman!"] (42). Unfortunately for Don Lino, Haruko sends a wistful letter to him in September 1941 saying she had married a Japanese man a year earlier and now was expecting a child (95). At the roughest level of interpretation, there goes the symbolic option of a successful union between the Philippines and Japan. This takes place just three months before Japanese war planes fly over Manila and so is a foreshadowing of harsher divergences to come.

With an actual maternal role absent among the Robles, motherhood is substituted metaphorically by a conflated array of feminized personas and personifications all treated as virginal purities: Natalia, her dead mother, Marta, Mary, and the Philippines. These five characters are described with similar discourses, each a sort of prelapsarian Eve, each being pristine regardless of whether they have produced offspring or not. Haruko incarnates an orientalized version of the same. But the prelapsarian Eve does not leave the Garden in this novel: she, or rather the archipelago, or rather Natalia, instead gets violated by the Japanese. This is where *The Birds of Fire* varies from the tendencies of Filipino novels in Spanish dating back to the first one, *Nínay* by Paterno. In many of those other texts, the trajectory of virginal figures ends in real or symbolic passing from this world, such as with death or removal to a nunnery. Yet in those predecessors, mass sadism is never so explicitly the cause. The house of Robles does not fall in *The Birds of Fire*; it is obliterated with sexual ferocity.

Meanwhile, Ramón, the lone blood survivor of the Robles clan, is not only an heirless bachelor but also does not like women at all. There is no chance of procreation in his future either. Don Lino notes that his brother is an "enemigo de los placeres, indiferente a la mujer, seco y frío como un árbol sin ramas y sin nidos" ["enemy of pleasures, indifferent to women, dry and cold like a tree without branches and without nests"] (52). The alleged asexuality of Ramón competes in this case with a cast flush with equally allegedly asexual female figures. Again, this is irrespective of whether the latter prove able to conceive. Fruitfulness may be attributed in *The Birds of Fire*, but it does not necessarily mean deflowerment, such as in the case of Mary, whose pregnancy is immaculate, or Natalia, whose pregnancy is purported but inapparent. The deceased wife of Don Lino did produce two children but manages to remain angelic to the point where "su cuerpo parecía tener luz. Su alma era el alma de las arpas que cantan" ["her body seemed to give off light. Her soul was the soul of the harps that sing"] (92). The same holds true for the Philippines, whose landscape is routinely described as Edenic. Marta, the indigenous peasant stand-in, is so pure that, as Balmori memorably puts it, "exhalaba ella un vago aroma virginal que la envolvía toda" ["she gave off a vague virginal aroma that enveloped all of her"] (30). This remarkable scent does not preclude Fernando from then paraphrasing her body language as follows: "¡Tómame! ¡Sórbeme!—parecía clamarle en suspiros y en sollozos—; ¡que la savia de mi vida te caliente las venas! ["'Take me! Slurp me!' she seemed to cry out to him in sighs and sobs; 'may the sap of my life heat up your veins!'"] (31). The earlier virgins in Paterno and Rizal are not nearly as sexualized as Marta, but she fits easily among them with her angelic religiosity, melodramatic emotional displays, and enduring chastity.

Modern women with autonomous lives have no place in Balmori. Nor do modern peasants, at least not if Balmori can help it. He does give space for Filipino lower classes to emerge as guerrillas in reaction to Japanese atrocities, but he cannot stomach the social upheaval that they embody and augur. Balmori not only implies that soap opera love should triumph over the desire to fight oppression (to wit, the fate of Fernando) but so should Christian theology. The family priest of the Robles thus tells the workers and peasants in arms that killing is unethical and recommends the following: "Someteos al orden, aprended a sufrir, resignaos a esperar. Es por la voluntad del Altísimo que suceden estas cosas" ["Submit yourselves to order, learn to suffer, resign yourselves to waiting. It is due to the will of the Highest that these things happen"] (180). Balmori upholds with such positions the primacy of class, family, and the church. He supports thereby a trinity of a terrible status quo.

Balmori is the most reactionary of subversives. Every disruption of every kind against established hierarchies, whether that hierarchy be Japanese or Filipino, is criticized by him. A key example is that of Pablo, the foreman of the Robles estate, who takes to the hills with his fellow laborers to fight against the Japanese. In *Trust in Me*, de la Rosa depicts irregulars in a positive light and surely would have represented Pablo as heroic. In *The Birds of Fire*, however, as a foreman who has abandoned his old position to fight for freedom, Pablo is portrayed as a diabolical upstart. When the priest implores him to resign himself to Japanese atrocities and not fight back, Pablo tells his men, "Atadle a un árbol y dejad que allí se lo coman las hormigas. Si le damos libertad, nos venderá" ["Tie him to a tree and let the ants eat him up there. If we give him liberty, he will sell us out to the enemy"] (180). Balmori, however, immediately has Pablo's own men disobey the order and liberate the priest. And later, when Pablo works for Fernando as the foreman of the latter's guerrilla army—the peacetime hierarchy of the Robles reappears here in wartime—Pablo shoots a Japanese prisoner against Fernando's wishes and the young patrician yells, "¿Y quién es Pablo para dar órdenes contrarias a las mías?" ["And who is Pablo to give orders contrary to my own?"] (198). The cardinal sin in Balmori is threatening not the Japanese but the presumptive superiority of his protagonizing bluebloods.

The antediluvian ideology of the novel pervade its portraits of Japanese fronts such as the Greater East Asia Co-Prosperity Sphere and the puppet Philippine Republic. The medium for these representations is Andrade, the reporter who is a quisling and, more importantly, a member of the professional class that Balmori detests:

> Elevaron al pobre diablo de Andrade al puesto de director de "La Linterna". Y Andrade, sintiéndose más japonés que Tokio, se dedicó desde el primer instante a loar en todos los estilos y por todos los medios las fantásticas glorias del Asia oriental más grande. Empezó públicamente a comer en cuclillas, renunciando a los cubiertos por los asiáticos palillos. . . . Un buen día. "La Linterna" amaneció repicando todas sus campanillas y todos sus cascabeles. El Japón se aprestaba a dar la independencia a Filipinas. Oh, corazón inmenso y generoso! Oh, nación bendita y alabada! Lo que nunca quiso hacer América! Lo que jamás pensó hacer España! Ya teníamos república, redención, libertad! (183–85)

[They elevated the poor devil Andrade to the position of director of *The Lantern*. And Andrade, feeling more Japanese than Tokyo, dedicated himself from the first instant to praise in all ways and by all means the fantastic glories of the Greater East Asia. He began publicly eating by squatting, renouncing cutlery for Asian chopsticks. . . . A good day. *The Lantern* dawned, ringing all its hand bells and all its jingle bells. Japan was preparing to give independence to the Philippines. Oh, immense and generous heart! Oh, blessed and praiseworthy nation! What America never wanted to do! What Spain never thought to do! Now we had a republic, redemption, liberty!]

Although Balmori satirizes here the imperial shells that are the Greater East Asia Co-Prosperity Sphere and the Philippine Republic, they are not his real target. He could have put those same sentiments in the foreboding, pragmatic voice of Don Ramón. Instead, he adopts the mode of irony so he can show that Andrade never had acceptable politics in the first place. Rather than grumbling about the society page wedding of Natalia and subsequently glorifying the institutions celebrated by Japan, Andrade should have done the opposite. What is venerable he takes wrongly to be vacuous and vice versa.

The whole array of ancillary figures, from Sandoval and Marta to Pablo and Andrade, is never substantively linked with the United States. None of them speaks a lick of English despite nearly half a century of English teachers foisted on the archipelago. Yet even if the myopic Robles family managed to block out post-1898 historical reality, surely the secondary characters could not have walled themselves off so readily from American impact in the archipelago. That Balmori casts them as almost as untouched amounts to a repression of such radical proportions that it results in revolution. More than forty years of massive American influence on daily Philippine life are, in *The Birds of Fire*, just about vaporized out of existence.

This astonishing subversion of the American century is worth contrasting to versions presented by Americans themselves of how the Philippines fit into the manifest destiny of the United States. As just one example, M. E. Beall, the likely translator of the Paterno short story "The Honorable Taft and His Successor Governor Wright" from 1904, published the following four decades before Balmori wrote *The Birds of Fire*:

The instinct to go west that has been operative among the people of America ever since the colonization of Jamestown and Plymouth, and which has carried the waves of population across the Connecticut, over the Alleghenies, up and down the Mississippi valley, into the fastnesses of the Rocky mountains and over their summits to Pacific tidewater, has not been extinguished.

The nation is still young, its youth is still daring, and the west still beckons onward. Oceans no longer separate, they unite, distant lands, and today Manila rather than San Francisco is the western city of the United States. (5)

Decades of American presences in the Philippines had succeeded such statements at all levels of archipelagic society and culture. Uneven colonial politics, to be sure, had allowed Filipinos to undertake substantive leadership roles from time to time, such as the Filipinization strategy of the Woodrow Wilson years (this policy increased the percentage of governmental roles filled by islanders) and, later, the creation of the Commonwealth. Yet the ultimate hard power of the United States over the archipelago never ceased, and its soft power became ever more profound and ubiquitous. The impossibility of extricating America from the Philippines in the time of Balmori is manifest in the way de la Rosa, his contemporary, could conceive only of a future in which the two lands were forever wedded. Nonetheless, Balmori manufactured a mock-up of the archipelago in which, military power aside, the United States played no obvious role whatsoever.

With this American century in which America is essentially absent, Balmori stands out from his earlier peers too. Although Paterno always put Filipino characters at the forefront of his operas, he did so in constant negotiations with the American colonial presence. He attempted to carve out space for united Filipinos to act independently despite their context of imperial duress. Balmori laments the lack of such space, though without any popular touch, by identifying colonial oppression with a different empire, that of Japan, while silently exiling to an unidentified abyss a half-century of American influence in the Philippines. Guillermo Gómez Windham, writing in the chronological middle of the American occupation and in a comparatively stable historical moment, does not dwell on mass conflicts such as those that permeate the operas of Paterno and the novel of Balmori. His texts therefore do not draw their dramatic energies from tensions of war and colonization. His protagonists can seek autonomy in their lives amid relative peace. Yet their seemingly greater opportunities to exercise free will do not liberate them from the contours of America at all. In the stories and novellas of Gómez Windham, the United States even when backgrounded appears as a mix of major forces that offer promise and punishment at once. His characters Cándida and Bert aspire to Americanization and respectively fail and succeed in life as a result. His protagonist Sing-A both rises and falls in contexts highly contingent on American power. Balmori diverges from this literary lineage for the extremes of his determination to ignore as much as possible the assorted Americanizations of the Philippines.

The Birds of Fire, therefore, overturns the history of America and of the world. This is true despite the decades of anonymity of the text, despite its inaccessibilities still today, despite the fact that its principal concerns, so many of them tied to an elite class, may no longer be those of its land of origin and perhaps never were. Southeast Asian literature composed from and about a center of the greatest conflict in history, written for that matter in a European language during an East Asian occupation over a North American colonizer, is not a phenomenon without planetary implications. *The Birds of Fire* is a most modern of texts with a least modern of laments, a most global of rebellions by a most insular of authors. That is why the novel should be read. In its multiple myopias, the novel rewrites America and remakes the century. Balmori was rooted beyond measure and yet uprooted more than his predecessors. And the purpose of art, after all, is not to leave us with the sense of our world that we already possess.

six

Space-Age Subversions

Mariano de la Rosa's *La creación* (1959)

The only known Filipino science fiction novel in Spanish is a great and strange text. The powers of *La creación* (*The Creation*) by Mariano de la Rosa are at once marginalized and mighty, for from a space of oblivion the twists and obsessions of its plot reinvent the possibilities of American literature and of America itself. Time too in this novel is both out of joint and enjoining. By the time de la Rosa submitted *The Creation* for a national literary award in 1961, the Spanish empire that had left him the language in which he wrote had been dead in Asia for more than six decades. His novel was also anachronistic with respect to the American empire that had run the Philippines, the wartime Japanese occupation aside, between 1898 and 1946. The place-names in English that mark *The Creation*, the constant description of space exploration as a conquest, and the fact that the characters, none of whom is American, all speak to each other in English, testify to the continuing cultural colonization of the Philippines long after the formal U.S. occupation had ended. The most important component of this ongoing colonization is its unstated assimilation. Imperial American influences are ubiquitous in *The Creation*, and yet the history of the United States in the archipelago is never acknowledged explicitly. Despite the early introduction of a major character from the Niagara Falls region, continental America is absent as well until the last sequence of the novel. At that point, Washington emerges as the political capital of the Western Hemisphere and the vice president of the United States is selected as one of the first three formal representatives of humanity to the royal court of Venus.

The uniquenesses of *The Creation* are manifest. Within archipelagic traditions, it also seems singular, or virtually so, on several grounds. For instance, it may have been the last or next to last Filipino novel in Spanish to be printed as a bound book, since the only contemporaneous novel that seems to have so appeared is *La vida secreta de Daniel Espeña* (*The Secret Life of Daniel Espeña*) by the relatively well-known Antonio Abad in 1960. Other Filipino novels in Spanish may have seen light thereafter in serialized forms in periodicals, but the tradition of bound novels that begins in 1885 with *Nínay* by Pedro Paterno seems to draw to a close with the narratives of de la Rosa and Abad. Moreover, *The Creation* borders on nonexistence or, its corollary, invisibility. Only one copy of the book is known to be extant, and as of 2008 it was buried in a backroom library of a forgotten social club in Manila.[1] There is no known trace of its reception at the time of publication and, indeed, no known record of its having been read by anyone. Were it not for an extraordinary amount of exhaust fumes inhaled at a photocopy kiosk beside a Manila avenue named for William Taft, the former American chief of state of the Philippines and later of the United States, this would still be the case. There is no other known science fiction novel in Spanish from the Philippines, and there is probably no other novel on the planet that suggests that yellowish people are descended from inhabitants of Pluto, that white people are a mixed race product of Mars and Mercury, and that survivors of the sunken continents of Atlantis and Lemuria merged with Native Americans to form a community of aviation virtuosos by Niagara Falls.

In the breadth of world literature, *The Creation* stands out as perhaps the first novel in Asia or anywhere in the global South to focus on space exploration in the era of its birth. De la Rosa initiates the plot with a total lunar eclipse on July 26, 1953 (4). In fact, that eclipse was indeed visible from Manila at the times indicated by de la Rosa, and so it seems likely that he witnessed it.[2] The eclipse took place the same year he retired as a judge and appears to have been an immediate source of inspiration. A biographical note by Ramon Velayo that was published along with the novel states that de la Rosa began writing *The Creation* after he left the bench.[3] He seems to have finished it some six years later, for the novel contains a prefatory comment dated November 8, 1959. There is no publication date given for the text, but Lourdes Castrillo Brillantes lists it as a 1961 entrant for the Zóbel Prize for the best Filipino literature in Spanish (*81 Years* 218). The novel could have been submitted in manuscript form, however, with publication posthumous. The note by Velayo is written entirely in the past tense and includes phrases such as "those who knew him."

The dates of 1953 and 1959 that correspond to the lunar eclipse and the prefatory comment, along with the length of the novel—260 pages in fairly small typescript—and the multiple editings implied by the polish of the prose, suggest that de la Rosa was working on *The Creation* before and after the launch of *Sputnik* on October 4, 1957, terrified the Western world. Surely it is not a coincidence that the spaceship of his protagonists takes off from Earth in an earlier October, that of 1954, three years before *Sputnik* (113). In other words, Manila beats Moscow and Washington into space. The Soviet Union, however, is even more absent in the novel than the United States, for it is never mentioned at all. There is no space race of any kind in *The Creation*, whose primary feature from a dramatic point of view is the remarkable lack of adversity faced by its itinerant protagonists. No one is in a contest with anyone else in the novel, and there are no enemies to overcome. In this alone *The Creation* is a rarity for a space travel story. The main characters boldly go where no one has gone before, but foreigners of neither the earthling nor extraterrestrial kind ever stand in their way. Everywhere they travel they are greeted with spontaneous applause by solar system denizens for their heroic triumphs over nobody. And for all these reasons and more, the novel may very well seem to be representative of nothing. Yet its subject, literally, is everything: the origins of humanity and, beyond that, the entirety of space-time and the cosmos. By definition, the novel represents the universe. It also represents America. The optimism of the endeavor, the ebullience of the explorations, seem as singularly American an orientation as the multiracial utopianism advanced along the way by the author.

And They're Off!

Facts are scarcely relevant to those orientations. De la Rosa makes it clear from the outset that his is a work of imagination that intervenes where religion and science meet their terrestrial limits (2). *The Creation* offers itself as a supplement to both. More specifically, the novel suggests that Genesis and Darwin offer equally compelling accounts of the origins of humanity and indeed conjoin in promoting explanations that take Earth as the starting point (6–7). Without discounting the merits of either biblical or evolutionary narratives, de la Rosa raises the possibility that different races on Earth previously existed on various other planets and on the Sun and then arrived at their present locales through accident or intent. The primary spokesman for this "Teoría de la Diversidad del Origen del Hombre" ["Theory of the

Diversity of the Origin of Man"] is Mr. Pee Nam, a philosopher who hails from "la raza mongoloide" ["the Mongoloid race"] (7, 4). He constructs the hypothesis upon observing the colors of heavenly bodies during the lunar eclipse and articulates it to three eminent intellectuals and their families who are with him that night (9–11). The famous thinkers are the geologist Mr. Miguel Lapulapu of the Philippines, Dr. Astor Legrín of Europe, and Professor Elías Uganda of . . . wait for it . . . Africa. In attendance too are their wives and, more significantly for the plot, their children: Shiva, Baltazar, Lisa, and Pretorio, the offspring respectively of Mr. Pee, Mr. Lapulapu, Dr. Legrin, and Professor Uganda.

The novel eventually will bear out the conjecture of Mr. Pee by revealing that a chunk of Pluto, for example, was long ago ejected in a cataclysm and crashed into East Asia. This explains why everyone on the distant orb speaks a language akin to "mongol o chino" ["Mongolian or Chinese"] and "en la Tierra sería un espécimen de la raza mongoloide" ["on Earth would be a specimen of the Mongoloid race"] (127, 130). It also turns out that the early days of space travel between Mars and Mercury resulted in the occasional lost astroship ending up on Earth with a contingent of white people, who, naturally, are the mestizo offspring of aborigines from the other two planets. During the lunar eclipse, Mr. Pee does not know these details but guesses correctly that

> tu, Lisa, por tu color resultante de la claridad blanquísima de Mercu-
> rio, matizada por los rayos sanguíneos de Marte, desciendes de ambas
> estrellas; tu, Pretorio, vienes del Sol, que es ardiente fuego y envolvió
> en su negra humareda a tus predecesores al nacer; tu Shiva, perteneces
> a la línea recta, pura y sin mezcla de la descendencia de Pluto, cuya luz
> blanca amarillenta impregnó tu tez; y tu, Baltazar, procedes del coloso
> Jupiter, que con sus destellos bermejizos tiñó tu pigmento, dándote ese
> color tostado. (11)

> [you, Lisa, given your color that results from the very white clarity of
> Mercury tinged with the blood rays of Mars, descend from both stars;
> you, Pretorio, come from the Sun, which is burning fire and wrapped
> in its black smoke your predecessors at birth; you, Shiva, belong to
> the direct, pure, and unmixed line of the descendants of Pluto whose
> yellowish white light impregnated your complexion; and you, Baltazar,
> originate from the colossus Jupiter, which with its auburnish glimmers
> dyed your pigment, giving you that toasted color.]

This is quite a spot-on deduction. Notwithstanding such perspicacity, however, Mr. Pee, soon cedes his central space on the soapbox. The role of protagonist occupied collectively at first by him and the adult intellectuals is filled next by their rainbow children and, finally, by the sublimely beautiful Princess La of Venus. A denouement yields scenes in Washington, Paris, and Manila, followed by the debut of an interplanetary airline and the exchange of diplomatic representations between Venus and Earth.

The plot of *The Creation* is always creative. After the lunar eclipse, the four older intellectuals pledge to spend their wide travels the next year looking for evidence to support Mr. Pee's theory of the extraterrestrial origins of humanity. They agree to reunite thereafter in Manila to discuss their findings. Before the families disperse, however, they visit the mountain town of Baguio to relax while continuing their conversations. The younger generation also passes the time in Baguio by flirting, amid which there is a more or less literal cliffhanger in which Baltazar saves Lisa (26). The whole Baguio sequence takes up more than half of this first part of *The Creation*, a section that in total comprises six of the twenty-seven chapters and about a sixth of the overall length of the novel. The next, somewhat longer stretch of plot, in which the intellectuals split up across the globe and then gather again in Manila, is marked by racial and scientific discoveries that subsequently will make space travel possible. For example, while meandering near Niagara Falls, Mr. Pee comes across the hitherto unknown and technologically advanced Leatam people (66–67). They speak the tongues of the ancient continents of Atlantis and Lemuria that once sunk on either side of the Americas (69). The contemporary Leatams are descendants of the survivors of those two apocalypses who made it to the continent in between, where they mixed with the "primitivos pobladores de América" ["primitive settlers of America"], that is, indigenous people (69).[4] A Lemurian-speaking pilot, Mr. Allen, later will provide assistances of various kinds to the young spacefarers. Meanwhile, back in the Philippines, Baltazar discovers that a mineral specimen in the laboratory of his father remarkably possesses, thanks to its volcanic origins, an immanent property of endless propulsion (45).[5] This will be the motor force behind the spaceship that Baltazar starts building in his workshop and then soups up with the aid of the Leatams (92–93).

Throughout these initial episodes of *The Creation*, the colonial history of the United States in the Philippines is unaddressed yet ubiquitous. A massive American effort to turn the Philippines into an English-speaking country, and its popular culture into an American offshoot, began soon after the United States took the archipelago from Spain and local revolutionaries at the turn of the 20th century. The enduring impact of those policies is evident from the early pages of *The Creation* onward, such as in the following passage in which de la Rosa inserts English words and various other markers of American culture: "Baltazar llevó a sus amigos a uno de estos 'night clubs' del Dewey Boulevard. Se sentaron a una mesa desde la cual podían ver, sin obstáculo alguno, los 'floor shows' y oir distintamente a la 'crooner'" ["Baltazar took his friends to one of these 'night clubs' on Dewey Boulevard. They sat at a table from which they could see, without any obstacle, the 'floor shows' and hear distinctly the 'crooner'"] (15). The significant extent of the scenes in Baguio, a setting that also appeared in de la Rosa's wartime and much more explicitly American novel *Trust in Me (Philippines-America)*, likewise frames the Philippines as enmeshed with the United States. Baguio was built on the orders of the early colonial administration of William Taft. Soon after arriving to the heat and humidity of Manila, Taft had decided that a mountain resort would be a refreshing retreat for himself and for American soldiers tired from all the conquering. He plumped for Baguio. And shortly thereafter, Pedro Paterno represented Baguio as the powerful god of an invading army in his 1904 opera *Magdapio*. By 1916, the opening page of a tourist brochure by Thomas Cook and Son was describing Baguio as "a garden city that has, in less than ten years, progressed from a native village of rude huts to a highly developed mountain station and health resort" while twice referring casually to "the American occupation of the Philippines" (*Baguio* 5).

The Baguio chapter of *The Creation* duly opens by noting an array of local markers that bespeak alien origins: the Pines Hotel, Hogan Alley, Cabinet Hill, Justice Hill and Kennon Road (20). The persisting American presence also includes such historically charged places as "la reserva militar americana de Camp John Hay y las cuestas de los campos de golf" ["the American military reserve Camp John Hay and the slopes of the golf courses"] (20). Mentioned as well is Burnham Park, designed by the same Daniel Hudson Burnham who planned much of Chicago (including the 1893 World's Columbian Exposition there) and Washington. The park became the primary open space of central Baguio and still serves as such today. The United States supposedly decolonized the Philippines on July 4, 1946, but just as the choice of a Fourth of July implies, national sovereignty on paper hardly meant national independence from empire. A decade and a half later in the pages of *The Creation*, the soldiers in Camp John Hay remained along with the golf courses and the English and the nightclubs and crooners on Dewey Boulevard. And long after the novel by de la Rosa, as well as long before, Baguio would stand as the primary geographic reminder of the American presence in the Philippines. As Erlyn Ruth Alcantara writes, "By 1913, Baguio had the amenities of a typical twentieth-century American city: Camp John Hay operated as a rest and recreation center for the U.S. Army. . . . From the beginning and throughout much of its existence, Camp John Hay was an American turf. It had its own life. Baguio residents rarely wandered into the camp save for a few tourists with private vehicles going on a city tour. . . . Over the years the scope of the military reservation expanded, and when Camp John Hay was finally turned over to the Philippine government in July 1991, its area covered 1,672 acres (677 hectares or about one-eighth of Baguio's land area)" (213–14).

The explicitly American inheritances of a novel set in a country that fairly recently had been an American colony may not seem surprising. Nonetheless, alternate historical scenarios can be imagined, and probably played out elsewhere on the globe, in which decolonization would have been followed with decisions by locals to expel the military camp, close the golf courses, change the toponyms, and eschew the imperial language. Such a sequence of events is not remotely envisaged in *The Creation*. Many of the references to the United States that thread through the novel are instead seemingly assimilationist of empire, including such subtle markers as the unlikely focus on Pluto. This outermost planetary body is the one that cues Mr. Pee into thinking that he and his "raza mongoloide" ["Mongoloid race"] are of extraterrestrial origins; the key is its "luz blanca amarillenta" ["yellowish white light"] (4, 11). Pluto is also the first destination of the youths when they blast off, which is odd because as the most distant of planets from Earth it would seem to be the most challenging to reach. Surely most science fiction protagonists who launch a space age first head to the moon or Mars or Venus. Yet it is Pluto that provides initial proof of Mr. Pee's theory when his daughter Shiva, serving as radio-telephone operator of the spaceship, picks up signals from the planet in a "mongol o chino" ["Mongolian or Chinese"] language akin to her own (127). "Mongolian" and "Chinese" and "Mongoloid" are just about synonymous terms throughout *The Creation*, all referring vaguely to inhabitants of mainland East Asia. Soon after arriving on Pluto, the space travelers learn from its royal family that "millones de años atrás un cataclismo desprendió una porción de nuestro territorio, llevándose un número considerable de nuestra población y a la princesa Ku, presunta heredera del trono, recién casada" ["millions of years ago a cataclysm detached a portion of our territory, carrying with it a considerable number of our population and Princess Ku, presumptive heir to the throne, recently married"] (132). Shiva is identified by court intellectuals as a direct descendant of Princess Ku, and the ejected chunk of Pluto is recognized to now be East Asia (133). This explains why people who look and talk like Mr. Pee exist, for Princess Ku crash-landed on Earth and multiplied. But it does not explain why Pluto is foregrounded in the plot ahead of the nearer planets known for millennia and why other faraway planets, Uranus and Neptune, are bypassed altogether in the novel.

The answer has to be that Pluto, from the perspective of de la Rosa, was a novelty of the United States as much as the 20th-century Philippines. Discovered in 1930 by the young astronomer Clyde Tombaugh at an Arizona observatory, Pluto was thus captured by an American while de la Rosa was rising professionally in the archipelago and while politicians in Washington had yet to settle on a decolonization plan. Since Pluto in *The Creation* is an insertion into China/Mongolia, it is a toponym just as indicative of American reach into Asia as Kennon Road and Justice Hill in Baguio. By contrast, Uranus and Neptune, discovered by Europeans in the late 18th and mid-19th centuries, would imply older and Old World advances. The inner planets, all visible to the naked eye, would evoke in turn ancient times and technologies. From a Philippine perspective, it is not really the Plutonians who have traveled across vast spaces and spread across Asia so much as the Americans.

Such an allegory in *The Creation* fits easily into the strong allusive traditions of Filipino literature in general. For instance, in the operas written and produced by Pedro Paterno at the start of the American regime, 16th-century Moors and prehistoric Malays arrive to usurp the archipelago, symbolically, as 20th-century Americans. Paterno calls for Filipinos to resist that appropriation. De la Rosa, instead, embraces the Plutonian (American) power that makes a comparable move. The positive highlighting of Pluto in *The Creation* suggests an acceptance of modern American stretch and, to that extent, a certain assimilation of its alien presence. Shiva, declared a princess by the extraterrestrial royal court and told by the king of Pluto that "desde hoy gozas de los privilegios que corresponden a tu clase" ["from today on forward you enjoy the privileges that correspond to your class"], fills the role of a coopted terrestrial elite of the kind that de la Rosa, as a high-ranking judge in the American-overseen legal system, seems to have exemplified in his own career. The superficial thrust of his previous novel, *Trust in Me*, tends in these directions as well.

Yet just as in *Trust in Me*, an acquiescence to aliens in *The Creation* is not all that it seems. An interpretation of the Princess Ku narrative as ideologically assimilationist aligns awkwardly with the seemingly subversive swerve of the Leatams, a people of the Americas who are manifestly not "Americans." They too are a displaced people. Their ancestors, like those of Shiva, emerged from large land masses that suffered seismic violence and disappeared into an otherworld. Princess Ku and her people, however, recovered from their unwilling flight to found an ostensibly pureblood race in Asia; the Plutonians note that there is just "una sola raza" ["a sole race"] on their home planet (132). In contrast, the surviving Atlantans and Lemurians mixed with Native Americans to form a multilingual mestizo nation in the geopolitically interstitial space of Niagara. These Leatams are described approvingly by de la Rosa at every turn, making their narrative an extraordinary affirmation of the interracial despite the quest of the four young heroes of *The Creation* to unearth the origins of their own racial purity. But why laud the miscegenated, worldly (and otherworldly) Leatams and also a particular palette of primary human colors?

Notably, the presence of the Leatams in *The Creation* is entirely unneeded by the internal logic of the plot. On the scientific front, Americans of the U.S. kind (or, for that matter, of the German Alabaman kind) could easily have supplied de la Rosa with characters who could have offered technological expertise to the space travelers. On the racial front, the overriding concern of the novel is why real humans from known societies look different, not why made-up humans from unknown societies look different. Therefore, the only reason for the Leatams to exist in the narrative is to elide the United States. Technological supremacy, particularly the ability to travel great distances with fantastic sophistication, is characteristic here of Americans who are not Americans but rather an amalgam of pre-American Americans (that is, indigenes) and two groups of refugees from the oceanic, nonexistent continental flanks of the continental United States. These merged, miscegenated Americans from temporalities and spatialities exterior to the United States are the ones who assist Baltazar with his Philippines-based project, one repeatedly described as a "conquista" ["conquest"] of space.

Why the Leatams displace the obvious role of the United States in the novel is unclear, but subversions of dominant geopolitical narratives are evidently under way. A great many large bodies seem to have been in violent movement, sinking into seas or exploding off planets and embedding into Earth. A great many people seem to have been forced from their lands as well and to have inserted themselves into the lands of others. The rock of perpetual motion that will power the conquest of space was likewise violently hurled outward, a volcanic ejaculate that surfaces in the Philippines. Some combination of Freud and a bizarro Frederick Jackson Turner is needed to figure out what on (and off) earth, or, rather, Earth, is going on. Transferences and frontiers of all types seem to be radically emerging where least expected. Whole societies disappear in apocalyptic fashion only to reappear with new profiles somewhere else. The accumulating aggregate of aliens and alienations is astounding. Filipino history and literature, however, is filled with aliens who suddenly depart from some faraway place and incrust themselves into the archipelago: the Japanese, the Americans, and the Spaniards for starters, arguably the Chinese, the Moors, and the Malays too, depending on how a reading is chosen to be done. Perhaps in *The Creation*, the Earth at the end of the day is just the Philippines at the start of it, an unpeopled place peopled, the duty of the narrator then to unveil the violence that undergirds it all.

Alienations and Assimilations

The United States in particular is central in *The Creation* to all these dynamics of strangers in not so strange lands. This centrality is manifest by its explicit absence. *The Creation* is a novel flush with American influence in the Philippines despite formal archipelagic independence years earlier and despite the lack of direct authorial engagement with the colonial period. Moreover, the supplementary performance of the Leatams in the role of beneficent Americans intensifies the likely significance of the relative invisibility of the United States proper. The cosmopolitan, fair-trading, progressive society here is based not out of Washington but the Niagara borderlands. Any interpretation of the presence of Plutonian power in *The Creation* as indicating a broad acceptance of American assimilation in Asia therefore needs to be complicated by the sidestepping substitutions of the Leatams.

Surely key to any argument here is the overturn of geopolitical power that takes place every time the Philippines is elevated to a leading role. This happens often and in diverse ways throughout the novel, starting with the gathering of the intellectuals in Manila and peaking toward the end with the president of the Philippines welcoming, on behalf of all humanity, a Venusian princess to Earth. In *The Creation*, Manila stands on more than equal footing with Washington and Paris. These are the three capitals of the world that ultimately send representatives to Venus after hosting international diplomatic conferences about the interplanetary accomplishments of the multiracial youths. Plus, within the premises of the plot, Filipinos stand as one of the four major races of humans, a fairly impressive achievement. In the novel in general, people and places and products of the Philippines, rather than persist on peripheries, appear as actual or metaphorical planetary powers.

For example, Baltazar, the Filipino lad, is the one who finds and analyzes the perpetual motion mineral, builds the spaceship, and takes the role of leader of his peers and their expedition. En route from the sun to Venus, for instance, "Trazó una norma de conducta para todos" ["He outlined a norm of conduct for everyone"] (189). He also becomes the primary connection to the Leatams, who trust him so much that they teach him such advanced technology as the way to make airships invisible. Meanwhile, Baltazar is also a thoroughly grounded fellow who, thanks to his strength and dexterity, saves Lisa in the Baguio cliffhanger episode. Significantly, the "toasted" person bails out the white person here, not vice versa (11). Along similar lines, the biblical implications of his name suggest insights and powers that, say, Lisa, the representative of Europe, does not quite carry in hers. Such vaguely religious importance is attached as well to his father, Mr. Lapulapu. After all, he is the host of three wise men in Manila who are leaders from diverse realms drawn together by an astronomical event. And his own son will ascend into the heavens with a cloak of invisibility, lifted by a supernatural rock.

In terms of historical metonymy, every achievement by Baltazar arises amid the charged implications of the name of his father. The original Lapu Lapu was the indigenous leader who, in 1521, refused the political and religious evangelizations of Magellan, commander of the first European fleet to reach the Philippines. Magellan reacted to Lapu Lapu by assaulting him from the sea, whereupon Lapu Lapu reacted to Magellan by killing him (this is the shorthand version of events). There is no greater symbolic standard-bearer for Filipino sovereignty than Lapu Lapu unless it is José Rizal, the late 19th-century novelist who critiqued Spanish comportment in the archipelago. To name a Filipino father after Lapu Lapu at the start of a narrative is therefore to throw down a nationalistic mark from the beginning. To inaugurate, at the end of the same narrative, an interplanetary airline at Luneta Park, site of the execution of Rizal, is to double down on the position. The two vessels making the initial voyage of that route, prior to take off, "aguardaban posados ante la estatua de Rizal que, respaldándose a un obelisco de fino mármol, parecía recitar de su último adiós" ["waited sitting before the statue of Rizal who, backed by an obelisk of fine marble, appeared to recite from his last farewell"] (244). That obelisk still stands today in the same park over the remains of Rizal. "Mi último adiós" ("My Last Farewell") is the most famous poem in Philippine history, written by Rizal (whom de la Rosa refers to as a "mártir" ["martyr"]) the night before Spain executed him for alleged subversion (244). In other words, de la Rosa bookends his science fiction saga with the historical figures, Lapu Lapu and Rizal, who most signify Filipino autonomy in the face of Western power. The novel does not, consequently, represent the archipelago as on the receiving end of History. Rather, it constructs the Philippines and Filipinos as active world-historical agents. Meanwhile, the

United States, the actual world-historical power in the Philippines in the era of the plot and publication of *The Creation*, is displaced metaphorically (such as into Pluto) or pushed off center (such as via the Leatams) or eliminated from the map altogether.

All of this could be dismissed as so much narcissistic nationalism by de la Rosa. Doing so, however, would ignore the fact that he shows no signs in this or in *Trust in Me*, his previous novel, of being anything other than favorably disposed to the United States. The antihegemonic impulses that run through his fictions—whether the hegemony in question is that represented by Magellan or Spain or the United States or Europe—are counterintuitive tendencies that necessarily complicate any readings of the novels as assimilationist in orientation. The foregrounding of the Philippines in *The Creation* and the concomitant depriviledging of the United States betokens a shift in expected imperial hierarchies. And this movement is propelled not only by Filipino nationalism conveyed via symbolic links to Lapu Lapu and Rizal but also by the multipolarity of the georacial project at hand and of the solar system at large.

For instance, the non-Filipino characters in *The Creation* carry names and back stories that are often ridiculous but indicate an earnest attempt by de la Rosa at encompassing enormous areas of earthly geography, history, and culture. In effect, such multiplicity and scale further marginalizes the United States from a leading role in the action inside the novel, in the Philippines outside the novel, and in the 20th century at large. For example, repeated references to the race and language of the Pee family evoke both Mongolia and China, while the name "Shiva" also calls to mind India. Collectively, in other words, this family suggests the immense stretch of continental Asia. The name of Pretorio, the son of Professor Uganda, recalls in his name Pretoria, the capital of South Africa, with the final vowel changed to "o" from "a" in accordance with Spanish grammar to reflect male gender. When "Pretorio" is matched with his father "Uganda," a vast African breadth emerges metonymically just as a vast Asian breadth is incarnated by the Pee family. As for Professor Legrín and his daughter Lisa, their names do not imply any corresponding pan-European ethnicity, but their geographic roots do. Lisa turns out to be from Alsace-Lorraine, the swath of land that historically switched back and forth between French and German hands depending on who won given wars. This origin in a European borderlands locates her in an interstitial zone as much as the Leatams of Niagara. Yet these borderlands are the heartland of Europe as well, and so by synecdochical extrapolation she hails from a family as continental as the Pees and the Ugandas. The panethnicities inherent in each of these characters or character groups prove also to be literally microcosmic, for the multiculturalism of the protagonists parallels that of the solar system. This mirroring contrasts brightly with the shadows of the postwar domination of the United States (either taken alone or dialectically with the Soviet Union) in planetary reality on Earth and, particularly, in the Philippines both before and after the formal decolonization of 1946.

The travels of the young spacefarers after leaving Pluto further develop subjectivities that, in their inversion or decentralization of terrestrial realpolitik orders, rebut any premise of the Philippines as a dependent, peripheral state and of the United States as a monopolar force in the archipelago and in much of the world. The second destination on the itinerary is Jupiter, which by virtue of its mythological associations and status as the largest of the planets might well be expected to represent the prevailing power on Earth. The Jovians, however, turn out to be ur-Filipinos instead. They speak a language that is a "mezcla de malayo y los principales dialectos de Filipinas" ["mix of Malay and the principal dialects of the Philippines"] (141). In addition, the only Americans around are ur-Leatams, for it turns out that the ancestral community of Lemuria—the sunken continent in the Pacific Ocean whose survivors ultimately merged with Atlantans and Native Americans to form the Leatam people—populates at least one of the Galilean moons of Jupiter and, along with the Jovians/Filipinos, many nearby asteroids (139–41). The cast agrees that the commonalities of language and phenotype can only mean one thing: once upon a time, some of the more distant asteroids in the Jovian system were attracted by the gravitational pull of Earth, which "los absorbió al incrustarse en ella" ["absorbed them when they incrusted in her"] (141, 146). Respective asteroidal populations of Galileans and Jovians thus became the founders of the Lemurian (and subsequently Leatam) and Filipino races, much as a bunch of Plutonians accidentally ended up as mainland Asians.

The preposterousness of this plot is not nearly as important as its political function. As Shiva has explained earlier to a Plutonian, she and her peers speak with each other not in their own tongues but "en otro lenguaje que se llama inglés, y no es de ninguno de nosotros, porque nadie de nosotros es inglés, pero lo aprendimos en las escuelas" ["in another language that is called English, and it is not any of ours, because none of us is English, but we learned it in schools"] (130). Why the space travelers all learned English in school and now share it as their only lingua franca is unstated but obvious: the American century, the global reach of the United States, created that linguistic regime. Language has always been the companion of empire. The youths necessarily must communicate with each other in the politically dominant language of the world, a language native to none of them. They, not the extraterrestrials, are therefore the real aliens in the story. Yet on Jupiter, the United States and the modern prepotency of English is displaced while presumptively peripheral tongues assume a multipolar centrality. Baltazar chats in a pan-Philippine language with his Jovian relatives, Allen schmoozes in Lemurian, and Lisa kibbitzes in, of all things, "el antiguo dialecto alsaciano" ["the ancient Alsatian dialect"] (143). She can do this because some Martian-Mercurians, the mestizo race that yielded white people such as herself, circulate on Jupiter as well. Naturally, therefore, they speak old Alsatian. Lisa, as a European and the standard-bearer in the novel for white people, should symbolize some kind of hegemony, but even in her case there are insinuations of subversion. Her phenotypic pallor, the pigmentation that powers on planet Earth, proves miscegenated, while French and German, the major European languages that alternated over Alsace-Lorraine, vanish before the irredentist sovereignty of autochthonous Alsatian. The native triumphs over the imposed. In the Jupiter sequence of the novel, in other words, peripheral geographies and languages move collectively to focal spaces. And as the marginal becomes primary, the controllers of quondam conquest backtrack into backwaters. There is no revolution in *The Creation*, not a hint of disorder, yet everything turns upside down nonetheless.

The presence of marginalized indigenous people on the next planets to be visited, Mars and Mercury, therefore seems especially noteworthy despite the brevity of the references to them. The mestizo/white populations on these orbs, it is revealed, did not supplant altogether their pureblood native forebears. On Mars, the earthlings happen upon a squad of soldiers composed, as a Martian-Mercurian guide explains, of "aborígenes de nuestra población" ["aborigines of our population"] (151). Lisa observes that these individuals are "nuestros ascendientes" ["our ancestors"], and the guide points out that "nos ha dado de su pigmento rojo lo suficiente para teñir de rosa nuestros rostros" ["they have given us enough of their red pigment to tinge our faces pink"] (151). Lisa asks if these indigenes are good soldiers, and the guide responds, "Son peleadores, bravos y astutos" ["They are fighters, brave and cunning"] (151). A short spin through the solar system later, the earthlings come across a different group of natives on the dark side of Mercury.[6] This time they are not red but albino, "individuos completamente blancos, de los pies a la cabeza, hasta los ojos que solo se distinguían por su color ligeramente terroso" ["completely white individuals, from head to toe, even their eyes that only could be distinguished by their lightly earthy color"] (161). A local guide explains that "son los aborígenes y los expertos cazadores de los animales cuyas pieles les abrigan contra el frio glacial de esta zona" ["they are the aborigines and expert hunters of the animals whose skins shelter them against the glacial cold of this zone"] (161).

To be sure, the existence of red and white races in these places is not surprising given the internal logic of the novel. The red planet has red people and the colorless half of another planet has uncolored people. That Mars would have martial natives also seems stereotypically straightforward. Given the biopolitical history of Earth, however, such associations are troubling at best. The redskins seem to be redskins, who likewise are described in many an American frontier novel—a genre that surely includes *The Creation*—with phrases virtually identical to "fighters, brave and cunning." The albinos, inhabitants of a land of eternal darkness, are also "expert hunters." In both cases, there is a romanticization of strong, sharp-witted indigenous peoples who were profoundly displaced by a white superrace that paradoxically emerged from them. The dominance of the pinkish white Martian-Mercurians extended to Earth when their early interplanetary ships occasionally landed there after getting lost or being pulled in by "corrientes atmosféricas" ["atmospheric currents"] (149). True, the Martian-Mercurians did come in peace, and on their home planets they do generally seem like a nice lot. They are not the sort of extraterrestrials who would blow up Earth because it was obstructing their view of Venus. And yet they exist because they largely wiped out their predecessors. The enduring presence of marginalized natives on Mars and Mercury endows *The Creation* as perhaps the happiest postapocalyptic fiction in history. And this tension is what makes the text so truculent after all.

In the superficial thrust of the novel, sources of disorder are never contemporary with the protagonists, who move in well-ordered fashioned through a well-ordered cosmos. De la Rosa is intent on portraying a solar system filled with different races who live in harmony. Everybody in this novel gets along famously with everybody. Yet once upon a time in this (unintended and darkly) hilarious version of life, the universe and everything, whole worlds did suffer totalizing violence, one after the other. Princess Ku and her people were suddenly ejected out of Pluto. Lemurian speakers got incrusted into Earth after their home asteroids were separated from the Jovian system. Oceanic holocausts later consumed most of them as well as the Atlantans. And something unspecified but evidently horrible and massive befell as well the once-large population of indigenous Americans that now forms the other third of Leatam stock. In other words, the Leatams are a society constituted by refugees from three different apocalypses. And these devastations resonate with the sharply reduced numbers of native communities on Mars and Mercury, who have lost virtually all their land amid the rise of mestizos/whites. It is very hard not to see the post-1492 fate of indigenous people throughout the Americas in these original Martians and Mercurians, even though the redskins and albinos are not presented as distressed per se.

Again, there is no revolution proposed in *The Creation* but rather quite the opposite. Everything is pretty much great on Earth and elsewhere. Everyone is pretty much content with the way things are. Yet acutely eschatological events underlie the good cheer that everyone extends to everyone else on every single occasion in the novel. So many peoples are depicted as survivors of genocides, so many marginalized peoples and cultures are exalted, that some kind of mutiny against the prevailing order of things does seem to be rising after all. And what could be more seditious in the American century than the expulsion of America itself, ejected almost wholesale from the pages of the novel and replaced by the rest of the earth, the solar system, the cosmos?

The darknesses that detail *The Creation* diminish only apparently as the earthlings head to their final space destinations, the Sun and Venus. The evident rationale for this stretch of *The Creation* is to reconfirm the theories and motifs long established and, on Venus, to turn the text decisively toward the romantic comedy foreshadowed at the start. The discrete extraterrestrial origins of human races is reconfirmed as Pretorio indeed finds his ancestral community on the sun. More than that, he finds his ancestral continent. That is, Pretorio actually discovers on the sun a larger-scaled version of Africa itself (167–68). This solar Africa features the same cartographic contours as its earthly counterpart, plus the best version ever of the same African stew (made with fresh fish plucked from the nearby solar ocean) that Pretorio eats back home (170–71). Although geography and food reinforce here the immutable nature of human racial and cultural identity that Mr. Pee takes as a given, such presumed stasis contradicts everything the young earthlings actually have experienced both on and off their home planet. After all, two races, the Leatams and the Martian-Mercurians, are shown to have come into existence by miscegenation. And while Africa may appear on the sun as well as on Earth, other huge landmasses vanish or are otherwise radically transmuted all the time: Lemuria, Atlantis, Pluto, and assorted asteroids. Language too proves neither unchanging nor innate. Throughout the novel, the characters communicate with each other only in a tongue that is foreign to them all, English, a medium that has become therefore their own. This linguistic evolution parallels the various racial ones that surely will follow the inevitable final pairings of Lisa and Baltazar, Shiva and Pretorio. Almost no one is allowed to have sex in Filipino literature in Spanish, but offspring are always welcome. And in both de la Rosa novels, the next generation will be miscegenated. In other words, the doubled Africa of the solar sequence bolsters the premises put forth by Mr. Pee, but doing so only sharpens the gap between those premises and the manifest realities of the text. At no point is this paradox recognized by de la Rosa. His silence on this count matches his nonarticulation of why English is the common language of the earthlings. The plot pitches against its postulates all the time.

Planetary Bodies

The episodes that take place on Venus, the last planet to be visited, deepen the disjunction between the foregrounded attentions of the novel and the geopolitical actualities that wend through its background. Unlike the visits to Pluto, Jupiter, Mars, Mercury, and the sun, the Venus sequence never truly ends. When the earthlings finally return home, the transcendently beautiful Princess La, heir to the Venusian throne, travels with them as a diplomatic representative. She visits dignitaries in Manila, Washington, and Paris, and then returns to Venus with Baltazar as he leads the first official flight of the new Earth-Venus airline. The novel subsequently concludes with the pleasingly interracial nuptials of Baltazar with Lisa, and Pretorio with Shiva, on Venus itself. It is the ultimate destination wedding and everyone will live happily ever after, not just the couples but all denizens of the solar system. As de la Rosa explains, "Rompiendo tradiciones tribales y raciales, religiosas y sociales Baltazar y Lisa, Pretorio y Shiva, de diferentes razas y pueblos, creencias religiosas y credos familiares, se unen en dos parejas por el mutuo amor que de sus almas naciera, causa natural de la unión entre el hombre y la mujer" ["Breaking tribal and racial traditions, religious and social, Baltazar and Lisa, Pretorio and Shiva, of different races and peoples, religious beliefs and family creeds, unite in two couples due to the mutual love that from their souls had been born, the natural cause of the union between man and woman"] (255–56). As in *Trust in Me*, this heterosexual and interethnic and philosophical synthesis is meant to symbolize a broader harmony that is at once utopian and universal.

This Panglossian finale is implicit from the beginning of *The Creation* but accelerates notably upon the arrival of the youths on Venus and the appearance of Princess La. She is the only major character to enter the plot since the opening chapter except for Allen, the Lemurian-speaking Leatam pilot. Princess La, the "encarnación de Venus" ["incarnation of Venus"], increasingly dominates the scenes of the last fourth of the novel and is its ultimate protagonist as the personification of an atomized universe rendered whole (195). Her beauty and palpable virginity is equated with all that is true and good. She is reminiscent, depending on the stretch of text, of Mary, Venus de Milo, cherubim, innocent children, the smoothest imaginable diplomat, and, say, Venus (well, an immaculate Venus). All the waxing by de la Rosa about her ineffable exquisiteness and purity is paralleled by varied depictions of her home planet as a virgin land, one touched for the very first time. After all, the earthlings are the inaugural visitors to Venus. The royal gardens of the planet are Edenic too, with a touch of Versailles and telepathy thrown in for good measure. And as if there were not enough virginity in the Venusian air already, de la Rosa also places a renewed emphasis on the virginal femininity of Lisa and Shiva. Topping it all off are repeated implications of homosocial attraction among them and Princess La.

The Venus sequence is not the first time that the sublime states of female beauty and chastity are put forth as the supreme idealization of the universe. Shiva too is a planetary princess, and it is not a coincidence that the moment when the Plutonians decorate her as such is also the moment when de la Rosa appreciates "su rostro virginal" ["her virginal face"] and "su frente inmaculada" ["her immaculate forehead"] (133, 134). But such twaddle is not tweeted consistently during the subsequent space adventures, whereas the entrance of Princess La into the narrative puts dazzling virginity front and center. Simultaneously, the Venus sequence also features the clearest reminders of the brutal histories that lie behind its utopian images. The Venusians speak the language of ancient Atlantis, prompting Allen to recount to Princess La that "un gran número de habitantes de la Tierra hablaba el lenguaje de Venus, pero su continente, el Atlántida, se hundió en la profundidad del mar, y los pocos que pudieron salvarse hallaron refugio en el continente americano, con cuyos aborígenes y otros refugiados del continente lemuriano, que también se hundió, formaron el pueblo a que ahora pertenezco, en el que aún se habla el idioma atlántida, que lo aprendí de los descendientes de los refugiados atlántidas" ["a great number of the inhabitants of Earth spoke the language of Venus, but their continent, Atlantis, sunk in the depth of the sea, and the few who could save themselves found refuge in the American continent, with whose aborigines and other refugees from the Lemurian continent, which also sank, formed the people to which I now belong, in which the Atlantan language is still spoken, and which I learned from the descendants of the Atlantan refugees"] (197). The triple holocaust behind the ethnogenesis of the Leatams—the twinned annihilations of the peoples of two continents and the third decimation, by implied association, of aboriginal Americans—

stands in stark contrast to the family reunion of the Venusians and their Leatam relations that is now in the offing.

Most acute from the initial appearance of Princess La onward, then, are the oppositions of otherworldly quintessence and grim earthly reality. Her more perfect union moves in tandem with utterly imperfect violations. When Princess La asks Allen, "¿Es su raza lemuriana pura hasta ahora?" ["Is your Lemurian race pure up till now?"], he quickly responds by naming, for the first time, his community as "el pueblo *leatam* (Lemurio-Atlántida-Américano)" ["the *Leatam* people (Lemurian-Atlantan-American)"] (198). The belatedness of this announcement of what his people call themselves underlines the fact that their autodesignation is an indication of their postapocalyptic origins. Not only is his race impure, as opposed to the unadulterated Princess La, but its mestizaje bespeaks calamities unspeakable. Venus, "aquel paraíso" ["that paradise"], knows no such past (203). Certainly, de la Rosa does treat Allen and the Leatams with sustained respect. And he does attempt to promote interracial harmony in the universe. In reality, though, blood purity is always his pole star. The four youths and their parents, along with Princess La, are all unmixed exemplars of their respective races and are all, not coincidentally, associated with unblemished optimism. It would seem a bit awkward, at best, to be asking questions about racial purity to the descendants of holocaust survivors in the 1950s. Yet as in most other deeply dark spaces in the novel, de la Rosa blithely forges ahead anyway.

There is really only one time when any of the protagonists directly addresses the awful actualities of the human past and present. As the youths transport Princess La to Earth in her new role as diplomatic envoy, they relay to her the kind of information about terrestrial conflict and imperial history that hitherto has been thoroughly suppressed in the novel. For instance, as they spin above Asia, Lisa points out "la región mongólica, habitada por una raza fuerte y guerrera que dominó el resto del subcontinente y llevó sus guerras de conquista hasta la Europa oriental: ésa es la raza de Shiva que desciende de Pluto" ["The Mongol region, inhabited by a strong and warring race that dominated the rest of the subcontinent and carried its wars of conquest up to eastern Europe: that is the race of Shiva that descends from Pluto"] (219). And shortly thereafter, as the spaceship spirals westward, Lisa tells Princess La of "la Europa contiental, con Alsacia-Lorena, mi país, en su lado central oeste, entre Francia y Alemania que se disputan su posesión en sangrientas luchas, originando nuestros frecuentes cambios de nacionalidad, de acuerdo con el resultado de la guerra" ["continental Europe, with Alsace-Lorraine, my country, in its central west side, between France and Germany, which dispute its possession in bloody fights, giving rise to our frequent changes of nationality according to the result of war"] (219). Only now aside a perfect Venus are the postapocalyptic Leatams named at last; only now are the bloody implications of the national backgrounds of Shiva and Lisa addressed explicitly. Just in case the reader had not grasped earlier what Mongol or Alsatian origins might indicate about the gory history of Earth, de la Rosa now spells it out as his novel climaxes. And he does so only in juxtaposition to the virginities of Venus. Here at last is the unadorned truth: *The Creation* is not a search for heavenly enlightenment so much as a meditation on earthly darkness. The contradiction between the two is never resolved, just as the logical third romantic pairing never comes to be. That is, Princess La and Allen also should form a couple, the utopian purity of the one matched with the postapocalyptic miscegenation of the other, the Atlantan language as a common bond of communication. But such a melding is never even hinted at, much less realized as a copestone to the novel.

Absent too is the United States, at least during the main of the text. This is silently startling. Although Lisa refers to the historical powers of Mongolia, France, and Germany, the empire of the day is America. This fact is implicit again when Allen translates from Atlantan to English a written message from the king of Venus so that the president of the Philippines and everyone else can understand it (229). And there is just one reason why the archipelagic leader knows English, why all the African and Asian and European protagonists of the novel know it too: assimilation to the American century exacted it. Anyone on the planet who aimed to join the new world order from 1898 onward, not just 1918 or 1945 onward, and especially anyone in the Philippines, needed to learn English, whether through formal instruction or autodidactically like de la Rosa himself. The global reach of the United States, produced by American military might, produced global English speakers in turn. But while everything in *The Creation* suggests the presence of American power on a worldwide scale, nothing in the novel acknowledges it. Love and peace and harmony are the guiding principles of a wonderful present and future, yet it is loss and catastrophe and decimation that brought this utopia about. Things do not fall apart in *The Creation*. They already did. And yet tomorrow is as bright as a morning star. The contradictions of the novel are endless. The United States meets no resistance in its pages. Yet resistances drive it out of those pages over and over again.

De la Rosa does portray a global order in which Washington, Paris, and Manila ultimately emerge as the three hubs in which world leaders gather to welcome Princess La. Washington "fué escogido para la reunión de los jefes de estado de las Américas e islas adyacentes" ["was chosen for the meeting of the heads of state of the Americas and adjacent islands"], a kind of Monroe Doctrine hegemony thereby implied (230). Paris, evidently representing the epicenter of European colonialism, "se tuvo por la ciudad que ofrecía mejores perspectivas para la congregación de los soberanos y jefes de estado europeos, africanos y del medio oriente" ["was taken to be the city that offered the best prospects for the congregation of the European, African, and Middle Eastern sovereigns and heads of state"] (231). Manila achieves comparable standing, for "como punto céntrico entre los continentes e islas del Pacífico, fue seleccionada para la reunión de los soberanos y jefes de estado de Asia, Australia y Oceanía" ["as the central point among the continents and islands of the Pacific, it was selected for the meeting of the sovereigns and heads of state of Asia, Australia, and Oceania"] (231). This inverts global power realities in that the dependent, weak Philippines suddenly becomes the leader of the Eastern Hemisphere, on par with imperial metropoles of the West. And the casting of the Philippine government as the main player in Asia and the Pacific further challenges extratextual actuality by displacing the United States back to its pre-1898 presumptive sphere of influence, the Americas. The fact that the first state visit of Princess La after meeting the president of the Philippines is to the president of the United States (one idly wonders what she and Eisenhower had in common) does acknowledge the standing of Washington in the realpolitik order of the day but awards primacy to Manila nonetheless. Nixon must have been fuming.

Such subversions of the American century surface as well during the state banquet held at the White House when "un Presidente sudamericano" ["a South American President"] offers a subtly cheeky toast:

"Sr. Presidente, Princesa,
    Damas y Caballeros:
    La conquista del espacio interplanetario, acabada de realizarse, ha hecho posible la presencia de la Princesa La de Venus en esta blanca mansión, entre nosotros esta noche.
    La proeza fué llevada a cabo anónimamente, sin el patrocinio de ningún gobierno, asociación o persona particular, y sí por el solo esfuerzo de un puñado de jovenes intrépidos, pertenecientes a diversos pueblos y razas, pero unidos por la amistad y un común propósito . . .
    Levantemos nuestras copas y bebamos su vino en celebración de esá [sic] gran conquista por los exploradores Baltazar, de Filipinas, Lisa, de Alsacia, Allen, de América, Shiva, de Mongolia, y Pretorio, de Africa, que con nosotros comparten este banquete" (aplausos). (233–34)

["Mr. President, Princess,

Ladies and Gentlemen:

The conquest of interplanetary space, which was just realized, has made possible the presence of Princess La of Venus in this white mansion, among us tonight.

The feat was carried out anonymously, without the patronage of any government, association, or person in particular, and yes by the lone effort of a handful of intrepid youths who belong to diverse peoples and races but are united by friendship and a common purpose . . .

Let us raise our glasses and drink their wine in celebration of that great conquest by the explorers Baltazar from the Philippines, Lisa from Alsace, Allen from America, Shiva from Mongolia, and Pretorio from Africa, who with us share this banquet" (applause).]

In other words, there in the White House, in front of the president of the United States, cheers ring out for a space race decidedly won not by the United States—and not, to be sure, by the invisible Soviet Union, whose *Sputnik* moment never happens in the novel—but instead by the collective protagonists who represent everyone else. For them, it was not even a race to begin with. Their unified quest in the name of humanity rebukes inherently the war games model that guided American space policy from its postwar embrace of Nazi scientists to its post-*Sputnik* push toward supremacy in the solar system. It is true that the banquet ends with the somewhat sovereigns of the hemisphere picking the vice president of the United States to represent them on the inaugural diplomatic mission to Venus—too bad Nixon did not stay there, it was probably just what he needed—and that this choice acknowledges the dominance of American power in the Americas and its protagonism in the space race. Nevertheless, the "South American President" has already thrown down a gauntlet that undercuts the gesture. The conquest of space, he emphasizes, belongs to no nation and certainly not to the one hosting the fete in the "white mansion."

Subversions of the American Century

Where there is empire, there is sedition. When the 20th century began with the United States fighting to consolidate its control of the Philippines, opposition of the most explicit kind was obvious in the ongoing military efforts of anticolonial forces in the islands. Yet guns are not the only way to gain the upper hand. Antagonism to the American appropriation of the archipelago took an infinite number of forms and was inescapable among even the most lickspittle of locals. For total assimilation of imposition is impossible. Consciously or not, willingly or not, every single Filipino in the Philippines countered the command of colonialists with dissonances from below, phrasings of one kind or another that were not synchronized with the talking points issued from above. There were strident subversions and countless more sub-versions. It could not be otherwise in global America, in an American century that commences with Act 292 of the Taft Commission, which in 1901 legalized the execution of writers adversarial to the American occupation. The American regime made it very clear from the beginning that resistance was not to be tolerated. That posture made it just as clear that resistance was very much operative.

Teddy Roosevelt is still somewhere bellowing "Resistance must be stamped out" (188). But resistance is never stamped out. It merely presses on. The true stamp of the 20th-century Philippines was on the United States and, by extension, the world writ large, for after 1898 America bore the mark of island resistance, which is to say global resistance, forever. The military campaigns against American authority in the archipelago were crushed in the main before a decade had passed, but new subversions arose in the import of the dead and in the comportments of the living. Bodies in decomposition and bodies of composition transformed America across the Pacific. Antipodal America was now a fact. The antithesis now defined the thesis. And it is Filipino literature in Spanish, a great and barely known tradition, that most underlines empire by its language of creation, that most undermines empire by its layers of contestation.

The operas of Pedro Paterno in the first years of the 1900s are, in all senses, subversions of the American century that was just getting under way. For all his toadying, Paterno never toed the line. And the lines that run from his creative work at the start of the century to *The Creation* by de la Rosa six decades later are remarkably evocative. Here, at the end of the main thrust of Filipino literature in Spanish, is a creative text that decenters and upturns the United States in a world just as fantastical as, say, the Paterno opera *Magdapio*. Here too in *The Creation* is a counternarrative of America and the American century in an old imperial language, penned by another elite Filipino hardly prone to rebellion.

Yet it is relatively easy to argue that Paterno should be considered an author of America. During the time that he wrote his operas, he was an American subject and an American national. His texts engage dramatically with American power. They are foundational to the American colonization of the Philippines and, more broadly, to the rise of the United States as a global empire and as the most influential and enduring superpower of the 20th century. If the history of America cannot be rendered remotely accurately without consideration of its expansion from coastal settlements to transcontinental lands to overseas territories—and it cannot—then the literature of Paterno is as American as, say, the speeches of John Smith in Jamestown and the accounts of William Bradford in Plymouth. This is not to say that literature in Spanish by Paterno does not form part of collective identities other than the American. But the America we know today does not exist without him. Nor does modernity, if defined as the American century. Nobody knows this. Hence this book. Much of our world needs rewriting.

Whether the foray into science fiction by de la Rosa is also American literature pushes the argument further. At the creation of *The Creation*, unlike at that of his previous novel *Trust in Me*, de la Rosa was not an American national or an American colonial subject. The Philippines was granted independence in 1946, and he launched *The Creation* in 1953. Virtually his entire adult life, however, he was indeed an American national and an American colonial subject. His judicial vocation and literary avocation are therefore as definitive of 20th-century America as are the productions of Paterno. De la Rosa is a much more Americanized figure, in fact, than the hispanophile Paterno, who spent most of his adulthood as a Spanish rather than American subject and who died barely a dozen years after 1898. Paterno probably could not read English well or at all, but de la Rosa, due to the timing of his life, had no choice but to gain fluency in that language in order to succeed. Whereas Paterno presided over the constitutional congress of a nominally independent Philippines, de la Rosa worked for courts whose sovereignty explicitly and ultimately rested in Washington. That the formal independence of the Philippines precedes the composition of *The Creation* does not seem particularly relevant to considering the novel as American literature.

Given that American influence over the Philippines scarcely waned after the technical decolonization of the latter on a Fourth of July, de la Rosa never did exist outside Washington. No Filipino did. No Filipino does today. Still. In April 2014, in the latest repeat of history, the U.S. and the Philippine governments signed the Enhanced Defense Cooperation Agreement "authorizing access to Agreed Locations in the territory of the Philippines by United States forces on a rotational basis, as mutually determined by the Parties" ("Agreement" 2). There are Agreed Locations that the elite Parties determine, yes, but there are approximately one hundred million other parties, namely the Filipino populace, who may or may not be in agreement and who now, regardless, live even more profoundly within the American orbit.

The text alone of *The Creation* reveals it to be an American novel. For to be American is to be defined by American hegemony and to define it in turn. De la Rosa interacts with American power in myriad ways, sometimes accepting of it, sometimes contestatory of it, sometime silent on it, but always engaged with it, always defined by it and always defining of it. In this sense, the story of the American century scrolls forth even in this novel not written in English by this writer not from, allegedly, America. And so *The Creation* could be read as an alternative version of America alongside all those other great rewritings of America that likewise appeared between 1959 and 1962: William Burroughs's *Naked Lunch*, Philip Roth's *Goodbye, Columbus*, William Appleman Williams's *The Tragedy of American Diplomacy*, Harper Lee's *To Kill a Mockingbird*, Robert Heinlein's *Stranger in a Strange Land*, Bob Dylan's "Song to Woody," the Students for a Democratic Society's "Port Huron Statement," and so on. That would be a hell of a course, wouldn't it. *The Creation*, like all these texts, imagines an America qualitatively different from what it claims to be. That is the sublimity of sedition.

After de la Rosa, Filipino literature in Spanish largely disappeared. Its paradoxes and inspirations must be sought anew. Global domination is not an academic question. Washington still sends drones to the antipodes. Washington still occupies and claims to deoccupy all the time. Ask an Iraqi. Ask an Afghan. Ask, for that matter, a Native American. You may not always get an answer in the affirmative, but you will always get a subversion.

Twentieth-century Filipino texts in Spanish do not constitute a radical tradition. And yet they upturn an empire, a century, a planet. The people who wrote them were almost always elites with significant stakes in the status quo, a state of things set up, supervised, and surveilled by America. There is no Katipunan cloak of substance to drape on that Filipino class, their troupes and troops, their legacy. At most there is a t-shirt. Nevertheless, America was remade by them. And so American classrooms must be remade to feature these texts untaught everywhere. Twentieth-century Filipino literature in Spanish reveals America, and therefore modernity, for what it demonstrably is. These writings compel new approaches to the imperial modes in which America operates and always has, though almost no one reads them now and few ever did. From a space of apparent weakness—a seemingly peripheral archipelago on the other side of the world, a seemingly parochial phenomenon scarcely recognized to exist—Filipino literature in Spanish forces fundamental rethinkings of what American literature was, is and can be. What America was, is and can be. What our world was, is and can be.

This is not an academic question.

Epilogue

The Case of the Antipodal Archipelago

꿍

A shot rang out. A body fell. There is no mystery here. Who shot J. R.? A firing squad. Spain gave the order and a man leaned back, bowler hat already fluttering off, took one last look at the sky, fell. There is a photo. Apocryphal, perhaps, but accurate enough. There is always much that is apocryphal. A shot ran out, shots rang out, all of them at once, as a dog looked on. Also, a priest or two, garbed in black. A revolution, an occupation, and an obelisk later, the remains of José Rizal were put on display. You can visit them today. The park is renamed now in his memory. There is no mystery here.

But death is often a diversion. There was another body that day, one that was born. Its own life, decades later, was taken by a globalized orgy of violence. No one speaks of it today. No one took a photo of its execution. No one interrogated the witnesses. It is the body of Filipino literature in Spanish after Rizal. A hundred and twenty years have been spent exhuming the martyr, notwithstanding the abundance of facts about his life long since evident. But what if the real body in play that day was not that of Rizal? The firing squad never looked behind them after all. The ruse of History went unseen. The truest of subversives were perhaps not the visible victim after all. . . .

Who rubbed out those Filipinos? The ones who wrote after Rizal, the ones who proposed new polities on stage and in print after a new power from across the Pacific purloined the peninsulas and promontories of seven thousand islands from an imperial rival and anti-imperial rebels. A corpus arose in Spanish that contested the Americans and their anglophone impositions, a corpus that faced an imperial public that did not see it. Colonial governors looked on stage and right through a revolutionary body of work by Pedro Paterno as if it were not there. So did anticolonial historians, despite their dedication to the defeated and the dead. Only those who at the time could sense the undead could recognize the crimes of which the ectoplasm spoke. Only they could joust for justice, however quietly, however obliquely, however dull their blades and sharp their barbs. Directness when possible, misdirection when not.

After 1898, the pallbearers, smirking to themselves, threw dirt on a body and tried to turn away. No last look. Elevate the obelisk, sacralize the remains, circulate the circumscribed memories, bury the past. This was about America and Filipinos, about English and Tagalog. It was not about Spanish, about Spain. That was an old, evil empire. This was a new, benevolent nation. But Rizal was the red herring. The coffin did not contain the corpus after all. Rizal was the red herring. Safely dead, safely executed by others, safely ensconced in a struggle in which the United States was not on the scene. America had an alibi in 1896. After all, we were somewhere else. We could not have committed the murder. There are witnesses. There are receipts. There are the priests. We were somewhere else. We are not suspects. We have our alibis.

But of course America was there, lurking on the outskirts all the time, sizing up the situation, planting the trails to elsewhere, the plausible deniability, the surprise of the surprise ending. The perfect murder, of course, is the one in which the trigger is pulled by someone else. Annex another archipelago . . . Hawaii. Remember the *Maine* . . . in Manila. Many Americans had spent much of the 19th century agitating for assault on Cuba, whose own revolutionaries had spent decades battling Spain before 1898. It is the prospect of Cuban independence, not Filipino, that sparked the Spanish reactions to the Filipino fighters who rose in 1896. But killing Rizal for mistaken association would not finish off a rebellion any more than had killing his counterpart, José Martí, for unmistaken association in Cuba the year before. First for Spain and then for the United States, Rizal was the red herring. He rejected armed revolution in 1896 and always had. He was a great writer, ferocious in his language, remarkable in his risk taking, but all the while, demonstrably, a dedicated subject of empire till the very end.

It was not Rizal but Paterno, the aristocratic buffoon, who produced fictions that fought for freedom. And he did so in front of foreign power. Over and over again. Guillermo Gómez Windham, the cosmopolitan customs officer, is the one who condemned his most Americanized character. And he won a major Filipino literary prize in doing so. Jesús Balmori, the unenlightened aesthete, is the one who attempted perhaps the most anti-American effort of them all: ignoring more than seemingly possible nearly half a century of American occupation. And Mariano de la Rosa, a judge in a legal system overseen by a colonial power he manifestly liked, is the one who kept awarding primacy and power to the Philippines instead.

But all these voices were silenced. Almost no one has seen the Paterno operas in over a century.[1] Various texts by Gómez Windham are next to inaccessible. The novel by Balmori was lost after World War II. The fictions by de la Rosa are virtually unknown. All these voices were silenced. Who pulled the trigger? Is it enough to say that the vicissitudes of the 20th century wiped out these writers and leave it at that? The question is not who rubbed these authors out of the Philippines. The answer to that is easy: they wrote in a language that not enough elites in Manila after World War II still called their own. But who rubbed them out of America?

Once upon a time, Americans made a point of translating into English everything that Paterno wrote that smacked of subversion. A censorship regime headed by a future president of the United States demanded it. That future president literally used his own red pencil to cross out offending lines. He also legalized the death penalty for playwrights convicted of opposing American control of the Philippines. The present is obfuscated on these matters but the verdict of History is very clear. Once upon a time, Filipino writers mattered to the United States. Once upon a time, Filipino writers *wrote* the United States. For once upon a time, Filipino writers *were* Americans, so much so that if they dared to be un-American they would be subject by America to execution. Flash forward sixty years to an America engulfed in a space race and there is no author who rewrote the United States more than de la Rosa, no premise more important than the nonsense that he put forth and that nobody read. There in his preposterous prose, produced by a national of a purportedly independent nation, is what America has wrought. But no one in America knows that.

In that oblivion, paradoxically, is the greatest power of all: the power to change a narrative that everyone has accepted. Weakness, here, is strength. Marginalization, here, is metropolitan. The buried body of literature that stretches from Paterno to de la Rosa has a story to tell that redefines the United States. America begins in colonies, and that is a story everyone knows. But America ends in colonies too, and that is a story everyone does not. The time has come to dig up a coffin, scrape off the dirt, pry open the lid, interrogate what is there. It is not Rizal. It is a different corpus altogether.

The case of the antipodal archipelago. The contestation of the American century as it began. Where there is empire, there is subversion. Everybody should read Filipino literature in Spanish. The global power of America, which is to say, the modern world, makes no sense without it. We are all moderns now and so should learn from those who were so first. Filipinos. Yes. Filipinos. Their stories inform ours. We cannot understand ourselves without them. They are not them. They are us. We, together, are implicated in all this.

I, alone, your author, am implicated in all this. I've walked these alleys, marked the crimes, grabbed the onlookers by their lapels, and shaken them down. Each day is the same. Death over here, corruption over there, a line of moonshine in between. Broken sign over a bar on the far side of the street. Zoot suits bent over dice against the wall. A sharp laugh from a doorway. A flicker of a light. A car screeches past, turns the corner. Paterno walks by, reading a novel by Balmori. Gómez Windham follows him, eyes sweeping up to Pluto. De la Rosa huddles by an empty flagpole. Upton Sinclair, Jack London, Sherwood Anderson, Jean Toomer, Hart Crane, Sinclair Lewis, Gertrude Stein, F. Scott Fitzgerald, Ernest Hemingway, William Faulkner, Dashiell Hammett, John Steinbeck, Henry Miller, and Richard Wright are nowhere to seen. Pearl Buck? As if. Zora Neale Hurston? Come on. All the known informants have vanished. But the interrogation yet remains. A scream leaps out of a jagged window. A quivering hand stretches through, clutching a Filipino flag. Shots ring out. A dog watches. A priest stands in black. Confessions are not what they used to be. The flag flutters red, white, and blue to the cobblestone crud. A bowler hat sits in dust by its side. I, not alone now, testify. Guilty? Yes. Why? How? Me? Yes. You? Yes. You.

You are implicated. Do not think that you are not. You are now witness too. You cannot plead innocence. You are party to all this. You stand where you stand because of all this. You benefit from this death. You are responsible for it. You kill this body again every day that you do not do it justice. This is not some remote story in some remote language in some remote place on the other side of the world. This is your story. Your language. Your place. Look down at your feet. The other side of the world is where you tread. Don't tread on them. They are you, after all, and yet you are not them. You are implicated. You are witness. You are defendant and jury and judge. There are sentences you must consider. There are nooses that await. There are crimes and there are, perhaps, liberations. You are implicated, like it or not, knowingly or not. What will you do? You play all the parts. You are on stage now. There is a dead body before you. What will you do. The lights are on. The audience awaits. The conductor raises his wand. The librettist folds his hands. What will you do?

You.

Notes

☒

Introduction

1. This is one of two accounts of what Twain said to reporters on May 9, 1907. The other version, reported by the *Baltimore News*, was similar in substance: "We claim to be a democratic people—a square-dealing people—but we have bought our way into the Society of Sceptred Thieves by paying $20,000,000 to a country that didn't own it for an island group that we had no right to purchase. It was the stupendous joke of the century when the United States, after conquering Spain and acquiring the islands by right of conquest, gave Spain $20,000,000. What for? For the islands? Spain didn't own them. Then, what for? Why, just for this: An American goes abroad and sells his daughter to a title and buys his way into noble circles. Uncle Sam paid that $20,000,000 for his entrance fee into society—the Society of Sceptred Thieves. We are now on a par with the rest of them" (Twain 185).

2. Calculations of Filipino casualties during the war commonly refer to over a million dead, but sources are vague on how that figure was derived and when and where most of the fatalities occurred. The infamous and often researched episode of the Bataan Death March is somewhat of an exception to this tendency, but the numbers of dead associated with that atrocity are usually given as around ten to twenty thousand Filipinos and hundreds to two or three thousand Americans. Although the carnage of Filipinos in the Death March vastly exceeds that of Americans, the scale is still not nearly enough to account for the general assumption that a million or more Filipinos died in the war. Once the Japanese took full control of the archipelago, Filipino deaths at their hands were frequent, but there was no mass slaughter on the quantitative level of Bataan. Therefore, if the prevailing premise of over a million Filipinos killed in the war is accurate, the overwhelming percentage of those fatalities happened during the end of 1944 and the start of 1945 as a direct result of the needless decision by MacArthur to engage Japanese forces in the islands.

Chapter 1

1. Section 1 of Act 292 reads, "Every person, resident in the Philippine Islands, owing allegiance to the United States or the Government of the Philippine Islands, who levies war against them, or adheres to their enemies, giving them aid and comfort within the Philippine Islands or elsewhere, is guilty of treason, and, upon conviction, shall suffer death or, at the discretion of the court, shall be imprisoned at hard labor for not less than five years and fined not less than ten thousand dollars" (*Public* 346). Frank Hindman Golay notes that Act 292 was "of dubious legality when passed, and never tested in an American court" (77).

2. Spain still possessed colonies and territories along African coasts after 1898, so it was hardly postimperial at that point, notwithstanding the common assumption otherwise.

3. The only two lengthy, published studies of Paterno seem to be *Brains of the Nation* by Resil Mojares from 2006 and *Panahon at pagsasalaysay ni Pedro Paterno, 1858–1911: Isang pag-aaral sa intelektwalismo* by Portia L. Reyes from 2011. Monographs on Taft are nearly just as scarce, with recent scholars acknowledging that the primary text continues to be an authorized biography by Henry Pringle from 1939 (Gould xi; Lurie xiii).

4. Arthur MacArthur felt Paterno to be a comically self-aggrandizing but potentially exploitable colonial subject. In an anecdote he retailed for laughs during testimony before the U.S. Congress, MacArthur drily noted that "the first interview I had with Paterno was very interesting, I think, and perhaps the committee would enjoy it, because I can repeat it in a moment. He said to me, 'I am permeated with the spirit of European cabinets; I am therefore prepared to discuss the Filipino question on the highest basis of statesmanship'" (*Affairs* 1966). MacArthur, despite his amusement, decided that Paterno "was a highly educated man, with a flowery, poetical imagination, and he had considerable hold on his people by reason of his ready oratory" (*Affairs* 1965). MacArthur also pointed out to Congress that when Paterno proposed to him the banquet and public fiesta to celebrate the general amnesty in July 1900, "he was very flowery in his own behalf" (*Affairs* 1965). Elsewhere in his testimony, MacArthur explained that Paterno was "flowery in imagination, and has a great desire to shine as a diplomatist. Aside from his little vanity he is a pretty good specimen of what education will do" (*Affairs* 909–10).

5. Maximo Kalaw, author of an early book about Filipino politics of the era, asserts that Paterno had urged other orators at the banquet to give similar addresses: "Secretly, Paterno had told some of the Filipino leaders to prepare speeches in favor of independence under the protectorate of the United States" (266).

6. For the texts of the letters, see Maximo Kalaw (267–68).

7. According to Jaime de Veyra, "Antonio Medrano" was the pseudonym of a well-regarded Spanish journalist (212).

8. The only phrase in this passage that Taft nixed as too politically problematic was "y defenderé" ["and I will defend"] (Medrano 569). See Mojares for a separate treatment of this passage and its context (*Brains* 33–35). An English translation of

the speech is available in the U.S. Senate proceedings of the Committee on the Philippines (*Affairs* 1966–68).

9. *The Dreamed Alliance* was the first Filipino opera but not the first Filipino play in Spanish. Previously Manuel Xeres-Burgos had written *Con la cruz y la espada* (*With the Cross and the Sword*). This drama is available in an English translation in Lapeña-Bonifacio, along with a letter of dedication by Xeres-Burgos to then U.S. president William McKinley (67–87). Xeres-Burgos expresses hope in the letter that McKinley was not about to repeat the oppressive practices of the Spanish empire in the Philippines (68). The translation of *With the Cross and the Sword* also includes a note by Xeres-Burgos indicating that the play premiered (most likely in Manila) in Spanish on January 1, 1900 (68). The language of performance distinguishes that production from the operas by Paterno, which were staged in Tagalog translations. There likely were other Filipino playwrights of the era who also wrote in Spanish. Lapeña-Bonifacio indicates that Aurelio Tolentino, the most important author of anticolonial plays in Tagalog, wrote texts in Spanish as well as Pampango throughout a prolific career (51). Whether he wrote dramas in particular in Spanish, though, is unclear. Prior to the era of Xeres-Burgos and Tolentino, there probably were various 19th-century theatrical texts that, if not full-length plays in Spanish, integrated some elements of Spanish beyond just loan words. For instance, *La filipina elegante y el negrito amante* (*The Elegant Filipina and the Amorous Negrito*), a short play in Tagalog by Francisco Balagtas (1788–1862), carried a title in Spanish and included two songs sung in that tongue (238). The term "Negrito" refers to a person of the Aeta or Ita ethnic group, about whom Paterno wrote in his 1890 historical tome *Los itas* and in his 1904 opera *Magdapio.*

10. Most of the music for the opera was composed by Ladislao Bonus, but the score did include other songs such as the American national anthem and "*Sampaguita* (*La Flor de Manila*), a popular melody of the period, which was composed by Paterno's sister, Dolores" ("Sangdugong Panaguinip: The First"). A sampaguita is a white flower that is a common literary symbol of Filipino national identity. The title "Sampaguita" also evokes *Sampaguitas*, a book of poetry that Pedro Paterno published in Madrid in 1880. It was the first chapbook in Spanish by any Filipino. The full text of *Sampaguitas* is available online at Google Books.

11. Mojares suggests that Lapu is also a stand-in for Paterno himself: "In Lapu, Paterno writes himself into the text: a hero whose 'intelligence' and 'inventions'— cryptic writings on a board and a secret philter for the blood compact—aid the people in their liberation" (*Brains* 39).

12. The next lines, spoken by the youth Tarik, reinforce the godlike elevation of Lapu / Lapu Lapu: "Sabio Lapu, todos los días vengo à suplicarte no me abandones" ["Wise Lapu, every day I come to beg you not to abandon me"] (11).

13. An indigenous and homophonous character named Taríc is an important narrator in Paterno's 1885 novel *Nínay.*

14. Structurally, this poison may counterpoint in some way the philter.

15. This homage to Mrs. Taft replaced the dedication to his father in the original version of the novel, the europhile *Nínay*, which was published in Madrid in 1885.

16. Riggs completed the book, entitled *The Filipino Drama*, in 1905 but never published it. The manuscript surfaced in a Washington used book store in 1965 and was published in 1981 (Laya viii–ix). Along with commentary by Riggs, it includes the English translations of various seditious plays, two of which had been lost in their original Tagalog. In his most bigoted and cantankerous account of the era, an article written half a century afterward, Riggs explains, "As a correspondent and daily newspaper editor in Manila from midsummer of 1902 to the summer of 1904, it was my fortune to be in close daily touch with every event that made news. The seditious plays made news of the most sensational type . . . the plays were the handiwork of a fifth column of saboteurs who strove to drive all Americans into the sea for the sake of their own personal benefit and glorification . . . the seditious drama marked a definite period in American history" ("Seditious" 202). Riggs later identifies the *Manila Freedom* as the newspaper of which he was editor ("Seditious" 205).

17. In a footnote, Riggs notes that *The Dreamed Alliance* "has even been attributed by some natives to the Moro-Moro class. This, however, seems to be incorrect" (*Filipino* 55). It is correct. The footnote implies that Riggs was getting at least some of his information about the play from Filipinos who were more cognizant than he of the theatrical and ideological argots of the opera.

18. It seems fair to assume that the "M." in "M. Paterno" stands for either his father Maximo, his brother Maximino, or his half brother Mariano.

19. Reyes translated into Tagalog at least three operas for Paterno, including *Magdapio* in 1903 and *Gayuma* in 1905. Also in 1905, he translated into Tagalog the zarzuela *Ang Buhay ni Rizal* (*The Life of Rizal*) that Paterno wrote first in Spanish; this show appeared before the Manila public on January 14, 1905 (Mojares, *Brains* 533). In 1908, Reyes produced the Tagalog translation of *Nínay*, the Paterno novel from 1885.

20. For a detailed biographical account of Loving, see Cunningham.

21. The multiple Spanish and English renditions of *alianza*/alliance in the fifth act are parallel and unambiguous save for two exceptions. First, the initial spoken line of the epilogue in Spanish refers to "nuestra alianza" ["our alliance"] in a context that clearly defines that alliance as strictly Tagalog (27). The English translation instead offers the phrase as "our alliances," which in its pluralization admits that there are actually two distinct alliances at hand, one among Filipinos and one between Filipinos and Americans (21). Second, the penultimate sentence of the opera in Spanish is given as "Brille eterna nuestra alianza fraternal con la gran República democrática" ["May our fraternal alliance with the great democratic Republic shine eternal"] (28). The English libretto renders this as "Shine forever, our eternal alliance, with the Grand Republic of the United States of America!"] (22). These phrasings allow for different interpretations according to the proclivities of the reader, for the alliance celebrated here could be taken as that of united Filipino villagers, who now form a collectivity, or that of Filipinos and Americans, who now form a transpacific partnership.

22. Recent and reputable considerations of the early 20th-century Philippines overlook *The Dreamed Alliance* and the Paterno operas that followed it. Alfred W.

McCoy's *Policing America's Empire: The United States, the Philippines, and the Rise of the Surveillance State* of 2009 mentions Paterno just once, as the head of a political party (106). Paul A. Kramer's *The Blood of Government: Race, Empire, the United States, and the Philippines* of 2006 acknowledges Paterno only once in a post-1898 context and does not include him in a one-paragraph description of the seditious dramas. That summary is pulled largely from the Lapeña-Bonifacio monograph of 1972 and from Vicente L. Rafael's *White Love and Other Events in Filipino History* of 2000. The pages on the seditious plays in Rafael, however, lean very heavily on Riggs and Lapeña-Bonifacio (39–51). Reliance on Riggs and Lapeña-Bonifacio, though less exclusively, also characterizes the section on the seditious plays in Michael Cullinane's *Ilustrado Politics: Filipino Elite Responses to American Rule, 1898–1908*, of 2003 (113, 115–24). Cullinane repeatedly references Paterno throughout his study but only as a political figure, not as an author of operas or fiction. The lone anglophone text to treat Paterno's operas as significant seems to be Resil Mojares's *Brains of the Nation*. Mojares, however, dismisses the operas in strong terms and denies them anticolonial heft (39–41).

Chapter 2

1. The program announces that "el maestro Ladislao Bonus ha compuesto sobre motivos de esta ópera una notable composición musical titulada 'MAGDAPIO' (two steps) con la que se terminara la función" ["the maestro Ladislao Bonus has composed based on the motifs of this opera a notable musical composition titled 'MAGDAPIO' (two steps) with which the performance will end"] (Riggs, *Filipino* 338).

2. The Allen translation into English weakens the agency of antiliberty forces by rendering "nadie" as "nothing" instead of "nobody" (340). In effect, this attenuates any association of that "nadie" with the American occupation.

3. In the English translation by Allen, Mapalad has a short role in this scene in which he announces, "Prepare yourselves, miserable and shameless Malays!" (342). In the Spanish version, the only parties who appear are the collectivities of Aetas and Malays and their respective gods. A typo in the Spanish transcript indicates that the second speaker in the scene is the chorus of Aetas, but it is clear from the line that the speaker is actually Arao.

4. Allen mistakenly represents Magdapio as conscious while being led to the court (346). It is clear in the Spanish original that she remains in a faint until arriving there.

5. Allen renders this last line as "the Queen and Pearl of the Oriental Sea" (348). The addition of "and Pearl" evokes the sobriquet of Manila as the "Pearl of the Orient." That locution appears most famously in the second verse of "Mi último adiós" ("My Last Farewell"), a poem composed by the national hero José Rizal the night before he was executed by Spain in 1896. The phrase "the Queen," for its part, disappears in the *La democracia* review of the premiere of *Magdapio*, which says that the heroine is proclaimed "Perla del mar de Oriente" ["Pearl of the Oriental sea"] ("Espectáculos" 4).

6. The O'Lantern review eventually was cited in the primary academic analysis of the anticolonial plays of the era, a study by Amelia Lapeña-Bonifacio from 1972, and from there made its way into an important 2006 text by Resil Mojares, *Brains of the Nation* (Lapeña-Bonifacio 47; Mojares 39–41).

7. *Magdapio* was not actually a "coda" to Paterno's oeuvre. Mojares himself notes that afterward Paterno "continued to write Spanish-language novels and plays," including the opera about Taft (*Brains* 41). In 1910 and 1911 alone, Paterno produced a bevy of short narratives, several of which won thousands of votes in newspaper contests. For a study of Paterno's short stories of 1910–11, known collectively as *Aurora social*, see Lifshey, *The Magellan Fallacy*.

8. O'Lantern refers to an article in the *Manila Cablenews* from weeks earlier in which descriptions appeared of the costumes of the characters in the premiere. Unfortunately, that article is not known to be extant due to gaps in the microfilms of the newspaper that are archived in the Library of Congress.

9. The Allen translation was reissued in a book by Castillo y Tuazon in 1937 and from there synopsized, act by act, in an article by Rodell in 1974 (197–210; 110). Riggs reproduces the Allen translation in *The Filipino Drama*, a book finished in 1905 but not published until 1981 (339–48).

10. Alternatively, Michael Cullinane depicts the Philippines Constabulary as "a national peace keeping force manned by Filipino soldiers and led initially by American officers. The Constabulary was created in July 1901 and, as the United States Army withdrew and 'outlaws' (which included many military officers of the Republic who refused to surrender) continued to operate in the countryside, it became the only effective police force in the provinces. . . . The senior inspectors and district commanders worked closely with Filipino and American civilian officials, and in many provinces became influential figures in nearly all areas of municipal and provincial affairs" (145).

11. A review in *La democracia*, a pro-American Filipino newspaper, confirms the presence of actual Aetas in the premiere: "El autor del libreto, metido á naturalista, nos exhibió a los *itas* de Bataan, en el traje primitivo" ["The author of the libretto, acting as a naturalist, exhibited to us the *Aetas* of Bataan in their primitive clothing"] ("Espectáculos" 4).

12. The original board was composed of "Dr. William P. Wilson, director of the Philadelphia Commercial Museum, Dr. Gustavo Niederlein, his assistant, and Señor Pedro A. Paterno, who had had much to do with a Filipino exhibit at Madrid" ("Philippine Exhibit" 519). In addition, "Señor Leon M. Guerrero, a Filipino of high scientific attainments, was made secretary of the board" ("Philippine Exhibit" 519). Niederlein, according to Paul Kramer, "was a German botanist and veteran of colonial expositions; he accepted the Philippine appointment following work for a French colonial exhibition" (239). Guerrero was a member of an extended family that made prominent contributions to Fil-Hispanic culture throughout the 20th century. His older brother Lorenzo, described by Benedict Anderson as "a well-known professional artist, and the teacher of the Philippines' most famous painters," apparently had collaborated with Paterno on his previous opera (248).

According to Raymundo Bañas, "A painting showing the background of the first scene of the opera [*The Dreamed Alliance*] was done by Lorenzo Guerrero, a noted Pilipino painter, with the title *Sandugong Panaginip* written in ancient Tagalog letters" (204). Lorenzo Guerrero later would design the cover of a 1910 short story by Paterno, "La braveza del bayani" ("The Valor of the Hero"). The "ancient Tagalog letters" to which Bañas refers are surely *baybayin*, a precolonial archipelagic writing system that Paterno enlisted in the dedication to his 1885 novel *Nínay* despite his likely inability to read or write that script with competence. The Bañas description is reproduced elsewhere without acknowledgment by Felipe P. De Leon (2342).

13. Curtis refers to this delegation as "another exhibit of human documents consisting of fifty representative men, who have been selected as honorary commissioners from the islands" (3). Paterno, no doubt to his considerable dismay, would have found himself labeled, like the Aetas, a human document.

14. As of this writing, no known source mentions a performance of *Magdapio* as taking place in St. Louis. It seems unlikely that it would have been staged without Paterno present.

15. Molina played the lead role of Magdapio.

16. The article "See Magdapio Monday Night" from January 27, 1904, in the *Manila Cablenews* thus states that the opera "will have its second performance on Monday evening next, the occasion being in honor of the induction into office of Governor Wright, whose inauguration is set for the morning of that day" (3).

17. Riggs may have been O'Lantern. If not, it seems likely that he read the latter's review and lifted from it adjectives such as "reminiscent" to depict the score and "disgusting" to describe the hoochee-hoochee dancing. Ergo, Carluen was probably not the only plagiarist in the theater the night of the gala performance.

18. The tenth section reads in full, "Until it has been officially proclaimed that a state of war or insurrection against the authority or sovereignty of the United States no longer exists in the Philippine Islands, it shall be unlawful for any person to advocate orally or by writing or printing or like methods, the independence of the Philippines Islands or their separation from the United States whether by peaceable or forcible means, or to print, publish or circulate any handbill, newspaper, or other publication, advocating such independence or separation. Any person violating the provisions of this section shall be punished by a fine of not exceeding two thousand dollars and imprisonment not exceeding one year" (*Public* 348–49).

19. There were numerous kinds of Katipunan flags, many of which featured a dominant blood-red field and a sun with rays emanating from it. Most of the suns were white, although at least one version of the flag did show a red sun on a white background.

20. Identifying the invaders as Malays, a term associated broadly with a spectrum of brown-skinned people who would come to predominate in Filipino demographics, is a feint. It is a faint one at that. Paterno would have been seen as mostly Malay himself, so perhaps he strategized that the seeming self-criticism would leave him just enough plausible deniability to escape the wrath of Wright.

21. Just to be sure about the feebleness bit, Riggs passed the libretto and the

texts of two other anticolonial plays to Dr. Albert Ernest Jenks "for an expert opinion in his official capacity as chief of the Ethnological Survey" of the Philippines (*Filipino* 49). Jenks deduced that the dramas "show the pitiful shallowness of the native mind . . . *Magdapio*, it is true, is the best expressed of the three, but it, too, is very shallow. . . . The plays helped me materially to form a more complete understanding of the native character. They are absolutely puerile and weak, where one would most naturally look for something strong and essentially virile" (Riggs, *Filipino* 48–49). Jenks also served on the "official staff of the board" of the Philippine Exposition in St. Louis as the chief of its "Department of Ethnology" (*Report of the Philippine Exposition* 7).

22. Mojares discusses *On the Arrival of Taft* in the main of *Brains of the Nation* but does not list it in the Paterno bibliography at the end. The zarzuela was a heterogeneous theatrical genre that included both spoken dialogue and singing.

23. The possibility seems low that two different men named "Beall" were officially involved in translating Filipino documents at the time. As of this writing, however, M. E. Beall is not known to have been in the Philippines in August 1904, that is, when the Paterno parable appeared in Spanish and probably was translated within a day or two. Consulted documents all locate Beall in Washington in those years. He was, however, an experienced writer. In 1902, Beall coauthored with Taft and others, including the former U.S. governors of Cuba and Puerto Rico, a book titled *Opportunities in the Colonies and Cuba*. And in September 1903, the *Los Angeles Herald* reported that one "Marion E. Beall, an unbonded clerk in the bureau of insular affairs," traveled with three million dollars in a suitcase from Washington to New York because "Under the direction of the insular department the mints of this country and the bureau of printing and engraving here [the article is datelined in Washington] have been making money this summer for use in the Philippines. To Beall was assigned the duty of overseeing the shipment of the money to the island possessions. The bureau of printing and engraving turned out $3,000,000 in crisp $1000 bills. The insular department wanted to get the money to New York" ("Carries" 2). Although the *Herald* headline refers to Marion E. Beall as a "Young Government Clerk" while the *Official Handbook of the Philippines* cites M. E. Beall as "chief of the compilation and translating division," a plausible conjecture is that the references are to the same individual at the Bureau and that his oversight of the delivery of currency to the Philippines eventually led him to Manila and therefore available to translate the Paterno story in August 1904 ("Carries" 2; *Official* 13).

24. This plot description is cited almost verbatim in the 1972 monograph by Lapeña-Bonifacio on the anticolonial plays and from there resurfaces in paraphrased form in the 2006 book *Brains of the Nation* by Mojares (Lapeña-Bonifacio 50; *Brains* 41).

25. The last stories by Paterno were published in 1910–11 and known collectively as *Aurora social*. For analysis of these texts, see Lifshey, *The Magellan Fallacy*.

26. "Don" is a Spanish honorific. Its use in this article shows that the journalist, unlike those in other *Manila Cablenews* articles, respected Paterno or at least recognized his status.

27. The official program shows that both roles were represented by José Buenviaje (Riggs, *Filipino* 338).

28. Mojares indicates that Alejo Carluen also collaborated with Paterno by scoring two zarzuelas for him, *Ang Buhay ni Rizal* (*The Life of Rizal*) in 1905 and *Los amores de Rizal* (*The Loves of Rizal*) in 1906 (*Brains* 533). Paterno surely wrote both shows in Spanish and probably had them performed in Tagalog, as with his operas.

29. A bibliographic reference by Mojares indicates that *Gayuma* was "staged at Teatro Zorrilla in 1902," which would place it in the same year as *The Dreamed Alliance* (*Brains* 533). This seems unlikely. Since the published Tagalog translations by Reyes of *The Dreamed Alliance* and *Magdapio* followed quickly their originations in Spanish and appeared about the same time as the performances themselves, the odds of a 1902 staging of *Gayuma* not yielding a published Tagalog translation by Reyes until 1905 seems doubtful. Mojares is a seminal scholar and his Paterno bibliography seems to be the most extensive and detailed in existence, but it does contain occasional inaccuracies. For instance, he misidentifies the English translator of *Magdapio* as "E.F. Allen" and does not include *On the Arrival of Taft* despite discussing it in the first chapter of his book (*Brains* 533, 41).

30. The earliest known reference to such a staging is by Felipe P. De Leon, who wrote in the 1970s that "another opera, *Gayuma*, in three acts, by Gavino Carluen, with libretto by Pedro A. Paterno, was also premiered in the *Teatro Zorrilla*" (2342). Nevertheless, De Leon is not a particularly accurate source in general. Plus, he wrote three-quarters of a century after the alleged performance in question. He acquired his information from somewhere, but the whisper-down-the-lane methodology that appears in so many secondary sources on Filipino literature in Spanish is not the same as credible scholarship. It seems highly unlikely that De Leon did original research, and the same goes for whatever writer from whom he pulled his details. The earliest known reference to the mere existence of *Gayuma* is from a February 1912 obituary of sorts—Paterno had died nearly a year previously— written by Jaime C. de Veyra, a prominent man of letters who tried to list the work of Paterno in all genres: "Como autor dramático, son conocidas sus operetas *Sang̃dugong̃ panaginip* [i.e., *La alianza soñada*] y *Magdapyo*, más otra que estuvo en preparación bajo el título de *Gayuma*" ["As a dramatic author, his operettas *The Dreamed Blood Compact* [i.e., *The Dreamed Alliance*] and *Magdapyo* are known, plus another that was in preparation under the title *Gayuma*"] (210). The uncertain scope of Filipino literature in Spanish in the early American colonial period is particularly striking here, for de Veyra was an accomplished, Spanish-speaking, Filipino contemporary in Manila and yet even he could not put his finger on the Paterno oeuvre. He mischaracterizes the first two operas as operettas; he misspells *Magdapio*; he remains unaware of *On the Arrival of Taft*, which was definitely written even if not performed; and he can only note that *Gayuma* was "in preparation." This last comment signifies that de Veyra was unaware of its published Tagalog translation and of the Spanish original that probably also saw print.

31. Elements of *Gayuma* likewise appear in much earlier texts by Paterno. His

1885 novel *Nínay*, for example, is structured with nine chapters in accord with the nine-day mourning period that also surfaces in *Gayuma*. And Bathala is a figure of note in many of the (quasi) historical writings of Paterno that followed *Nínay*. The circumstances of the archipelago after 1898, however, lend new imports to these tropes of antecedent origination.

32. Japan defeated Russia in a war that began on February 8, 1904, that is, one week after the *Magdapio* performance for Wright. The war ended with a treaty in early September 1905, that is, one month after *On the Arrival of Taft* was presumably staged. According to Michael Cullinane, "In early November [1905], only a month after Taft's return to Washington, Wright was recalled by President Roosevelt and discreetly appointed ambassador to Japan" (111).

Chapter 3

1. The first Zóbel competition is considered to have been held in 1921 but yielded no winners (Brillantes, *81 Years* 54). Gómez Windham was therefore the inaugural winner of the Zóbel award despite being a contestant in the second Zóbel competition, held in 1922.

2. Early in the colonial period, the United States sent hundreds of English teachers to the Philippines.

3. The university is indicated in the story by its earlier name of "Boston Tech" (18).

4. With regard to the general impulses of his shorter texts, Gómez Windham takes stands against totalizing philosophies of life. For example, he rejects stoicism in "El espectador" ("The Spectator") and gluttony in "Suicidio espiritual" ("Spiritual Suicide"). In similar veins, he disfavors unadulterated honesty in the fairy tale "El príncipe cruel" ("The Cruel Prince") and vegetarianism in the theatrical dialogue "Incompatibilidad de paladares" ("Incompatibility of Palates"). In terms of his overall genre tendencies, his dominant inclination is to produce character studies. These often appear in the form of sketches framed by a first-person narrator who is seemingly interchangeable with the author, a style that blurs distinctions between fiction and reportage. His longer character studies are compressed bildungsromans, such as those of Cándida and Sing-A, that are relayed in a more or less omniscient third person.

5. Spanish laws went into effect in 1863 that allowed more Filipinos to study the imperial language. The percentage of Filipinos who knew Spanish remained very small regardless, with most estimates ranging in the low single digits. Those Filipinos who did speak Spanish, however, constituted the bulk of the political, cultural, and economic elite.

6. Hiligaynon/Ilonggo has millions of native speakers but is less broadly dominant in the central Philippine islands than Cebuano. The narratives of Gómez Windham refer to the vernaculars of his characters as "bisaya" ["Visayan"], a term that technically encompasses many related languages but popularly usually refers to Cebuano. In this case, however, "bisaya" would seem to indicate Hiligaynon/Ilonggo.

7. By 1920, certainly, his English was very good, as evidenced by an open letter he published in that language (Gómez Windham, "An open" 11). Its complex sentences, however, one of them nearly 150 words long, have a bookish, learned feel to them, with syntaxes that would sound more natural in Spanish than in English.

8. The gradual and inevitable disappearance in the Philippines after 1898 of the Spanish language and associated culture is often taken as a given, but Florentino Rodao argues strongly that this is a misreading of history: "El declive de lo hispano en Filipinas no fue el resultado del final del periodo de colonización española: la lengua española tampoco desapareció con las personas educadas bajo su colonización y los ricos no fueron los únicos hispanistas. Este libro muestra que el declive del hispanismo en Filipinas, antes bien, fue motivado por factores ajenos a esos hispanistas, y que la Guerra Civil española fue decisiva en ello, aunque hubo otras razones" ["The decline of Hispanic things in the Philippines was not the consequence of the end of the period of Spanish colonization: the Spanish language also did not disappear with the people educated under its colonization, and the rich were not the only hispanized people. This book shows that the decline of Hispanic culture in the Philippines instead was caused by factors external to those hispanized people and that the Spanish Civil War was decisive in that, although there were other reasons"] (xvii).

9. The byline on the text in Spanish is "Lourdes Brillantes" and on the version in English is "Lourdes Castrillo Brillantes." The two books concur that the prize was established in 1920 and that the first competition was held in 1921 but that no winner was declared either that year or in 1923; Gómez Windham won it in 1922. The explanations given in the two books for the unawarded years, however, are somewhat contradictory. The award lay fallow in 1921, according to *80 años*, "al no haberse presentado obra alguna total o parcialmente inédita" ["since no totally or partially unpublished work had been submitted"] (58). *81 Years* says that "The reason was because the entries were not published during the year" (54). As for 1923, references to the competition of that year seem to have been spliced in both books into the passages explaining the 1922 award: a few paragraphs that discuss Gómez Windham lead into a list of what appear to have been the nonwinning entries in 1922, followed by more paragraphs about Gómez Windham and his texts. Nevertheless, *80 años* implies that those nonwinning entries are actually from the 1923 competition, which was declared void when not enough submissions were received to make for a respectable contest (62). This clarification is absent in *81 Years*, leaving the impression that the mentioned texts competed against those of Gómez Windham in 1922; no explanation is given for the lack of a prizewinner in 1923. The two books also diverge on whether there were five or six entries among the list of nonwinners for what was either the 1922 or 1923 contest; the lists are identical until the end, whereupon some bibliographic confusion arises involving a three-act drama.

10. Hornedo does discuss fictions by Pedro Paterno that are much shorter and simpler than the novellas of Gómez Windham, so length and complexity cannot be the reasons for their noninclusion in his study.

11. In other texts that mention Gómez Windham, there is often a unique additional factor at play, namely the frequent input of his relative and 1975 Zóbel

honoree Guillermo Gómez Rivera. Gallo writes that "al fallecer sin hijos Guillermo Gómez y Windham en 1957, nombró heredero a su sobrino-nieto Guillermo Gómez y Rivera, al que dejó el 27% de su fortuna" ["when Guillermo Gómez y Windham died in 1957 without children, he named as heir his great-nephew Guillermo Gómez y Rivera, to whom he left 27% of his fortune"] ("Guillermo" 23). Gómez Rivera holds in high regard his great-uncle. In a 1978 essay, he kvells about Gómez Windham as one of the two best Filipino short story writers in Spanish, as a playwright who "gave the local dramatic craft maturity," and as one of a number of "great" essayists writing after World War II ("Who's" 1859–60). A fervid writer, Gómez Rivera has spent decades extolling the historical role of the Spanish empire and the Catholic Church in the Philippines and their persisting cultural legacies. Correspondingly, he has decried the post-1898 formal and informal regimes of the United States in the islands. These dual positions have led him to the highly unusual stance of lambasting the national hero José Rizal, who was liquidated by Spain in 1896. For instance, Gómez Rivera has written that

> Como siempre hemos dicho, José Rizal fue re-inventado por los invasores WASP usenses para sus fines bastardos sobre Filipinas. Pero ni aun esa reinvención de Rizal podrá salvarle de sus flaquezas humanas. . . . Pues, por encima de esta su señalada flaqueza, ha sabido volver a la verdad y morir con grandeza retráctandose de todo lo que escribió en contra de la Iglesia Católica y en contra de España. Esa retractación es la que, al fin y al cabo, le hace grande a Rizal. Pues, arrepentido, resulta ser un buen modelo a seguir en esta vida. Pero los enemigos de la Iglesia y de lo hispano en Filipinas quieren seguir usándole a José Rizal para sus fines francamente injustos. ("El caso")

> [As we always have said, José Rizal was reinvented by the U.S. WASP invaders for their bastard aims regarding the Philippines. But not even that reinvention of Rizal could save him from his human weaknesses. . . . Well, beyond this mentioned weakness, he knew how to return to the truth and die with greatness by retracting everything he had written against the Catholic Church and against Spain. That retraction is that which, at the end, makes Rizal great. Because, repentant, he turns out to be a good model to follow in this life. But the enemies of the Church and of Hispanic things in the Philippines want to continue using José Rizal for their frankly unjust aims.]

The literary judgments and personal archives of Gómez Rivera have informed directly, whether explicitly or implicitly, some of the most well-known texts that consider Filipino literature in Spanish, such as *Letras en filipinas* (*Letters in the Philippines*) by Pedro Ortiz Armengol from 1999, *Estampas y cuentos de la Filipinas Hispánica* (*Sketches and Short Stories of the Hispanic Philippines*) by Manuel García Castellón from 2001, and possibly the two texts by Brillantes from 2000 and 2006. For example, Ortiz Armengol writes, "Citamos también la incansable lucha de nuestro amigo filipino Guillermo Gómez Rivera, en defensa de la presencia de la lengua española en su país" ["We cite also the untiring fight of our Filipino friend Guillermo Gómez Rivera in defense of the presence of the Spanish language in his country"] (168). García Castellón thanks Gómez Rivera before anyone else in his acknowledgments page. Brillantes drew the information for her texts in part from her communications with living Zóbel recipients and with the family of deceased winners. Gómez Rivera fits into both categories and so seems likely to have been consulted.

12. The bulk of chapter 4 of "The Adventure of Cayo Malínao" was also published in the Manila newspaper *El debate* in August 1924 under the slightly altered title "Aventura de Cayo Malinao" ("Adventure of Cayo Malinao") and with the following lead: "(A continuacion reproducimos un trozo de una de las ultimas obras selectas del Sr. G. Gomez Windham, "La Aventura de Cayo Malinao". En el nuestros lectores tendran un exquisito ejemplo de la preciosa obra del nuevo academico") ["In the following we reproduce a bit of one of the latest select works of Mr. G. Gomez Windham, "The Adventure of Cayo Malinao." In it our readers will have an exquisite example of the precious work of the new academician"] (5). The designation of "academician" refers to his standing as indicated in the byline: "Correspondiente de la Real Academia Espanola de la Lengua" ["Correspondent of the Royal Spanish Academy of the Language"] (5). The excerpt of fiction appeared alongside three other texts under a banner headline, "Las cuatro mejores producciones literarias del año" ["The Four Best Literary Productions of the Year"], whose subsequent prose described Gómez Windham as a "cerebro cultisimo y temperamento franco" ["a brain of very high culture and a frank temperament"] (5). The writers featured alongside Gómez Windham were Manuel Bernabe, Buenaventura Rodriguez, and Maria Paz Zamora. The first two shared the Zóbel Prize in 1924; Bernabe won it again in 1926, this time sharing it with Jesús Balmori (Brillantes, *81 Years* 62, 68). Paz Zamora published the short story anthology *Mi obolo* (*My Contribution*) in 1924 and in so doing became possibly the first Filipina to publish original fiction in Spanish.

13. Gómez Windham suggested that the translation of *Don Quijote* was important because of "the democratic spirit that pervades the work; for it reflects the thoughts and aspirations of the common people. Filipino writers, as part of a people growing increasingly jealous of their democratic gains, may well bear this point in mind if their works today and in the future are to be saved from the triviality of mere literary exercises. Obviously it is not enough to write well" (Mangahas 100).

14. In this essay, Gómez Windham proposed that Don Quixote is "algo simbólico para nosotros, pues también, como él, profesamos los filipinos un ideal alto y sublime, y sufrimos igualmente de cortedad de medios, no ya para lograrlo, sino para afirmarlo y conservarlo. La diferencia está en que el ingenioso hidalgo no se daba cuenta de su pequeñez y de su poquedad, al paso que nosotros nos percatamos de nuestras limitaciones y nos preparamos a remediarlas y a suplirlas" ["somewhat symbolic for us, for, like him, we Filipinos also profess a high and sublime ideal, and

we suffer equally from a shortness of means, not anymore to achieve it but rather to affirm it and preserve it. The difference is in that the ingenious gentleman did not perceive his smallness and his littleness, whereas we realize our limitations, and we prepare ourselves to remedy them and make up for them"] ("El Quijote" 85).

15. In this same review, Gómez Windham explains his preferences for a text that "describe con honrada fidelidad artística un trozo de nuestro pasado reciente, pues hallo encanto especial en estos estudios retrospectivos, pareciendome que son sin genero de duda los mejores temas para la novela de costumbres. El presente es demasiado fugaz y estamos demasiado interesados en el personalmente para que podamos juzgarlo con alguna ecuanimidad; el futuro es asaz incierto y problemático . . . en cambio, el pasado, especialmente el pasado inmediato, es absolutamente nuestro, y podemos analizarlo, estudiarlo y observarlo a nuestro sabor, extrayendo de el la vision plena de 'lo que ha sido' con perfecto realismo y completa verdad" ["describes with honest artistic fidelity a bit of our recent past, for I find a special charm in these retrospective studies, it seeming to me that they are without any kind of doubt the best themes for a novel of customs. The present is too fleeting and we are too interested in it personally to be able to judge it with some equanimity; the future is exceedingly uncertain and problematic. . . . On the other hand, the past, especially the immediate past, is absolutely ours, and we can analyze it, study it, and observe it to our taste, extracting from it the full vision of 'what has been' with perfect realism and complete truth"] ("Siembra" 2).

16. The predominant pattern of writings on 20th-century Filipino fiction in Spanish is archaeological and philological in orientation. This leads to anthologies and annotated editions more than to interpretations and theoretical interventions. It also swings the scholarship ideologically, at least at times, because philological projects are associated more with normative Spanish academic practices than with the argumentative approaches favored in the United States. The seeming neutrality of a choice of scholarly strategies therefore can transpose into a posture that retroactively opposes the American colonization of the archipelago and its impacts not by celebrating Filipino resistance thereto but by praising the previous Spanish colonization and its legacies. Academic approaches then become proxies for pontificating whose empire was best for the Philippines.

17. For the 1924 Zóbel contest, Gómez Windham entered and then withdrew "The Adventure of Cayo Malínao" (apparently just that novella and not the tripartite volume in which it was published), "dejando el campo libre por razones de delicadeza" ["leaving the field open for reasons of tact"] (Brillantes, *80 años* 69). There seems to be a backstory here but its details are unclear.

18. The designation of "bandit" both before and after 1898 was political in nature and not descriptive of an objective reality. For instance, Raymond Ileto writes of "the myth, created by the declaration of the 'Bandolerismo Act' in 1902, that all remaining 'troublemakers' in the new colonial order were plain bandits, or *ladrones* . . . this identification of any armed resistance with banditry provided the government and its Filipino allies with the needed justification to use harsh measures against recalcitrants" (172).

19. She gains her honorific after moving to San Pedro: "Tía Pasia, como empe-

zaron a llamarla cuantos la conocían porque con su traje de luto, su manto de viuda y su pelo que encaneció prematuramente parecía tener derecho a este respetuoso tratamiento" ["Aunt Pasia, as they began to call her all those who knew her, because with her mourning attire, her widow's cloak, and her hair that prematurely grayed, she appeared to have a right to this respectful treatment"] (140).

20. Pedro Paterno used the nine days of Pasiam as the structure for the nine main chapters of his novel *Nínay*. Nine days of bereavement also appear at the end of his opera *Gayuma*.

21. This fourth section of "Aunt Pasia" is available in the 2001 anthology *Estampas y cuentos de la Filipinas Hispánica* (Gómez Windham, "Tía" 217–26).

Chapter 4

1. Hard numbers and specific proof of how many Filipinos perished during the war is scarce. Most commentators, however, give the death count as over a million. See note 2 in the introduction for further details.

2. The byline of the article is militarized: "By Commander A.S. Riggs, Retired Naval Officer and Historian" ("Seditious" 202). An italicized teaser declares above the headline, "Today, Filipinos may turn again to this tool of revolution" ("Seditious" 202). In the piece, Riggs mentions in passing both *Magdapio* and *The Dreamed Alliance* and reaches the general conclusion that "in the present conditions in the Islands, with strong Communist influences openly at work, and the Communist-inspired and munitioned Hukbalahap forces raiding, intimidating, murdering, threatening, it comes as no surprise that again the seditious play is being used in some instances to inflame the peasant mind" (204, 205, 207).

3. This event is positioned at the front of the novel in a brief, unpaginated passage entitled "La bandera" ["The Flag"].

4. The narrator characterizes the charm here as an "idolo" ["idol"] (74). Later, the narrator refers to it as an "amuleto" ["amulet"] (127).

5. The lone footnote of *Trust in Me* appears right after a passage about the bombing of Pearl Harbor and reads "Escrito durante la guerra" ["Written during the war"] (105).

6. The lodge was called "Isarog" after a mountain of that name in Camarines; "Isarog" means "The only beloved" (Kalaw, *Philippine* 214).

7. The translation of the Spanish sentence into English does not capture the moment when de la Rosa inserts "leader" in English in the original.

8. See Lifshey, *The Magellan Fallacy*, for an analysis of the texts by Gerardo.

9. WorldCat, the global library catalog, inaccurately gives the author of *Trust in Me* as "Manuel de la Rosa." A search for the novel using "Mariano de la Rosa" therefore yields no results.

10. Personal copy. Reproduction of the dedication available upon request.

11. Mariñas says the novel was published in 1950, but if so, the turnaround from the Briones prologue in December to the publication of the entire manuscript would have been extremely quick (77).

12. The current president is Benigno Aquino. His paternal grandfather of the

same name collaborated with the Japanese. His father of the same name led opposition to the dictator Ferdinand Marcos and was assassinated as a result; his mother was Corazon Aquino, who became president after Marcos was overthrown and whose purported policies of redistribution made little headway, partly due to the landed wealth of her own family in the sugar sector of the economy.

Chapter 5

1. Alinea's description of its plot suggests a firsthand familiarity with the novel, though the summary theoretically could have been lifted from another, unknown source (97–98).

2. In the summer of 2008, intrigued by the idea of the lost text, I searched major Manila archives for it and found it the moment I checked the library of the Ateneo de Manila University. The staff there kindly made me a copy of it, which I took back to the United States in order to write an essay about it. That article was published in the journal *Kritika Kultura* of the Ateneo de Manila University in 2011, that is, shortly after an annotated edition of the novel appeared in 2010. In the summer of 2008, however, when I came across the typescript, there was no published version of the novel and no public record of anyone else having located it. My conversations at that time with literature faculty of the University of the Philippines, De La Salle University, and other institutions in greater Manila also suggested that the text in the Ateneo library was not known by anyone to exist. The timing of the independent rediscovery of the novel that led to the published edition of 2010 is not known by me.

3. Isaac Donoso Jiménez also concludes that Hornedo is "F.H.H." (lxii).

4. The other text is a short story collection by Adelina Gurrea, a Filipina who published in Spain.

5. As recently as 2010, Donoso Jiménez wrote that *The Birds of Fire* "se trata de la única novela en español sobre la Segunda Guerra Mundial en el Pacífico escrita por un asiático contemporáneamente al conflicto" ["is the only novel in Spanish about World War II in the Pacific written by an Asian contemporary to the conflict"] (1). Hornedo, writing thirty years earlier, stated that *The Birds of Fire* "is the only known [Filipino] novel in Spanish written in and about World War II" ("Notes" 412).

6. The wording by Brillantes seems to be a paraphrase of the introduction to the bilingual 1987 anthology *Cuentos de Balmori* (*Short Stories by Balmori*) edited by Mariño, who therein writes, "In his third novel *Pájaros de Fuego*, the protagonist does not only accept the existence of a supreme creator but also the limitations of society. Written during his forced retirement during World War II, this novel, distinctly patriotic in content, is considered the most important prose work of Balmori" (xv). This description in turn may be a paraphrase of comments by Alinea (97–98).

7. The last page of the novel indicates a manuscript completion date of September and October 1908 (360). In scholarship, the publication year is given regularly as 1910.

8. This consensus is unlikely to hold for much longer, as many other texts that could be called novels probably appeared in periodicals during the years between Rizal and Balmori.

9. The roofs of traditional Filipino huts were thatched with leaves of the nipa tree. The nipa hut generally stands in Filipino literature as a national symbol.

10. The Executive Committee of the party included other important cultural figures such as León M. Guerrero and Rafael Palma ("Partido" 8).

11. See note 2 to the introduction regarding the number of Filipinos estimated to have died in the war.

12. During the Bataan sequence, a passage appears that fulfills in both content and vocabulary the foreshadowings of the military parade and Quezon speech that open the novel: "Y en tanto el enemigo se dispersaba acosado, derrotado, los pabellones de América y Filipinas confundían unidos en el viento sus colores, al par que confundían su sangre los hombres de Filipinas y de América muriendo por la misma causa y por el mismo ideal" ["And as long as the enemy dispersed under pursuit, defeated, the flags of America and the Philippines mixed together, their colors united in the wind, just as the men of the Philippines and America mixed together their blood, dying for the same cause and the same ideal"] (161). Once again, the American presence in the Philippines is portrayed as strictly of a military nature. And once again, the counterfactually shared ideal is liberty.

13. Donoso Jiménez states inaccurately that Sandoval "se venderá como colaboracionista del mando japonés" ("sells himself as a collaborator to the Japanese command") (liv).

14. The characters are "all doctors" in the sense of having university degrees. One is a physician and another is a dentist, but the group also includes a lawyer, an optician, a professor, and a veterinarian (85).

Chapter 6

1. The social club is the Casino Español de Manila, whose membership was constituted by Fil-Hispanic elites. Their book collection more or less ceased acquiring new titles in the 1960s, that is, about the time *The Creation* was published ("Catálogo" 2). Most of its holdings are in Spanish by authors from Spain, but there are also some texts in English and a few in French. The library catalog notes that "es escasa la presencia de la literatura hispanofilipina" ["the presence of Filipino Hispanic literature is scant"] ("Catálogo" 3). On chronological and authorial counts, therefore, the survival of the lone known copy of *The Creation* within this archival context is something of an outlier. The copy appears to have been transferred there at some point from a different institutional archive, since the front pages of the book are marked by two stamps that read, "Propiedad de la Embajada de España Manila" ["Property of the Embassy of Spain Manila"] and three stamps that read, "Centro Cultural de España" ["Cultural Center of Spain"] and give information on where to find the book on the shelves. The collection of the Casino Español de Manila is overseen today by staff in the adjacent and much more visited library of the Cervantes Institute of Manila.

2. De la Rosa writes that the total eclipse lasted from 7:00 p.m. sharp to 9:11 p.m., a fairly accurate depiction (4). In reality, totality began at 7:31 p.m. and ended at 9:10 p.m. ("Local").

3. Velayo writes that de la Rosa retired as "Associate Justice of the Court of Appeals" and that "only the constitutional age limit of 70 years prevented his further promotion to the Supreme Court, the highest tribunal of the land."

4. In *Trust in Me*, Max suggests that the indigenous inhabitants of Baguio, the Philippine mountain city, are blood relations of Native Americans because the two populations were likely connected geographically by Lemuria before it sank in the Pacific Ocean (64).

5. The specimen was found in the plains near the Isarog volcano (45). About four to five decades earlier, de la Rosa had cofounded a Masonic lodge named for that volcano (Kalaw, *Philippine* 214).

6. De la Rosa avails himself here of the long-held assumption that one side of Mercury always faced the sun while the other side existed in perpetual darkness, with a sliver of transitional land in between.

Epilogue

1. Probably the only production of a Paterno opera since 1905 is a version of *Gayuma* that was staged by Club Filipino of Georgetown University in March 2014 based on the translation by Jemm Excelle S. Dela Cruz.

Bibliography

Affairs in the Philippine Islands: Hearings Before the Committee on the Philippines of the United States Senate. April 10, 1902. Vol. 31. Washington, D.C.: Government Printing Office, 1902. Available on Google Books as *Elihu Root Collection of United States Documents Relating to the . . . , Volume 31* by Elihu Root. Print.

"Agreement between the Government of the Republic of the Philippines and the Government of the United States of America on Enhanced Defense Cooperation." *Document: Enhanced Defense Cooperation Agreement between the Philippines and the United States.* Web. August 4, 2014. Available at http://www.gov.ph/2014/04/29/document-enhanced-defense-cooperation-agreement/.

Alcantara, Erlyn Ruth E. "Baguio between Two Wars: The Creation and Destruction of a Summer Capital." *Vestiges of War: The Philippine-American War and the Aftermath of an Imperial Dream, 1899–1999.* Ed. Angel Velasco Shaw and Luis H. Francia. New York: New York UP, 2002: 207–23. Print.

Alinea, Estanislao B. *Historia analítica de la literatura filipinohispana (desde 1566 hasta mediados de 1964).* Manila: Imprenta Los Filipinos, 1964. Print.

Allen, Henry T., trans. *Magdapio or Fidelity Rewarded.* By Pedro Paterno. *The Filipino Drama [1905].* By Arthur Stanley Riggs. Manila: Ministry of Human Settlements, Intramuros Administration, 1981: 339–48. Print.

Anderson, Benedict. *The Spectre of Comparisons: Nationalism, Southeast Asia and the World.* London: Verso, 1998. Print.

Baguio and Northern Luzon Philippine Islands. Manila: Thos. Cook & Son, Official Passenger Agents to the Philippine Government, 1916. Print.

Balagtas, Francisco. "The Elegant Filipina and the Amorous Negrito." *Philippine Magazine* November 1932: 237–40. Print.

Balmori, Jesús. *Bancarrota de almas.* Manila: Imprenta y Litografía de Juan Fajardo, 1910. Print.

Balmori, Jesús. *Los pájaros de fuego: Novela filipina de la guerra.* Ed. Isaac Donoso Jiménez. Manila: Instituto Cervantes de Manila, 2010. Print.

Balmori, Jesús. *Los pájaros de fuego: Novela filipina de la guerra.* [1942?]–1945. TS. Available at the Library of the Ateneo de Manila University.

"Banqueros Are Heroes." *Manila Cablenews* August 6, 1905: 12. Print.

Bañas, Raymundo C. *Pilipino Music and Theater.* Quezon City: Manlapaz Publishing, 1969. Print.

Bascara, Victor. *Model-Minority Imperialism.* Minneapolis: U of Minnesota P, 2006. Print.

Beall, M. E. "Opportunities in the Philippines." *Opportunities in the Colonies and Cuba.* By Leonard Wood, William H. Taft, Charles H. Allen, Perfecto Lacoste, and M. E. Beall. New York: Lewis, Scribner, 1902: 5–122. Print.

Ben-Aben. "Nuestras entrevistas." *Excelsior: Revista decenal ilustrada* November 30, 1931. Print.

"Bonus, Ladislao." E. Arsenio Manuel. *Dictionary of Philippine Biography.* Vol. 2. Quezon City: Filipiniana Publications, 1970: 106–8. Print.

Brillantes, Lourdes [Castrillo] [de]. *80 años del Premio Zóbel.* [Manila?]: Instituto Cervantes y Fundación Santiago, 2000. Print.

Brillantes, Lourdes [Castrillo] [de]. *81 Years of Premio Zóbel: A Legacy of Philippine Literature in Spanish.* Makati City: Georgina Padilla y Zóbel Filipinas Heritage Library, 2006. Print.

Bulosan, Carlos. *America Is in the Heart.* Seattle: U of Washington P, 1973. Print.

Campomanes, Oscar V. "Casualty Figures of the American Soldier and the Other: Post-1898 Allegories of Imperial Nation-Building as 'Love and War.'" *Vestiges of War: The Philippine-American War and the Aftermath of an Imperial Dream 1899–1999.* Ed. Angel Velasco Shaw and Luis H. Francia. New York: New York UP, 2002: 134–62. Print.

"Carluen, Alejo." E. Arsenio Manuel. *Dictionary of Philippine Biography.* Vol. 2. Quezon City: Filipiniana Publications, 1970: 106–8. Print.

"Carries Millions in His Suit Case." *Los Angeles Herald* September 30, 1903, morning ed.: 2. Print.

Castillo y Tuazon, Teofilo del. *A Brief History of Philippine Literature.* Manila: Progressive Schoolbooks, 1937. Print.

"Catálogo de la biblioteca [del] Casino Español de Manila." Manila: n.p., 2000. Available at the library of the Cervantes Institute of Manila. Print.

"Las cuatro mejores producciones literarias del año." *El debate* August 10, 1924: 5. Print.

Cullinane, Michael. *Ilustrado Politics: Filipino Elite Responses to American Rule, 1898–1908.* Quezon City: Ateneo de Manila UP, 2003. Print.

Cunningham, Roger D. "'The Loving Touch': Walter H. Loving's Five Decades of Military Music." *Army History: The Professional Bulletin of Army History* Summer 2007: 4–25. Print.

Curtis, William E. "Coming from Manila." *Evening Star* [Washington, D.C.] May 28, 1904, part 2: 3. [Datelined "Special Correspondence of The Evening Star and Chicago Record-Herald. Manila, April 26, 1904"]. Print.

"Dastardly Japs Attack Colonially Occupied U.S. Non-State." *Our Dumb Century.* Ed. Scott Dikkers. New York: Three Rivers P, 1999: 60. Print.

Dela Cruz, Jemm Excelle S. *Gayuma [Love Charm]: Filipino Opera.* By Pedro Paterno. Washington, D.C.: n.p., 2014. Print. Available on request. Translated from *Gayuma: Operang Filipina*. By Pedro Paterno. Trans. Roman Reyes. Manila: n.p., 1905. Print.

de la Rosa, Mariano L. *La creación*. Quezon City: Novel Publishing, [1959?]. Print.

de la Rosa, Mariano L. *Fíame (Filipinas-América)*. [Manila?]: n.p., [1946? 1951?]. Print.

De Leon, Felipe P. "Manila Welcomes the Opera." *Filipino Heritage: The Making of a Nation*. Ed. Alfredo Roces. Vol. 9: *The American Colonial Period (1900–1941) Under the School Bell*. [Manila?]: Lahing Pilipino, 1977–78: 2340–46. Print.

De Veyra, Jaime C. "Un polígrafo filipino." [Bylined as "J.C.V."] *Efemérides filipinas*. Ed. Jaime C. de Veyra y Mariano Ponce. Vol. 1. Manila: Imprenta y Librería de I.R. Morales, 1914: 209–12. Print. Originally published in *El ideal* on February 27, 1912. Print.

Donoso Jiménez, Isaac. Introducción. *Los pájaros de fuego: Novela filipina de la guerra*. By Jesús Balmori. Ed. Isaac Donoso Jiménez. Manila: Instituto Cervantes de Manila, 2010: vii–xciii. Print.

"'The Dreamed Alliance' a Brilliant Success." *Manila Freedom* August 28, 1902: 1+. Print.

"Espectáculos." *La democracia* January 9, 1904: 4. Print.

Fernández, Tony. "La hispanidad y Don Guillermo Gómez Wyndham, primer ganador del Premio Zóbel." *Revista Filipina* Summer 2000. Web. July 30, 2011. [Consists principally of a reprint of an article first published in *El debate* on January 9, 1966].

"Filipino Comic Opera." *Manila Times* January 9, 1904: 2. Print.

Foreman, John. *The Philippine Islands: A Political, Geographical, Ethnographical, Social and Commercial History of the Philippine Archipelago Embracing the Whole Period of Spanish Rule with an Account of the Succeeding American Insular Government*. 3rd ed. New York: Charles Scribner's Sons, 1906. Print.

Gallo, Andrea. "Guillermo Gómez Windham: Líneas bio-bibliográficas y unos poemas." *Humanities Diliman* 7.2 (2010): 1–33. Print. Available at http://journals. upd.edu.ph/index.php/humanitiesdiliman/article/viewArticle/1985.

Gallo, Andrea. "La novelística de Guillermo Gómez Windham: una 'comedia humana' filipina." *Transmodernity* 4.1 (2014): 136–53. Available at https://escholar ship.org/uc/ssha_transmodernity?volume=4;issue=1.

García Castellón, Manuel. *Estampas y cuentos de la Filipinas Hispánica*. Madrid: Clan, 2001. Print.

Gerardo, Félix. *Justicia social y otros cuentos*. [Cebu?]: n.p., [1941?]. Available at the National Library of the Philippines, Manila. Print.

Golay, Frank Hindman. *Face of Empire: United States–Philippine Relations, 1898–1946*. Madison: U of Wisconsin P, 1998. Print.

Gómez Rivera, Guillermo. "El caso de José Rizal frente a los dominicos españoles." *Revista Filipina* Summer 2011. Web. July 30, 2011.

Gómez Rivera, Guillermo. "Who's Afraid of a Romantic Language? Filipino Works in Spanish from Age to Age." *Filipino Heritage: The Making of a Nation*.

Ed. Alfredo Roces. Vol. 7: *The Spanish Colonial Period (Late 19th Century) The Awakening*. [Manila?]: Lahing Pilipino, 1977–78: 1854–61. Print.

Gómez Windham, Guillermo. "Aventura de Cayo Malinao" [Excerpt from the fourth chapter of "La aventura de Cayo Malínao"]. *El debate* August 10, 1924: 5+. Print.

Gómez Windham, Guillermo. *La aventura de Cayo Malínao. Los ascensos del inspector Rojo. Tia Pasia. (Novelas filipinas contemporáneas)*. Iloilo: Editorial Catalana, 1924. Print. Available at the Filipinas Heritage Library in Makati, Manila.

Gómez Windham, Guillermo. "La carrera de Cándida." Cuentos Escogidos por GUILLERMO GOMEZ de la Academia Española. *"Informaciones" Suplemento Al Número Del Sábado, 11 De Marzo De 1933*. Print. Possibly available at the Lopez Museum and Library in Manila.

Gómez Windham, Guillermo. *La carrera de Cándida: Novelas cortas: cuentos: artículos*. Iloilo: 1921. Print. Available at the Filipinas Heritage Library in Makati, Manila.

Gómez Windham, Guillermo. "'Incompatibilidad de paladares' y 'El príncipe cruel.'" Cuentos Escogidos por GUILLERMO GOMEZ de la Academia Española. *"Informaciones" Suplemento Al Número Del Sábado, 25 De Febrero De 1933*. Print. Possibly available at the Lopez Museum and Library in Manila.

Gómez Windham, Guillermo. "Marinos y navieros son como el fuego y el agua: Tienen que asociarse para producir el vapor que da fuerza, movimiento y progreso." [Bylined as "Por GUILLERMO GOMEZ De la Real Academia de la Lengua] *El debate* July 12, 1925: 8. Print.

Gómez Windham, Guillermo. "La odisea de Sing-A." Cuentos Escogidos de GUILLERMO GOMEZ de la Academia Española. *"Informaciones" Suplemento Al Número Del Sábado, 1.o De Abril De 1933*. Print. Possibly available at the Lopez Museum and Library in Manila.

Gómez Windham, Guillermo. "An Open Letter to the Girls and Boys." [Bylined as "Guillermo Gomez"] *The Independent* February 28, 1920: 11. Print.

Gómez Windham, Guillermo. "El Quijote en Filipinas." [Bylined as "Guillermo Gómez"] *Literature under the Commonwealth*. Ed. Manuel E. Arguilla et al. Manila: Philippine Writers' League, 1940: 83–87. Print.

Gómez Windham, Guillermo. "'Siembra de vientos' por Manuel Ma. Rincon un nuevo libro filipino." [Bylined and datelined at end as "Guillermo Gomez, Iloilo, Diciembre 20, 1923"] *El debate* December 25, 1923: 2+. Print.

Gómez Windham, Guillermo. "Sr. Gregorio Nieva." [Letter to the editor dated March 7, 1916.] [Bylined as "Guillermo Gomez"] *The Philippine Review/Revista filipina* 1.4 (April 1916): 67. Print. Available via www.hathitrust.org.

Gómez Windham, Guillermo. "Tía Pasia (fragmento)." *Estampas y cuentos de la Filipinas Hispánica*. Ed. Manuel García Castellón. Madrid: Clan, 2001. Print.

Gould, Lewis L. *The William Howard Taft Presidency*. Lawrence: UP of Kansas, 2009. Print.

"Governor Taft Assists in Starting a Filipino Conservatory of Music." *Manila Cablenews* August 28, 1902: 1. Print.

Hernández, Tomás C. "The Emergence of Modern Drama in the Philippines (1898–1912)." Philippine Studies Working Paper No. 1, Asian Studies Program, University of Hawaii, June 1976. Print.

Hontiveros-Avellana, Daisy. "Philippine Drama: A Social Protest." *Brown Heritage: Essays on Philippine Cultural Tradition and Literature.* Ed. Antonio G. Manuud. Quezon City: Ateneo de Manila UP, 1967: 668–88. Print.

Hornedo, Florentino H. "Notes on the Filipino Novel in Spanish." *Saint Louis University Research Journal* (Baguio City) September 1980: 383–422. Print.

Hornedo, Florentino H. [F.H.H.]. "To The Reader." Preface. *Los pájaros de fuego: novela filipina de la guerra.* By Jesús Balmori. [1942?]–1945. TS. Available at the Library of the Ateneo de Manila University. Also available in Jesús Balmori. *Los pájaros de fuego: Novela filipina de la guerra.* Ed. Isaac Donoso Jiménez. Manila: Instituto Cervantes de Manila, 2010: lxi. Print.

Ileto, Raymond. *Pasyon and Revolution: Popular Movements in the Philippines, 1840–1910.* Quezon City: Ateneo de Manila UP, 1997. Print.

Isaac, Allan Punzalan. *American Tropics: Articulating Filipino America.* Minneapolis: U of Minnesota P, 2006. Print.

Jones, Gregg. *Honor in the Dust: Theodore Roosevelt, War in the Philippines, and the Rise and Fall of America's Imperial Dream.* New York: New American Library, 2012. Print.

Kalaw, Maximo M. *The Development of Philippine Politics (1872–1920).* Manila: Oriental Commercial, 1926. Print.

Kalaw, Teodoro. *Philippine Masonry: Its Origin, Development, and Vicissitudes up to Present Time (1920).* Trans. Frederic H. Stevens and Antonio Amechazurra. Manila: McCullough, 1956. Print.

Karnow, Stanley. *In Our Image: America's Empire in the Philippines.* New York: Ballantine, 1989. Print.

Kramer, Paul A. *The Blood of Government: Race, Empire, the United States, and the Philippines.* Chapel Hill: U of North Carolina P, 2006. Print.

Lapeña-Bonifacio, Amelia. *The "Seditious" Tagalog Playwrights: Early American Occupation.* Manila: Zarzuela Foundation of the Philippines, 1972. Print.

"Lawshe Arrives from Manila." *St. Louis Republic* August 28, 1904: 5. Print.

Laya, Jaime C. Preface. *The Filipino Drama [1905].* By Arthur Stanley Riggs. Manila: Ministry of Human Settlements, Intramuros Administration, 1981: vii–ix. Print.

Lifshey, Adam. *The Magellan Fallacy: Globalization and the Emergence of Asian and African Literature in Spanish.* Ann Arbor: U of Michigan P, 2012. Print.

"Local Times for Eclipse in Manila on Sunday, July 26, 1953." *Eclipse Calculator—Solar Eclipses in Manila, Philippines.* Web. December 25, 2013. Available at http://www.is.timeanddate.net/eclipse/in/philippines/manila?iso=19530726.

Loving, W. H. [Walter Howard], trans. *The Dreamed Alliance: Philippino Opera in One Act Divided into Five Scenes.* By Pedro Paterno. Manila: Imp. de la "R. Mercantil" de J. de Loyzaga y Ageo S. Jacinto, 1902. Print.

Lurie, Jonathan. *William Howard Taft: The Travails of a Progressive Conservative.* Cambridge: Cambridge UP, 2012. Print.

"'Magdapio.'" *La democracia* January 18, 1904: 4. Print.

Mangahas, Federico. "Notes on a Literary Anniversary." *Philippine Magazine* January 1940: 100, 109–11. Print.

"Manuel C. Briones." *Senate of the Philippines.* Web. December 21, 2011. Available at http://www.senate.gov.ph/senators/former_senators/manuel_briones.htm.

Marcus, Greil, and Werner Sollors, eds. *A New Literary History of America.* Cambridge: Harvard UP, 2009. Print.

Mariñas, Luis. *La literatura filipina en castellano.* Madrid: Editora Nacional, 1974. Print.

Mariño, Pilar Eugenia. Introduction. *Cuentos de Balmori.* By Jesús Balmori. Trans. Pilar Eugenia Mariño. Ed. Edgardo Tiamson Mendoza. Manila: National Book Store, 1987: ix-xvi. Print.

McCoy, Alfred W. *Policing America's Empire: The United States, the Philippines, and the Rise of the Surveillance State.* Madison: U of Wisconsin P, 2009. Print.

Medrano, Antonio. "Pedro A. Paterno: Recuerdos de un periodista." *Cultura filipina* March 1911: 546–70. Print.

Mojares, Resil B. *Brains of the Nation: Pedro Paterno, T.H. Pardo de Tavera, Isabelo de los Reyes and the Production of Modern Knowledge.* Manila: Ateneo de Manila UP, 2006. Print.

"Molina, Juana." E. Arsenio Manuel. *Dictionary of Philippine Biography.* Vol. 2. Quezon City: Filipiniana Publications, 1970: 284–87. Print.

Official Handbook of the Philippines and Catalogue of the Philippine Exhibit. In two volumes: Part 1. Published under authority of the civil governor of the Philippine Islands by the Philippine Exposition Board: William P. Wilson, *President.* Gustavo Niederlein, *Member.* Pedro A. Paterno, *Member.* León M. Guerrero, *Secretary.* Manila: Bureau of Public Printing, 1903. Print. Available on Google Books.

O'Lantern, Jack. "Gave Play for Wright Last Night." *Manila Cablenews* February 2, 1904: 5. Print.

"La Opera del Sr. Bonus." *La democracia* August 4, 1902: 3. Print.

"Opera to Be Repeated." *Manila Times* January 15, 1904: 4. Print.

Ortiz Armengol, Pedro. *Letras en Filipinas.* Madrid: Dirección General de Relaciones Culturales y Científicas, 1999. Print.

"Partido 'Union Nacionalista.'" *El nacionalismo* December 8, 1906: 8. Print.

Paterno, P. A. [Pedro Alejandro]. *La alianza soñada.* Manila: Estab. Tipográfico de M. Paterno y Comp, 1902. Print. Available at the National Library of Australia and the National Library of the Philippines.

Paterno, P. A. *The Dreamed Alliance: Philippino Opera in One Act Divided into Five Scenes.* Trans. W. H. [Walter Howard] Loving. Manila: Imp. de la "R. Mercantil" de J. de Loyzaga y Ageo S. Jacinto, 1902. Print.

Paterno, P. A. *Gayuma [Love Charm]: Filipino Opera.* Trans. Jemm Excelle S. Dela Cruz. Washington, D.C.: n.p., 2014. Print. Available on request. Translated from *Gayuma: Operang Filipina.* Trans. Roman Reyes. Manila: n.p., 1905. Print.

Paterno, P. A. *Gayuma: Operang Filipina.* Trans. Roman Reyes. Manila: n.p., 1905. Print.

Paterno, P. A. "The Honorable Taft and His Successor Governor Wright." Trans. [M. E.? Marion?] B[e?]all. [August?] 1904. Print. Available in the William Howard Taft Papers at the Library of Congress, series 3, roll 45.

Paterno, P. A. "El Hon. Taft, y su sucesor el Gobernador Wright." *La patria* August 13, 1904: 1. Print. Available in the William Howard Taft Papers at the Library of Congress, series 3, roll 45.

Paterno, P. A. *Los itas.* Madrid: Imprenta de los sucesores de Cuesta, 1890. Print.

Paterno, P. A. *Magdapio ó La fidelida premiada: Opera en 4 actos.* Manila: La Patria: 1903. Print.

Paterno, P. A. *Magdapio: Operang apat na bahagui.* Trans. Roman Reyes. Maynila: La Patria, 1903. Print. Available at the National Library of the Philippines.

Paterno, P. A. *Magdapio or Fidelity Rewarded.* Trans. Henry T. Allen. *The Filipino Drama [1905].* By Arthur Stanley Riggs. Manila: Ministry of Human Settlements, Intramuros Administration, 1981: 339–48. Print.

Paterno, P. A. "La nueva era." *La patria* August 13, 1903: 1. Print.

Paterno, P. A. *Sangdugong Panaguinip: Operang Filipina.* Trans. Roman Reyes. Manila: n.p., 1902. Print.

"[Pedro Paterno's opera]." *Manila Cablenews* February 3, 1904: 4. Print.

"Pedro Paterno's Peace Festival." *Scranton Tribune* September 11, 1900: 4. Print.

"The Philippine Exhibit at the Louisiana Purchase Exposition at St. Louis." By The Civil Governor and the Heads of the Executive Departments of the Civil Government of the Philippine Islands (1900–1903). *Reports of the Philippine Commission.* Bureau of Insular Affairs: War Department. Washington, D.C.: Government Printing Office, 1904: 518–20. Print. Available on Google Books.

"The Play and the Presentation." *Manila Times* August 29, 1902, morning ed.: 1. Print.

"Program Is Complete Now." *Manila Cablenews* August 4, 1905: 3. Print.

Public Laws and Resolutions Passed by the United States Philippine Commission during the Quarter Ending November 20, 1901. Manila: United States Philippine Commission, 1901: 346–56. Print.

Rafael, Vicente L. *White Love and Other Events in Filipino History.* Durham: Duke UP, 2000. Print.

Report of the Philippine Commission to the President. Vol. 2 (Testimony and Exhibits). Washington, D.C.: Government Printing Office, 1900. Print.

Report of the Philippine Exposition Board to the Louisiana Purchase Exposition and Official List of Awards Granted by the Philippine International Jury at the Philippine Government Exposition World's Fair, St. Louis, MO. St. Louis: 1904. Print. Available on Google Books.

Reyes, Portia L. *Panahon at pagsasalaysay ni Pedro Paterno, 1858–1911: Isang pag-aaral sa intelektwalismo.* Quezon City: Bahay Saliksikan sa Kasaysayan/Bagong Kasaysayan, 2011. Print.

Reyes, Roman, trans. *Gayuma: Operang Filipina.* By Pedro Paterno. Manila: n.p., 1905. Print.

Reyes, Roman, trans. *Magdapio: Operang apat na bahagui.* By Pedro Paterno.

Maynila: La Patria, 1903. Print. Available at the National Library of the Philippines.

Reyes, Roman, trans. *Sangdugong Panaguinip: Operang Filipina.* By Pedro Paterno. Manila: n.p., 1902. Print.

Riggs, A. S. [Arthur Stanley]. "The Drama of the Filipinos." *Journal of American Folk-Lore* January–March 1904: 279–85. Print.

Riggs, A. S. *The Filipino Drama [1905].* Manila: Ministry of Human Settlements, Intramuros Administration, 1981. Print.

Riggs, A. S. "Seditious Drama in the Philippines." *Current History* 20:116 (April 1951): 202–7. Print.

Rodao, Florentino. *Franquistas sin Franco: Una historia alternativa de la guerra civil española desde Filipinas.* Granada: Comares, 2012. Print.

Rodell, Paul A. "Philippine 'Seditious Plays.'" *Asian Studies* 12 (1974): 88–118. Print.

Roosevelt, Theodore. "The Strenuous Life." *Theodore Roosevelt: An American Mind. Selected Writings.* Ed. Mario R. DiNunzio. New York: Penguin, 1994: 184–89. Print.

"Sangdugong Panaguinip: The First Tagalog Opera." *Filipinas Heritage Library.* Filipinas Heritage Library, n.d. Web. March 12, 2013.

Schlimgen, Veta R. "Neither Citizens nor Aliens: Filipino 'American Nationals' in the U.S. Empire, 1900–1946." Diss. U of Oregon, 2010. Print.

"See Magdapio Monday Night." *Manila Cablenews* January 27, 1904: 3. Print.

"Speeches at the Palace." *Manila Cablenews* August 6, 1905: 1. Print.

"Taft Honored by Liceo de Manila." *Manila Times* August 10, 1905: 1. Print.

Tiongson, Antonio T., Jr. "On Filipinos, Filipino Americans, and U.S. Imperialism: Interview with Oscar V. Campomanes. *Positively No Filipinos Allowed: Building Communities and Discourse.* Ed. Antonio T. Tiongson, Jr., et al. Philadelphia: Temple UP, 2006: 26–42. Print.

"Tolentino, Aurelio." E. Arsenio Manuel. *Dictionary of Philippine Biography.* Vol. 2. Quezon City: Filipiniana Publications, 1970: 371–432. Print.

"El trece de agosto." *La patria* August 13, 1904: 1. Print.

Twain, Mark. "The Stupendous Joke of the Century." *Mark Twain's Weapons of Satire: Anti-imperialist Writings on the Philippine-American War.* Ed. Jim Zwick. Syracuse, NY: Syracuse UP, 1992: 184–85. Print.

Velayo, Ramon M. "The Author." *La creación.* By Mariano L. de la Rosa. Quezon City: Novel Publishing, [1959?]. Print.

Wood, Leonard, et al. *Opportunities in the Colonies and Cuba.* New York: Lewis, Scribner, 1902. Print.

Xeres-Burgos, Manuel. "Con la cruz y la espada." *The "Seditious" Tagalog Playwrights: Early American Occupation.* By Amelia Lapeña-Bonifacio. Manila: Zarzuela Foundation of the Philippines, 1972: 67–87. Print.

Index

𝕏